Timeless Years

With

Shri Ramakant Maharaj

Timeless Years

With

Shri Ramakant Maharaj

2012 - 2022

by

Ann & Charles Shaw

© 2022 Ann & Charles Shaw

First Edition: 1st March 2022 (*Shivaratri*)

ISBN: 978-1-9993578-2-5

Published by "Selfless Self Press"

www.ramakantmaharaj.net

admin@ramakantmaharaj.net

www.selfless-self.com

admin@selfless-self.com

Contents

Foreword

It is my immense pleasure to say a few words about the new book *Timeless Years with Shri Ramakant Maharaj*.

Both Charles and Ann are blessed disciples who had the opportunity to spend quality time with Maharaj. Their dedication and devotion to Shri Maharaj has been simply exemplary. Maharaj had a lot of respect for the profound work both Charles and Ann put in to spread the ultimate truth to the broader society through the release of his book *Selfless Self*.

In 2018, when Ann brought the Bible form of *Selfless Self*, he was very delighted. He also requested Ann to "proofread" *Ultimate Truth*, such was his confidence in Ann's understanding of his teachings.

This book is straight from the heart and shows the love and dedication of Ann for Shri Maharaj. Maharaj used to say that the Sadguru graces his disciples to become like him. That grace is surely conferred on Ann.

Anvita Sawant   *10th January 2022*

(Disciple of Shri Nisargadatta Maharaj   *Mumbai*
  and Shri Ramakant Maharaj's wife)

Introduction

In today's spiritual supermarkets, few seekers use discrimination and discernment when they approach a spiritual teacher, even when they are asked to pay for the guidance! It is a fact that authentic, fully realized Gurus/Masters are very rare indeed. Ramana Maharshi was one such spiritual beacon and the great sage, Nisargadatta Maharaj, was another one. Importantly, neither of them charged money for imparting knowledge that is innately our own!

Spiritual teachers can only guide students as far as the limits of their knowledge. What is the difference between an authentic Guru/*Jnani*/Self-Realized Master, and an ordinary teacher? The journey of the Guru is founded on demolishing the ego and transcending knowledge. If the teacher has not fully hammered the ego and not yet penetrated the confines of knowledge, then his teachings will only convey mere words, lacking in power. There will not be a transmission of energy because the ego is still in the way; he is separate from the Source. Put simply, he does not teach from the unlimited Source, but the limited mind!

In 1962, 21-year-old, Ramakant Maharaj met his Guru, Nisargadatta Maharaj, who immediately saw the purity and destiny in this young man. He began the work of remoulding him, chiselling and removing the worldly add-ons, and drawing Shri

Ramakant closer and closer to himself. Shri Ramakant followed his Guru's instructions and became deeply devoted to him. Subsequently, he started to initiate seekers with the Lineage *Naam Mantra*, thereby for the first time, generously spreading the "Master Key" to western seekers. He stressed the importance of *Naam Mantra* meditation which clears away all the illusory concepts. This process of undoing makes for a perfect foundation, which in turn, enables the permanent establishment of Truth.

Out of those timeless years spent with Nisargadatta Maharaj, Ramakant Maharaj's teachings would evolve to become one of the most direct, hard-hitting and refined teachings of Non-Duality to date. He rejected every concept, including spiritual concepts, which he frequently referred to as the "polished words", and dispensed with Indian terminology, for the most part. His effective method of teaching leaves no room for the mind to be entertained.

These absolute teachings, combined with the powerful tool of the *Naam Mantra*, is proving to be the shortest cut to Self-Realization that continues to awaken endless seekers! His book, *Selfless Self*, hailed as a spiritual classic, has been compared to Nisargadatta's *I Am That*. The late Alan Jacobs, (President of the "Ramana Maharshi Foundation UK") reviewed it, saying: "*Selfless Self* is a marvellous, outstanding book that will help many of Sri Nisargadatta Maharaj's followers and others. This is truly a great book and a worthy successor to the much-celebrated 'I AM THAT' written by Shri Ramakant's own Master, Shri Nisargadatta Maharaj. I greatly admire the content. Wonderful! I have no doubt about Sri Ramakant Maharaj being a *Jnani*, (Self-Realized Master)".

The Teachings of Shri Ramakant Maharaj are unique because they are so simple, direct and potent! His emphasis on hammering the ego and removing all the concepts and knowledge, including spiritual knowledge, in other words, purifying the ground before planting the seeds, is essential. The cleaning, purification or purging process has been overlooked by most modern-day teachers. Yet, if the ground is not cleared first, the foundations will not be solid, and, consequently, whatever knowledge is shared, will not be permanently established. Instead, it will rest on shaky ground.

As Maharaj often says, "Knowledge on top of ego is useless and will crumble". Overlooking the first stage of "Self-Enquiry" and thereby, bypassing the demolition process of the ego, will not bring about liberation. It will only ensure the continuation of those endless spiritual supermarkets!

Many readers will be able to relate to our search for Truth. Our journey started at a young age, and reached its culmination when we discovered Shri Ramakant Maharaj! From childhood onwards, we both asked the ultimate questions, such as:

"Who am I?" and "Where have I come from?" We both felt we were misfits in the world, lacking sufficient interest in pursuing our careers, or other such material goals. So great was our discontentment with worldly affairs, that at some point in our lives, we both even tried to "escape to the Monastery!" While Charles hoped to join a Tibetan Buddhist Monastery, I set my sights on entering a Convent! Fortunately, we were not accepted! When we found out that we shared this identical biographical detail, we burst out laughing, because neither of us was answering a true calling. We were only seeking refuge to hide from the pressures of the world!

The search for meaning and Truth continued throughout our lives. When we eventually met one another, (after we had freed ourselves from ill-matching relationships), we knew that together, we would become a mighty force and scale the heights of the spiritual mountain! For the next twenty years or so, we searched, read, studied and shared everything from Jiddu Krishnamurti, the *Upanishads*, Ramana Maharshi, Buddhist texts, to Yogananda, the mystics, etc.

Some years later, when we discovered Nisargadatta Maharaj and his wonderful Lineage, we let out a sigh of relief, and over the next x number of years, we studied the books and meditated.

Fast forward to 2012, Charles was now in his sixties and I was in my late 50's. It was time to demolish the ego for good and be established in our true nature permanently. We looked for authentic teachers in the west, but drew a blank, so, we actively turned our attention to India, in search of a Guru who could help us.

Timeless Years With Shri Ramakant Maharaj uncovers the sacred and unique relationship between the Guru and his disciple, or the Master and the student. The Guru is not a person. He is the impersonal, unmanifest Absolute in manifest form.

This book reveals how the association with an authentic Guru - following his instructions, listening and meditating on the transcendental knowledge – all lead to the Conviction that one is unborn, which in turn, results in freedom from suffering.

The "relationship of oneness" removes the ego, the sense of separation, and enables a merging in the pure and impersonal love of the Guru. What was the impact of being with Shri Ramakant Maharaj? Freedom from our little selves and causeless, unquantifiable happiness and peace, coupled with unending gratitude!

What follows is a detailed account of our timeless years with our Guru, Shri Ramakant Maharaj, including extracts from journals, diaries, reflections, and experiences, as well as many discourses from Maharaj.

Ann Shaw   *1ˢᵗ January 2022*
                                                                      London

Biography

Who is Shri Ramakant Maharaj?

Shri Ramakant Maharaj (8th July 1941 to 31st August 2018) was a direct disciple of Shri Nisargadatta Maharaj (17th April 1897 to 8th September 1981) and spent 19 years with him. He was an Indian spiritual teacher of Advaita, Nonduality, and a Guru, belonging to the Inchegiri branch of the Navnath Sampradaya. He offered Initiation to this Sampradaya.

Ramakant Sawant was brought up in rural Phondaghat, Gadgesakhal Wadi. In 1965, he attended the prestigious establishment of Elphinstone College, Bombay, at the behest of Nisargadatta Maharaj. Following this, he graduated from Bombay University in 1972, (M.A in History and Politics). In 1976, he obtained his LLB qualification, from Siddhartha Law College, Bombay. He worked in banking, in the Legal Department, from 1970 until his retirement as Manager in 2000.

He was married to Anvita Sawant, also a long-standing disciple of Shri Nisargadatta Maharaj. They had two sons.

In 1962, Ramakant Maharaj was introduced by relatives to his future Guru, Shri Nisargadatta Maharaj. After spending a few months with the Master, he took the

Naam Mantra, the Guru Mantra, on 2nd October 1962. From then on he attended faithfully and listened to Nisargadatta Maharaj's discourses regularly. He was present at his Master's *Mahasamadhi* on 8th September 1981.

For over a decade, at the Ashram in Nashik Road, (Nashik, Maharashtra), Shri Ramakant Maharaj introduced students, disciples and devotees from around the world to these teachings and, on occasion, initiated them into the Inchegiri Navnath Sampradaya Lineage. About his life, Maharaj used to say, "I know my past and where I have come from. I am a miracle. All thanks to my Master, Shri Nisargadatta Maharaj".

Shri Ramakant Maharaj attained *Mahasamadhi* on 31st August 2018.

"It is by the Grace of my Master Shri Nisargadatta Maharaj, that I am sharing this Knowledge with you, the same Knowledge He shared with me."

Shri Ramakant Maharaj

2012

July – When we bought our *Finca*, comprising of 12 acres of land, and a cottage in Spain, Charles said, "I feel as if I've died and gone to heaven!" We were now free to live "the dream", the simple life, away from civilization, without electricity, gazing at the stars, just being and abiding. That said, our real intention was to awaken from the "long dream of life", meditate, contemplate and fully absorb the Teachings of Shri Nisargadatta's Lineage, the "Inchegiri Navnath Sampradaya".

As often happens in life, things do not work out according to plan. It looks like we came to Spain at the wrong time of year! The grass is growing fast and the sun is belting down. The dream is quickly turning into a mini-nightmare. We decide to let the sheep take over the grass-cutting and return to the UK for a few months, planning to come back in the cooler weather.

Beginning of October – We return to Spain for a long and serious Retreat. We are currently reading Shri Siddharameshwar's classic, *Master of Self-Realization* (MSR). We love it, especially Part 2! It's so alive, inspiring and uplifting. Siddharameshwar was Nisargadatta's Guru.

We bring great pictures with us of the Lineage Masters and stick them on the walls of our humble cottage. It feels like they are always looking at us, inside us, and following us around. We both experience strong energy coming from the images, especially from Nisargadatta and Siddharameshwar. We ease into a rhythm of reading, contemplation and meditation. The Presence of the Masters is very strong, sometimes, even emitting a fizzing or sizzling sound!

22nd November – Magical things are happening in our cottage. Whenever we light a fire, the flames take various fascinating forms. We can see the Masters dancing in the fire, as well as divine shapes, like figures bowing and various other prayerful poses. Today is the second time we have seen the "*OM*" symbol emerging from the fire!

We are scribbling lots of phrases from the "MSR" book on the walls. One wall is already covered with Nisargadatta quotes from our previous stay.

December – It's Thursday! I had read that in India, Thursday is regarded as "Guru day" and, therefore, auspicious. It is today! Charles had been out for a walk this afternoon at the other end of the field when suddenly, he came running towards me with tears in his eyes. "What's wrong?" I ask, "Nothing is wrong!", he replies. He is crying with joy, telling me he has just seen Siddharameshwar who raised his hand and blessed him. We start jumping up and down like children, laughing aloud… so very happy, happy!

I feel we are being called to go to India. Last night, I had a dream where Siddharameshwar appeared and offered me flowers in abundance. Both of us seeing Siddharameshwar on the same day is to be taken as an important sign, a calling – at least, that's what I think!

Today I say the same thing I'd been saying to Charles for more than 20 years: "We need a Guru". Whenever I said "We need a Guru", he always said, "No, we don't". And then I said, "Yes we do!", and so it went on, and on! Maybe now, after seeing Siddharameshwar, he will finally relent. I hope and pray! (Interestingly, over 20 years ago, Charles sketched a drawing of a Guru/Master who appeared in a dream. And 10 years ago, a Vedic astrologer predicted he would meet his Guru within the next decade!)

2013

January – Our *Finca* is the perfect place for *sadhana*/practice. We are off the grid. Life is simple! Here, all we need is food, water, exercise for the body, and study and meditation for the Spirit.

We read that Nisargadatta only knew his Guru, Siddharameshwar, for three years but that touch or transmission was more than enough, for Nisargadatta who was ripe. We also read that the instructions he received included devotion to his Guru, as well as the singing of *bhajans*/devotional songs, four times a day. All the disciple needs is faith in his Guru. The Guru's words are true. Nisargadatta often said: "My Guru told me I am Ultimate Reality, therefore, I am Ultimate Reality" – end of story!

We discuss how, in the various Nisargadatta books to date, references to his Guru are hardly mentioned. The concept of "devotion" is almost completely omitted. This is probably intentional to avoid discouraging readers – but then again, maybe not! Western seekers are interested in knowledge. They are not interested in, or know little, about devotion! We have an inkling that devotion is essential to bring the knowledge down, from the head to the heart. As we remain ignorant of the way devotion is expressed in this lineage, we just follow our inner promptings.

February – We start the day with our usual bows and prostrations, in front of the pictures of the Masters, thanking them for life, and asking them to bless the day. This is followed by meditation, before going out "to play" in the field. In this landscape, we feel like children, free and spontaneous. Today, after climbing to the top of the hill, and seeing Portugal in the distance, we stop for a picnic. We eat a simple fare: freshly baked bread and butter with fresh strawberries! As the heavenly food infuses the senses, it feels like the first taste ever! Big doses of innocent laughter echo through the mountains. In this beautiful space that has been gifted to us, we are taught how to appreciate the simple things in life. And from our eagle's perch, we see more clearly how, sometimes, we take things too seriously! When I forget that I am an illusion, Charles reminds me, and vice versa! We help each other with the practice of discarding illusory concepts. When either one of us gets caught up in illusory thoughts, we remind each other, saying, "Alert, alert!", often quoting Nisargadatta: "Everything perceivable and conceivable is nothing but an illusion".

March-April – What a beautiful spring! Everything is fresh on both the outside and the inside… not that there is an outside and inside! Everything is just space. We feel renewed and invigorated after our period of sweet isolation. However, even though we both agree that now we have more clarity than ever before, we still feel that something is missing. We know what that something is…. While reading the various Nisargadatta books, we kept coming across references to the "*Naam Mantra*". We need to receive the *Naam Mantra*. I feel it in my bones, and I'm certain it is going to help us. While I'm not sure how, I have a strong, gut feeling that it will!

May – We return to the UK at the beginning of May before the temperature starts to rise. As soon as we arrive home, we hang the pictures of our Masters - our faithful travelling companions - back on the walls, in their usual place. Many years ago, we put all our books to good use for loft insulation. We had finished with books, apart from the lineage ones! And now it looks like we have reached a point where we both feel we have done enough reading, including the lineage books!

As the days pass by, we experience intense energy emanating from the Masters' pictures. Some days, I can see Siddharameshwar and Nisargadatta coming out of the pictures, and approaching me closer and closer, before they dissolve into this formless form.

June – We continue with our silent meditation, at times wondering if we are making any progress! It doesn't feel like it some days. It is often said that the Guru/Master will appear when the disciple is ripe. We feel ripe and ready. Charles often said that there must be a living disciple of Nisargadatta … but where? We search online again, looking for disciples of Nisargadatta, but we don't find anything. It is said that the Master will find us and not the other way around. We hope he finds us very soon! We long for a Master!

July – We contact a devotee of Shri Ranjit Maharaj, (Shri Nisargadatta's co-disciple of Shri Siddharameshwar Maharaj). He informs us of a long-standing disciple of Nisargadatta, currently teaching in Nashik. His name is "Ramakant Maharaj". Again, we start jumping up and down with pure joy! Yes! Yes! At long last, we have found a Guru, a Master! We feel we have struck gold.

15th July – Now that we have a phone number, we are getting closer and closer. Finally, finally, after searching for a Guru for years, it is happening, our time has come! Charles phones, and Ramakant answers. He tells him we are looking for a direct disciple of Nisargadatta. Ramakant says, "I was with my Master,

Nisargadatta, for nearly 20 years!" We cannot believe our good fortune. Ramakant suggests we Skype tomorrow. That's cool! He is a hip guru! We are feeling very excited, but slightly nervous. What is he going to be like? How will he be dressed? What should we wear?

16ᵗʰ July – It is Tuesday morning, the BIG DAY! Maharaj will call us at 4 pm. We remind each other: "When the disciple is ready, the Guru appears". So, we are ready! My heart is longing to see and hear my Guru, my Master, but my gut is making me sick with nerves. Charles is feeling anxious as well. He tells me he has a big knot in his stomach!

Tuesday afternoon – Shri Ramakant appears on time! He looks normal, wearing a simple white dhoti. There are no frills. He may look ordinary, but his Presence is powerful. His energy is very light. He has a beautiful smile and radiates kindness and warmth. We feel the same way about him as Jean Dunn felt about Nisargadatta, when she saw him for the first time: "Loved him on sight!"

I try to impress him, saying, "I've always known that there is an underlying reality". Maharaj quickly steps in, "Who has always known?" I find myself momentarily lost for words, dumbstruck. After a pause, I say, "I don't know", smiling. The Master smiles back, affectionately.

He asks us which books we have read? We say, "a whole library". And then, he asks: "What is your conclusion after all your reading?" Drumming up a little courage, I say: "I am God!" The Master smiles approvingly, but then adds, "Yes! But we don't say it!" (I am unsure if I had given the "right" answer!) He tells us that we need to forget about all the book knowledge, that his approach is "direct knowledge" – from the "invisible speaker" to the "invisible listener", (from Presence to Presence).

Shri Ramakant starts talking about how people come to spirituality because they are afraid of death. Charles interrupts him, saying, "No! We are not afraid of death", so, the Master does not pursue this line further. We explain that our interest in spirituality grew from a passion, drive and need to find Truth. We had been searching for truth all our lives, separately, before we met, and after that, together. We tell him that our search is over, but we wish to stabilize and be established in Truth.

We bring up the subject of the *Naam Mantra* and ask if we can receive it? Maharaj says: "Come here to Nashik, and you will be initiated". It was a short session but we feel very happy, and think he is lovely! He tells us that he spent many years with Nisargadatta and we feel the deep love he has for his Master, as he speaks about him with great tenderness. He says we will Skype again next week.

We swam towards the Guru, and he cast his net! The fisherman had just caught two fish. We are happy to be caught. Finally, we are trapped! He is not going to let us go! We will not be able to wriggle out of Shri Ramakant's net, nor do we have any wish to escape from it. He can chop off our heads, cut us up into little pieces, and devour us, so that we can be like him, a part of him, and eventually, become one with Him!

After the call, we both feel very elevated. We like his fresh approach, his spontaneous talking and how he manages to convey powerful truth, using few words.

Maharaj has agreed to give us the *Naam Mantra* when we go to India! Our nerves have settled down and in their place, there is deep peace. Today is a momentous day: we both know we have found our Guru, our Master!

Tuesday, following week – The scary ego is back! There is the same feeling of nerves that surfaced before our first Skype call with Maharaj: We both feel a sense of dread, even a little nauseous as 4 pm approaches. Could it be that the mind/ego is afraid of this *Satsang*, this meeting in Truth, and so, it just wants to hide? It is like sitting in the dentist's waiting room, dreading the treatment that awaits and wanting to run away! But we know we must take the medicine, whether it is bitter or sweet.

Afternoon – We explain to Maharaj how we have been looking for a Master to guide us for many years, but there was no one to be found! He responds: "You are at the destination! Now is the time". He is kind and gentle, though, at times, he looks at us very sternly, as if he is looking right through us. Enthusiastically, he asks us when we are coming to Nashik? We explain that we need time to prepare. And even though he replies with an "of course", we have a strong feeling he wants us there, a.s.a.p.

Evening – Charles and I share how we feel about Maharaj's piercing gaze. It is uncomfortable, but at the same time, we know it is good for us, even a blessing. He is digging deep to see what garbage he can pull out, from under the heap of illusion. We also know he is transmitting energy to purify us. We are excited! At long last, we have found our Guru, Master and Guide who will light the way!

Months later – After weekly Skype sessions with Maharaj, we are finally preparing for our great adventure. We don't know what's going to happen, but at the same time, we know it's going to be life-changing because we have been divinely led to Maharaj. We are certain that everything that happens is meant to happen! We have been guided on our spiritual journey up until this point. No doubt about that! And now we are on the cusp! We are convinced that what awaits us will end in the culmination of our spiritual quest!

Dreams and visions of the Masters are happening more frequently, messages, too. It feels like they are calling us, beckoning us forward, encircling us, and sometimes we also hear them clapping with joy, to welcome us. Our experiences are now more intense. We are eager to travel to India, but first, we must attend to certain things, practical issues, responsibilities, etc.

We decide to go for six months. We feel very happy to have found Maharaj. We have a plan: we will go and see him first, receive the *Naam Mantra*, and then, we will continue our travels to Tiruvannamalai, where we can practise meditation in peaceful surroundings. I have always felt a strong connection to Bhagavan Ramana Maharshi, and over the years, he has appeared in dreams and during the waking state, too. I feel he has been protecting me, so, I would love to have the opportunity to prostrate to him in Tiruvannamalai, to, at long last, express my heartfelt thanks.

Tuesday – Skype session. These days, Maharaj no longer exchanges pleasantries, such as, "how are you?", or "how are your travel plans coming along?", etc. He dives right in, spontaneously teaching what we need to here at the time. He always hammers us with, "You are not the body. You were not the body. You are not going to remain the body". He is the master eraser… every concept has to be rubbed out! "I am not talking to you, I am talking to the "Invisible Listener" within you", he exclaims. His approach and teachings are so direct that we will be able to absorb them quickly. He leaves no room for the mind to play with words, as he uses vocabulary that is fresh and disarming to the mind. Our identity is, he says, "invisible, anonymous, unidentified". His teachings are beautiful and powerful!

This evening, we talk about Maharaj for a long time. We are convinced he will show us how to be liberated, permanently, from our small, false, egoic selves. We have complete faith in him! Today, he said, "I am removing the ash, so the fire can burn", meaning he is helping us to remove the layers of illusion that are covering our true nature.

Maharaj is very dear to us. He has already captured our hearts. Everything is falling into place, not through our efforts, but by his grace. All we need do is be earnest, determined and courageous.

We summarize what we have grasped so far from our "Skype Conferences" (as Maharaj likes to call them), and write it all down on a big sheet of paper, headed, "10 Point Teaching":

Summary

1. You are not the body. You were not the body. You are not going to remain the body.
2. There is nothing but Selfless Self. No God, no *Atman*, no *Paramatman*. You are That.
3. Your Presence is Spontaneous and the world is the Spontaneous Projection of your Spontaneous Presence.
4. Your Identity is an invisible, anonymous, unidentified identity.
5. You are prior to beingness - meaning the Stateless State, where there is no language, no concepts, no body, no knowledge, no nothing. You are like the sky.
6. Everything is an illusion. To erase the ego we need to listen, hear the knowledge, recite the *Naam Mantra* and sing the *bhajans*.
7. Listening to the Master. He is sharing Knowledge of our Reality which needs to be absorbed.
8. Spirit does not know itself, but it can through the body-form.
9. The fear of death disappears when you know you are unborn. Suffering disappears when the illusory "I" dissolves.
10. After liberation, there is complete happiness without any material cause. Devotion continues.

We are about to leave behind our familiar life with its daily routines and embark on a journey into the unknown. Although we both enjoy the sunshine and usually spend the winters in Spain, now the time has come to uncover the true Sun that shines, permanently, within us!

We both feel strongly connected to Maharaj. Maybe we knew him in a previous existence! We do not believe in reincarnation, but our gut says we have a connection. When we met him for the first time, we both felt as if we had always known him. It was the same when Charles and I met: we were instantly aware of, and in tune with, an eternal bond. More than thirty years ago, we even said to each other: "Where have you been all these years? I have been looking for you". We had both been in previous, challenging relationships which had intermittently interrupted and disturbed the spiritual flow.

On our own, we had not been doing so well, as far as functioning in the world, and climbing the career ladder were concerned. But spiritually, we had both continued searching, Self-enquiring, meditating and following a spiritual path. At the same time, we confessed to feeling weak, succumbing to various diversions along the way, and maybe not making much progress. But when we met, (or met again!), everything changed! We knew that, together we could, and would, reach the pinnacle of the spiritual mountain.

October – Tuesday Skype. It is only 2 weeks now before we leave for India! Yo! We are feeling Maharaj's Presence strongly. What is it going to be like when we meet? Explosive, I guess! Today I told Maharaj: "Your energy is very strong!" Immediately, he dismissed my comment, saying, "There is no 'my' or 'your' energy. There is only one energy. There is no difference between you and me, except for these bodies!" Maharaj echoed Nisargadatta's frequently used statement: "Except for Selfless Self there is no God, no *Atman*, no *Brahman*, no *Paramatman*, no Master". We had read all the Nisargadatta books and found it strange, that we had never come across this quote! Maybe it had been omitted, or had not been translated accurately, from the Marathi language. When we told Maharaj we were excited and really looking forward to meeting him, he beamed his beautiful smile at us.

Charles is getting anxious about health issues. We had been to India before, mainly on holidays to Kerala and a visit to Bodh Gaya, (to attend a "*Phowa*" course on "Death and Dying"). Also, many years before, we had travelled to "see a Seer" and visit a famous Vedic astrologer, (who revealed many things, including the fascinating information that we had been married twice before!) Fortunately, we did not fall ill during those trips.

Now Charles is beginning to think that maybe he/we might get sick this time. Are we pushing our luck? I reassure him that the Masters will protect us, and that maybe, what is really going on is that he is trying to wriggle out of meeting Maharaj. He is experiencing a fit of the jitters! When I ask him if this could be what the anxiety is about, initially, he is in denial, but later on, he admits to maybe being a little scared. "Who is scared? You don't exist!" On hearing my words, he bursts out laughing and the fear subsides.

I reassure him that nothing untoward or harmful is going to happen. Soon after, his enthusiasm is reignited. Thank goodness! I am feeling a strong pull from Maharaj but know I can't travel to India on my own. I would not feel safe. So, by hook or by crook, I will take Charles by the hand, dragging him there if necessary, lol!

We can't let these worries about our bodily health deter us. As long as we see the Master first, then everything will be ok… and then, if we happen to fall ill, it won't matter. Nothing at all will matter after that! I have been looking for a Guru for years. So what if we get sick in India, at least we will have met our Guru and truly met our Self!

"Charles, are you listening to me? No more excuses! We must meet our Guru. Everything has led us to this point of travelling to India, to be in the Presence of Ramakant Maharaj".

"Look, Ann, I know we must. It is just the big hassle of going to India that bothers me, and the risks", he replies.

Tuesday – Our last Skype with Maharaj! "We will see you in 3 days", we exclaim. Maharaj eagerly says, "Yes, yes! Have a safe journey!" He gives us a taxi number to call from Mumbai Airport that will take us to Nashik.

October – Finally, we arrive in Nashik and are greeted by Maharaj and his wife, Anvita, who are both smiling. Instantly, we feel his great power! Maharaj exclaims: "Maurice Frydman and Jean Dunn have arrived! I have been waiting for you!", he says, cryptically. Then he teases Charles, asking him if he is older than him? Charles is taken aback, and half-laughing, denies it, saying, "I am only sixty-four!" Maharaj chuckles, then suggests that we have a look at the Ashram accommodation. If we find the room suitable, we can stay there, and if not, he will find us a hotel. At his home, we learn that Anvita and Maharaj have been looking after her father for the last ten years. After a short while, she leaves us to attend to him. Maharaj tells us to follow him into the kitchen, where he starts chopping some vegetables. They make a good team!

Our room is situated above the ashram. It is small and basic but sufficient for our needs. Maharaj tells us to, "take rest". We are exhausted after our travels and the long flight. It is about 11 am. He instructs us to come downstairs to attend the *bhajans*, and then listen to his discourse at 5.30 pm! After he leaves, we fall asleep until the next morning!

The next day, still jet-lagged, after an hour or so, we go downstairs to meet Maharaj. He does not look too pleased at all, and asks us why we had not attended the *bhajans* the night before? I tell him the truth, that we were sleeping. It wasn't so much that he was annoyed we had missed the *bhajans*, but that he was eager for us to start listening to his discourses!

It's our second day in Nashik, and we miss the early morning *bhajans* again. We will return at 11.30 am to listen to Maharaj talking. We still feel a little like two scolded children. We know we will have to behave, or else, get on the wrong side of the Master again. Once is enough! Lovely as he is, Maharaj can be quite stern. He had explained to us before on Skype, that everything is an illusion, and that all our concepts are illusory, including sleep! But concept or not, we are not youngsters anymore! We have just endured a 13-hour flight from the UK, and are still jet-lagged and exhausted! Surely, he can understand that! For a brief moment, we feel as if we have entered some kind of strict army camp. Finally, we stop complaining, laugh about it all, and have breakfast. We eat the cereal we brought with us, as we are not yet ready to face an Indian-style breakfast.

11.30 am - We enter the small, humble ashram with huge energy and sit down. Someone is reading, no, it is more like chanting, from the *Dasbodh*, a sacred text, for half an hour, while everyone else remains quiet. The large pictures of the Masters are imposing. In contrast, the altar is a delicate, humble affair. In the centrepiece, there is a small statue of Nisargadatta's Master, Shri Siddharameshwar, wearing a beautiful golden outfit. He is in his usual pose, often depicted in pictures, with his legs crossed, holding a cigarette.

I do not understand a word of the chanting, as it is in the Marathi language, but I am still strangely touched by the vibrations. At one point, when I open my eyes to look at the pictures of the Masters, suddenly, Shri Bhausaheb Maharaj appeared to fly out of the picture. He is standing right in front of me! The message he conveys is, "Welcome back!" before quickly disappearing. I am left somewhat shaken, and still trying to decipher the message when, suddenly, everyone stands up to sing. I notice Charles has fallen asleep - Maharaj won't like that - so I start coughing loudly to wake him up. He gets the message and rises from the chair! The sound of the *bhajans* is very uplifting and transporting, even though we haven't a clue what they are singing about.

Maharaj sits in his big armchair, ready to talk. A few Indian devotees gather on the floor close to him. Maharaj tells us to bring over a couple of chairs, as we are not used to sitting on the floor. We appreciate his thoughtfulness! He wants us to be comfortable.

Maharaj states: "You have come here because you want to know the Reality. Correct?" We nod. "What is Reality? Here we give commando training. (We smile at each other, thinking "so it is an army training camp after all!") By listening to these discourses, meditating and singing the *bhajans*, all the garbage will be cleared out. In our lineage, we give a Mantra, the *Naam Mantra*, which will help you forget everything".

This is the first time we hear Maharaj speak in Nashik! Here is the amazing discourse:

"**Maharaj**: If you are strongly dedicated, it is not difficult to absorb the teachings. This external identity is not going to remain constant. Conviction is essential for spirituality. Some Spirit is there, through which we are talking. Some power is there, working. We are looking, we are hearing, all the activities are for the body. Some power is there, some strength is there, some Spirit is there, just like electricity. It is invisible, anonymous and unidentified. It is "That" with which we feel, without which, you cannot utter a single word, without which, you cannot raise your hand. Without its power, there can be no movement. That Spirit is called *Brahman*, *Atman*, *Paramatman*, God, *Parabrahman*. We have created these words. What is the content of the Spirit? It is not your death or your birth... just that, just that!

What remains after the death of the body? There is no experience, no experiencer, no knowledge, there is nothing. Simple, simple! What remains after the disappearance of the body? Nothing! Everything comes out of nothing and everything dissolves back into nothing. Out of nothing, there appears to be something. They are interrelated. We are using some words, just for conversation

We have to have the conviction that, "I am totally unconcerned with the world". There are all these relations, conditions, sensations, expectations and needs. These are all bodily related things. All body-related! But, "I am totally unconcerned with the world".

We want peace. Who does? We want happiness and more happiness. Who wants that? We want a tension-free life. A tension-free life, happiness, peace, we did not know about any of these things prior to beingness. They came along with the body. They are bodily requirements, not Spirit's requirements. The body will dissolve one day. We fear that, because of our attachment to it! No one wants death. Everyone is afraid of death. But when you come to know the Truth about death, there will be no fear.

There is the story of the rope and the snake. You are afraid of the snake. As a matter of fact, there is no snake, it is a rope. Similarly, we are afraid of death. Who is dying? Who is taking birth? When you realize nobody is taking birth or dying, you will be totally unconcerned, totally indifferent. This Presence is spontaneous, just like the sky. Out of Presence, the entire world is projected – a merging takes place. Without Presence, we cannot see the world, we cannot see anything. That anonymous, that invisible, unidentified identity has been called by many different names, *Parabrahman*, *Brahman*, *Atman*, etc., for which there is no death or birth and no need of salvation. The question of heaven and hell never arises. There is no *prarabdha* (the concept of accumulated deeds from previous incarnations, brought into the present life as *karma*), no religion. These are all body related attachments. 'This and that' - all have to do with the bodily state.

Prior to the body form, there was nothing there. Prior to beingness, to whom did these individual names belong? Religions and the principle of religion were formed just to stimulate a peaceful life. It is ok, but more importantly, you must know the secret of your life, the gist of your life. Understand and realize what it means! Only then, will you be completely fearless. You should ask yourself, "Why should I fear death when it is the same for everybody?" You say, "I can't escape from the concept of death". Find out, who is dying? Who is living? Just self-enquire. Nobody is dying, nobody is taking birth. We're thinking from the point of view of the body-mind, blindly accepting all these concepts, these illusory concepts, such as man or woman, this religion or that religion, last birth, next birth, present birth, rebirth… so many concepts! They are all illusions!

We've blindly signed and accepted all these illusions. You have not committed any crime, yet you sign, "I am a criminal". (The understanding here is that you are guilty of accepting a false identity, ie, as an individual person. You have taken your mind/body complex for real…unknowingly, this has made you a criminal in your acceptance of the false, the untrue.) The Masters say you have not committed any crime. The Master makes you enlightened. You were never a criminal, you are not a criminal.

Your Master is your reflection. As a matter of fact, there is no Master and no disciple because the sum total of this existence is a dream. All this is a dream which has come out of bodily relations, which you are not, which you were not, and which you are not going to remain, (ie, you never existed). So, how do you get rid of the body-based illusion? By knowing that you are the architect of your own life and realizing this life is a long dream! For example, say you are acting in a drama/movie as the hero, the heroine or the villain. While you are acting, you know better! For a few hours, two or three hours, you know you are playing a role. "I am playing my role, but there is no connection to that role". Similarly, we are acting out different roles, (these concepts) as a man or a woman, and accepting them without question. It, (Reality) has nothing to do with all these concepts.

You are unborn. To know this deeply, you have to undergo a basic discipline. Here, the same principle is placed before you, using different words, different ways, different angles and different dimensions.

Q: In order to hammer home the truth?

Maharaj: Yes! The message is the same: "Except your Selfless Self there is no God, no *Atman*, no *Brahman*, no *Paramatman*." That is the message, the only message. To establish that truth, we use some examples, just like when you tell a child a story, and place before them the principle of the story. If you want to convey something, you have to put it into story form. The mother or father puts it into a story form and then explains the principle of the story. Likewise, here, the Master is placing before you the Ultimate Truth in story form, using certain words and language.

Once the Conviction arises, you will know what to do, or not to do, because you know your Selfless Self best. Conviction, enlightenment or realization means becoming one with the Final Truth: "I was never born. Why fear death?" There is no fear. Fear is a concept. You are afraid because you think you are somebody. Here we are hammering you with Reality. This is direct hammering!

Q: Sometimes, one can listen and maybe not hear what is being said, and then at another time, when one listens, suddenly, there is an emphatic "Yes", a click of understanding!

Maharaj: The invisible listener within you is listening quietly and calmly. Reality is engraved in the invisible listener. It cannot be removed. Perhaps you are not aware, you may not understand some things, but the silent listener is accepting it all, just like a recorder. Silently, the process of recording is going on, the process of analyzing is going on, without your knowledge. There is no ego, no intellect, no mind, too. These are all external layers.

Q: They try to block...

Maharaj: You can use them, they're not bad. If you wish, you can use them, but do not become their slaves. Excessive use of anything is poison. Excessive use of anything will be poisonous. If you take too much food, it is poison.

Q: Too much mind...

Maharaj: There is no mind at all! [Laughter] This is exceptional knowledge. This is Reality. It's not bookish knowledge. It's not literal knowledge. It is beyond everything, beyond knowledge, everything, beyond imagination. It is your knowledge. Nisargadatta Maharaj used to say, "the way you were prior to beingness, remain as it is". You are unaware of anything. You do not know anything.

It is like that. So, how were you prior to beingness? There was no knowledge. You were totally unaware of everything. You did not know anything. After manifestation, you started learning and knowing so many things. Therefore, the mind is body-based knowledge. What remains? The food body. Some day or other, willingly or unwillingly, you will have to leave the body. It's not your identity."

Halfway through the discourse, Charles and I look at each other, smiling, with a discreet, eye-popping expression that communicated: "This Talk is mind-blowing!"

Maharaj carries on a little longer, then looks up at the clock. It is time to eat! He asks us if we have any questions, and we tell him, "No!" He tells us to return at 5.30 pm for the evening *bhajans* and another Talk.

We are stunned by what we have just heard. Elated! We have four hours or so, to eat and rest, before returning for the evening *bhajans*. We know we have made the right decision to come here, even though it may resemble an army training camp! We have never heard such simple, direct, spontaneous, non-intellectual knowledge, transmitted before. Feeling blessed, we strongly feel this is the beginning of the end… the end of the beginning – without beginning, without end. We have reached the full stop! We are excited to hear Maharaj mentioning the *Naam Mantra*. That's what we are here for!

In the evening, we go to the ashram early, to make a good impression. The ladies are dressed in traditional saris. I am wearing a pair of loose white trousers, and a loose-fitting long top, which I think is appropriate, until one lady gives me the "evil eye". She looks at me from top to bottom with some disdain! I am the only western lady there. Sheepishly, I join them at the back of the hall. Ladies to the right and gentlemen to the left!

Maharaj enters, taking the utmost care to stop to bow at, all the pictures of the Masters, arranging the flowers on the way, with love and devotion. Anvita has kindly given us a couple of books, so we can sing the *bhajans*. The *bhajans* have been poorly translated into English, but at least now, we can follow them, as they have been written phonetically. There is a very old lady here who is smiling at me, and I mean, very old. However, when she starts to sing with such strength of devotion, she appears completely ageless!

As the *bhajans* continue, I experience a kind of flashback. There seems to be a recognition, a familiarity with some of them. And then, as I am singing, an intuition arises that I was part of the "*Navnath Sampradaya*" (which evolved from the "*Nath*"), many years before, when it existed more as a semi-closed, kind of esoteric sect. This is a bizarre consideration, but somehow, it rings true!

After the *bhajans*, Maharaj gives a short Talk. It is wonderful! Though, at the end of it, all we can remember is what Maharaj said at the beginning: "Master plants the plant of Reality in your Selfless Self". We don't try to remember. We know the seed has been planted!

I tell Charles that I recognize some of the *bhajans*. He says, that maybe I lived at the time of Shri Bhausaheb. I wasn't sure at first, as I did not feel any connection to him. In the last few years, I felt strongly connected to Nisargadatta and his Master, Siddharameshwar, but even though we had pictures of Bhausaheb next to them, I did not "sense" him. However, I am still feeling overwhelmed at what happened this morning, when Bhausaheb came towards me to welcome me back! Hopefully, clarity will come. Both exhausted, Charles sets the alarm for 5 am for our next commando training drill! We quickly fall asleep.

Sunday evening – It is an effort to get up so early, (especially when you are used to long Spanish *siestas* and *manana* - when "tomorrow" means nothing gets done for weeks!) We just make it downstairs on time! The ashram is packed - maybe because it's a Sunday. There are a few musicians here today, too. We self-consciously walk to the back of the ashram and find a spot.

Sunday evenings resemble social gatherings for the locals, where whole families get together. The musicians are there and the atmosphere is electric. We look at each other across the hall as time passes, and then we look at the clock. Exhausted, as usual, we wonder if it is ever going to end! We started at 5.30 pm and it is nearly 8 pm now! It feels like we are singing the same *bhajans* for a second round. (It turns out that we were!) After the session finishes, we see Maharaj pointing to us. He is telling a few devotees that we have travelled a great distance to meet him. He says, "Now two people have come who have a lot of knowledge!" We hear someone asking if England is close to Russia!

At the end of the *bhajans*, everyone lines up to bow before the pictures of the Masters, starting with Gurulingajangam Maharaj, then Bhausaheb, Nisargadatta, Siddharameshwar and Ranjit Maharaj: Then, one by one, we bow at the feet of Maharaj.

Bowing at his feet feels intensely sacred, holy, a privilege, yet at the same time, immensely scary because I question whether, in the face of the Absolute, I am humble enough to do so. I kneel down, and with the lightest touch, place my fingers lightly, on only one or two toes of His Holy Feet. I feel this is all I dare do at the moment. Maybe in time, "I" will become more courageous!

After the session, everyone wants to speak with Maharaj. There are also some ladies holding up their children for blessings. Maharaj is so patient and generous with his time, letting them chat for as long as they wish.

At last, we can crawl into bed. An exhausted Charles says, "I didn't come here for all this! I'm nearly a pensioner! This is ridiculous. We are not getting any free time!" I agreed, then reassured him, saying, "I know, but as soon as we receive the *Naam*, we will go elsewhere and relax… take things at our own pace". "I hope so!" he replies.

Monday – We get through the early morning session, and then listen attentively, to another Talk:

"**Maharaj**: Any questions?

Q: Maharaj, can you tell me a little about how you came to meet Nisargadatta Maharaj?

Maharaj: In 1962, I was staying with relatives. At that time, I was staying with my sister. I was unemployed, searching for work and in a little bit of poverty. So my sister said, "You are sitting here idle, come with me to see Maharaj". I wasn't sure about it at the time, but this is how it happened that I came to Nisargadatta Maharaj.

In those days, he did not give you the Mantra immediately. He used to observe you, to see how much devotion you had. So, after going to Maharaj's home, sitting on the floor, and doing meditation in the name of some God, about one month later, Nisargadatta Maharaj gave me the *Naam Mantra*, the Guru Mantra.

Subsequently, he came to know that I was very poor, that I had no job, so, he asked everyone and anyone, if they had a job for this "poor boy". He was just like a father asking for help on my behalf. When I got a temporary job for 3 or 4 days, he suggested I should have a bank account, and so he opened one for me. He also purchased a watch for me. His actions felt like parental love and affection. I continued to go every day - morning and evening. I was not able to understand what he was talking about because it was beyond me, but he used to say "listen to me, listen to me", and I did. He also helped by giving me many encouraging tips, and like that, slowly, silently, slowly, silently, I absorbed that knowledge to some extent. About 10 years later, on reflection, I came to know what he had been saying. And then, I took a job in a bank and got married.

When Nisargadatta came to my house, he would often say, "knowledge is part of you". He used to deliver lectures every day at 6.30 pm and then at 7.30 am. He was a very simple and straightforward, down-to-earth character. I changed my job so many times, starting my employment career at only one rupee. Back then, I used to walk 10 kilometres for 1 rupee. The only reason I am mentioning this is to impart knowledge, so that you know the importance of struggle and the vital role it plays. To struggle in life is very important - it is not easy, but in order to struggle, what is demanded is total involvement, you must have strong involvement. Likewise, you must struggle to know: "I want to know myself! I want to know who I am?". I keep telling people that casual involvement, casual spirituality, will not do, it won't work!

You must be driven. You must want to know the secret of "Who am I?" "Am I just a body?" As a child, some thoughts had arisen like, "Where was I prior to my birth?" This was around the age of 8/9 and 10. Some thoughts appeared, but answers were not forthcoming. So like that, you have to struggle and search within yourself. Then, finally, with true knowledge, real knowledge, the search will truly be over.

We are looking, trying to find answers outside of ourselves, yet the finder is the Self, the Ultimate Truth. What I am saying is very subtle. We identify with the body. We have a lot of attachment to the body, a lot of affection and attachment, even though we know the body is not going to survive for a long time. Everybody knows that! Yet still, we continue to go here and there, till the Spirit leaves, till this body cannot live any longer and is burnt like some common, ordinary material object.

The body is only alive because of the Spirit, the Power, the Energy which is called *Brahman*, *Atman*, *Paramatman*, God. Knowledge means just to know yourself in a real sense - that you are Ultimate Truth. I will repeat it again. Knowledge means just to know oneself in a real sense. Up until now, we have only known ourselves as body-forms. The body-form needs to dissolve completely. Knowledge must be absorbed. I was not a body, I am not a body, I am not going to remain as a body. It's the truth, the naked truth, open truth known by everyone, yet still, we prefer to ignore this truth. Every day we hear of so many people dying, true? One day, it will be your body that expires, so, wake up!

There should not be any kind of ego, like saying, "I have got a lot of knowledge, I am a spiritual master", etc. All of your knowledge will disappear with death, so what is the use of that knowledge? I ask the same question to many people who come here. They will say: "I have read this book, I have read that book. I have read this thing, I know *Vedanta*". So, I always ask this simple question: "For all your knowledge, lots of knowledge, will that knowledge help you when it's time to leave your body?" It is a simple question for you to address. You have a great deal of knowledge and imagination. You are a master of knowledge. But is that knowledge going to help you when the body is about to expire? And if it won't, then, what is the use of all that knowledge?

Say, you have a million pounds, but if the notes are fake, then what is their value? If you have one hundred pounds, these notes should be marketable, convertible. Similarly, your knowledge is meant to be marketable. It should help you know deeply, that "I'm not dying" when you leave the body. That way, there will be no fear of death around. "Death and birth only happen to the body, not to me!" This conviction is most important. And for that conviction to be established, you have to undergo a process of meditation, etc.

Accumulating knowledge is very easy. If you read many books, you can deliver lectures. It won't be difficult at all if you have the desire to impress others. And they will bow down to you, "oh great master", and you will be thrilled!

[Maharaj chuckles] But, ask yourself this most vital question: "Will the knowledge I have be useful when I leave my body?". This is the real test! Find out if the proof is in the pudding! There should not be any fear of dying, like "Oh, what will I do!" The fearless state at the time of death is real knowledge, pragmatic knowledge. That is Ultimate Truth. Knowing and being at one with Ultimate Truth, Ultimate Reality means there will be complete peace, causeless peace.

Generally, the three causes or sources of happiness in human life are publicity/power, money and sex. There are so many people going after publicity, that they will do anything to be famous. It is the same for money and sex. They will even kill for these. These are the three things from which human beings are trying to extract happiness and peace. But who is enjoying that peace? "Oh I am", you will say, but, that happiness is temporary, based on a material cause.

No material cause whatsoever is required for happiness and peace. There can be spontaneous happiness, spontaneous peace - without money, sex, publicity – just *Om Shanti*. This peace is not artificial, but spontaneous peace, with no worries, no tension. Why have tension? It is only because we have some degree of bodily attachment, that we have tension.

Nisargadatta Maharaj used to say that if it wasn't for his Master, Siddharameshwar Maharaj, coming into his life, he would have remained a common man, aimlessly running here and there. There is respect for the Guru, the Master. Saint Kabir says, "If my Master and God appear before me, I would give respect to my Master, for it is only because of Him, that I know God. Therefore you must give importance to the Master, the Guru. The Master is God's God. The Master is God's God".

You can see the lineage there, (Maharaj points to the pictures of the Masters, Bhausaheb Maharaj, Siddarameshwar Maharaj, Nisargadatta Maharaj, Ranjit Maharaj). They were ordinary people, but they had no egos whatsoever, no expectations.

If something unpleasant happens in your life, the mind grows restless and feels, "oh, something is wrong". The discipline is very easy, but, at the same time, it is very difficult because the body-based knowledge - the "food-body" knowledge must be dissolved completely. This knowledge is very simple knowledge. Your intellect will not help you because you are prior to the intellect.

How were you prior to beingness? You reply, "I don't know". You see, there is no ego, no intellect, no mind, no God, and it is only because you are in a body-form, that there appears to be a need for God. If there is "no-body", where is this God, this Master, this knowledge? This Knowledge of Reality is needed because you have forgotten your identity. I am inviting the attention of the silent, invisible, listener. I am drawing the attention of the silent, invisible listener. You are *Brahman*, you are *Atman*, you are God.

Changes will take place. It won't be difficult, with strong devotion, a strong will and a little sacrifice. This is a very important time. Every moment of your life is very, very important. Don't seek after the Ultimate Truth in a casual manner. Every day and every moment are important, so, keep it simple. Attend to your work! Be practical! Sitting idly, saying, "Oh, I am *Brahman,* I am *Brahman*" is not knowledge.

Nisargadatta Maharaj used to say, "learn something", "do something", "find out who you are".

This is the proper time for you, the right time. The ghost of fear is surrounding you, so break the vicious circle of the ghost of fear, and accept the truth: "I am not dying", "I am not born". Birth and death are only for the body, the food-body. That conviction is most important. In order to accept and deepen that conviction, a scientific process is taught.

Because of your bodily attachment and body relations, a discipline is required, a process is necessary - the reciting of the Guru Mantra. Why the Guru Mantra? Why a Master? It is a corrective procedure. At the initial stage, you have to undergo this. It is like giving a child a walker to assist him in learning to walk. After the child's legs have steadied, the walker is no longer needed. But, initially, during the first stage of meditation and concentration, there has to be self-involvement, therefore, devote some time to yourself. Out of 24 hours, take 2 hours for you, and be strict about it. Spend at least 2 hours per day on yourself.

Your life is so important, valuable and precious, but you are ignoring it. You don't know that your life has immense value. You remain unaware. The Master is directing your attention to your true identity: you are Ultimate Truth! Don't ignore it any longer! Be strict and self-disciplined! Nothing is impossible. Have courage! Nisargadatta Maharaj used to say, "After conviction, don't spend any time with undesirable people with negative influences, as they will only try to impress their own illusory thoughts on you."

I told you about a boy who came here with good knowledge of the Masters, but unfortunately, later on, he met up with his friends and his whole building collapsed!

Q: The foundations weren't strong enough?

Maharaj: The foundations must be very strong. Through meditation, you will develop unbreakable, strong foundations. People are coming with various thoughts, always trying to impress and impose their own thoughts on others. It is like the famous story of the blind group who go and see the elephant. Each blind person feels a different part… one says "oh it's just like a pillar", etc… but all of them could not see the entire elephant, the whole picture. So, it is advisable not to mix with people with "half-knowledge". The Master shows you the entire elephant, the Master places before you the Ultimate Truth, so you can "see".

When the mirror of knowledge has been given to you, you can see! But, even after such knowledge, devotees can still be distracted, due to weak foundations. I was very sorry because I had put a lot of effort into that boy. He had a sufficiently long stay here of 1 or 2 months, with daily lectures, until one day, he said – "this is not logical knowledge", and he went elsewhere.

This type of thing will happen if one's faith is not strong enough. So, what I am placing before you - you can either accept or not – it's up to you. Everyone can accept it, or not! I am sharing with you the same knowledge my Master shared with me, free of charge. You may be living anywhere in the world - in England, America or elsewhere. Wherever you are, your Presence is there. You are a Master!

You can see, verify it for yourself. It's an open fact that the body is not permanent, that some day or other, willingly or unwillingly, you will leave this body. Even if you employ the best doctors, the most you may get is to postpone death for a year or two. You must have the conviction: "I am not dying". There is no death. Nisargadatta Maharaj used to say "you are unborn". It's a fact, but at the same time, do not neglect your body. If you are ill, go to the doctor and take the prescribed medicines.

What is Conviction? It means, "I am not related to the body, prior to consciousness, prior to beingness, or after leaving the body". You are your own Master. Nisargadatta Maharaj would say, "I am not making you a disciple, I am making you a Master". Every sentence spoken by Nisargadatta Maharaj has the highest value.

When you wake up in the morning, the world is projected, so, the entire world is your spontaneous projection. It is a dream. During sleep, you dream and see everybody, as well as the sky, the moon, the ocean, so many different people. In that dream, you are acting, and the images and recordings of all the activity are captured. You are acting, but you are also sleeping, so, who is acting in that dream, who or what is capturing images of your each and every action? And, then, after coming out of that dream, what happened to all the people? Where did they go? Have they gone to hell and heaven? [Maharaj laughs] Think about it! Everything is within you. So, like that dream, this world is a dream-world, that without your

Presence, you can't even say "me", "they", etc. The entire world is the spontaneous reflection, the projection of your invisible, unidentified, anonymous identity, which you cannot see.

Don't become a victim of bookish knowledge. You can read spiritual books, but remember, the story you are reading is the reader's story, the invisible reader's story, "my story". It is not the body-mind's story. In other words, it is Final Truth, Ultimate Truth. The body is only the medium, the vehicle, like the fan on the wall which cannot work without electricity. But when the electricity starts, the fan spins. It is the spontaneous existence, invisible existence that is solely responsible for actions. It is behind every action. Without the Spirit, you can't even lift your hand. Your body is like a dead body. Without the connection to Spirit, the body is like a dead weight that will need a crane to lift it upwards.

That subtle, subtle knowledge, that Spirit, that very, very subtle Spirit, is what makes the big elephant walk. What is that power? Within you, there is exceptional power, strong power, but you are not using that power. Why go begging "Oh! Help me! Help me! Oh! Bless me, Bless me", when all the power is within you. So, without ego, make yourself realized! Self-realize! It's an open secret, open knowledge that you are ignoring.

You are searching for God somewhere else, searching for a God somewhere in the sky, who is administering the whole world. It's a concept that God is in the sky, ruling the entire world, punishing those who are doing bad things, and blessing those who are doing good. No religion is bad in itself, but the way religion is implemented by the so-called masters of religion has developed out of selfish purposes."

We love Maharaj's Talks! They are so fresh, enjoyable and unique! He uses many different analogies to convey the Ultimate Truth, sometimes employing computer language, business, medical, or financial language, as he did today!

After the Talk, Maharaj, out of the blue, announces he is going to initiate us. He asks Charles if he is ready? Charles panics and squeals, "No!" He thinks he is not ready for the execution. Lol! Then Maharaj asks me, and I shout, "Yes", enthusiastically. Charles gives me one of his disapproving looks. Anyhow, we have no choice in the matter. It is going to happen, as Maharaj has ordained it.

Maharaj tells me to wait outside of the ashram. Charles is going first! The men always come first in India! As I wait, a European lady starts chatting to me. I am curt with her, telling her I am about to be initiated and I express my wish to be quiet. She carries on yapping for a little longer until, finally, she gets the message. I am preparing myself and need to be silent. It feels like time has stopped during this waiting period. It feels as if Charles has been inside the ashram for a long, long time. Eventually, he emerges, wearing a "spaced-out smile" on his face.

It is now my turn! Maharaj explains the process. Like many others, I was worried that I would not be able to hear the *Naam Mantra* properly. I could understand the way Maharaj spoke most of the time, but I was a little anxious about not hearing it, at this incredibly special moment! What if "I don't get it"! What if "I miss it, or get it wrong!"

In a very serious tone, Maharaj states that in this lineage it is forbidden to reveal the *Naam Mantra* to anyone. I promise not to! I understand perfectly well that the initiation is sacred, to be respected and to be taken extremely seriously. Maharaj places his hand on my head and whispers the *Naam Mantra* in my ear. He tells me to bow to all the pictures of the Masters, after which he announces, "I am now your Master!" He beams one of his beautiful smiles; I grin back! Then he asks me to sit on the floor. He tells me how to practice it: with the first part of the Mantra, we inhale, and with the second, exhale. Then he tells me to start meditating with the Mantra, while he encircles me a few times. After that, Maharaj explains the requirements: a minimum of two hours per day, plus reciting the *Naam* without the breath throughout the day, like *Japa* – continuous repetition. Finally, he says: "Now you can go!" I thank him and bow.

As I open the ashram door, the thought arises, "go where?" When I step out of the door it is like stepping out into a vast universe. I feel lost and disorientated and can still feel the Master's hand on my head. Feeling unsteady on my feet, I sit down for a few minutes on one of the benches outside the ashram, before making my way back to our room. When I open the door, I find Charles chilling on the bed. All his previous anxiety and tension have melted away, and with a big smile, he asks me how it went? "Very well," I said. "It was very powerful. And you?" "Well, yes". We didn't know what to say about it, or couldn't say anything, so, we withdrew into meditation.

Thursday – "Guru Day". Many more local devotees appear on Thursdays! It has been a few days now since our initiations. With more energy, we are powering on, diligently following the 2-hour per day stipulation, and using the *Naam* throughout the day, at every available opportunity.

Today, during his Talk, Maharaj asks us how our practice is going? We tell him we are following his instructions to the letter and that we are already feeling re-energized. "Very nice", he replies. "You will both find it easy because I don't see any ego there. The *Naam Mantra* is the "*Master Key*" that will unlock the door to your Ultimate Reality".

After his discourses, Maharaj always expects us to stay behind to absorb the teachings, and all that he has conveyed. We usually meditate for about 30-40 minutes. Today I am again drawn to the picture of Shri Bhausaheb Maharaj. I feel a strong connection. As I close my eyes, I can see him clearly. Once again, he speaks to me and tells me he is happy that I have returned. Then, he communicates the following:

"You need to empty yourself completely". As the image of him vanishes, I hear his words: "Today I have prepared a pyre for you". The first thought I have is, "Oh, thank you, Master", with a little cynicism. But then, I understand that the pyre refers to the process of burning the ego, that Shri Ramakant often speaks about: the clearing away of all body-based knowledge, or the "garbage". After my initial reaction, or knee jerk, human response, I give thanks to Shri Bhausaheb.

Later on, when Charles and I are sharing and catching up with inner developments, he tells me that during today's meditation, he was amused when a set of windscreen wipers spontaneously arose. They were wiping continuously, thoroughly cleaning the very dirty windows that he was looking out of, so that he could have a clear view. His cleaning process has started as well! We both laugh at the appropriateness of the symbolism of the windscreen wipers, as Charles had been a driving instructor at one point in his life! As an artist pursuing his passion, he had to take many different jobs to simply survive!

In the afternoon, Maharaj asks us if we have any children. Charles is a little nervous about mentioning his divorce, aware that it carries a stigma in India! However, he went on to explain that he has four children from his first marriage! Maharaj exclaims, "four?" smiling, then laughing… We laugh as well. "You were a busy father!" he says. Then Maharaj turns to me and asks if I have any children? When I tell him, "No"! he smiles, saying, "Good! No attachments!"

This afternoon's Talk was dynamite! It was extra powerful as we received direct transmission of Truth. Pointing to us, Maharaj said, "You are Ultimate Reality! You are Ultimate Truth!" and the energy was, as if, transferred from his space to ours. Afterwards, I asked Charles if he felt it? He did strongly! "And did you see it?", I asked excitedly. He said that he could see the waves of energy vibrating, moving. And then, something touched his inner core. I felt the same! We meditated together for a timeless duration, both of us feeling we had gone deeper, transcending the known and reaching fresh depths.

Friday morning - Talk:

Maharaj: "There must be complete and total peace, without any material cause, inner peace. No disturbance of anything, not from the mind, the ego or the intellect. Even if the external atmosphere is not favourable and there is disturbance or chaos, the spiritual person, the enlightened, realized devotee, still has complete peace because he remains indifferent and unconcerned at all times. Total

Knowledge is absorbed in Oneness. There is no duality. Clouds are coming, clouds are going - the sun is as it is!

For that conviction, you have to undergo various processes (meditation etc.) Dry philosophical discussions will not help! We can go on discussing philosophy together, for hours and years. All you will get from that is spiritual entertainment, nothing more than that. So one should be very serious. Question yourself: "Why is there fear?" "Why am I fearing?" Why am I afraid?". Question yourself and Self-enquire. "Why am I not at peace?" Question yourself. "What is causing the disturbance of peace?", "Why am I always under tension?", "Why do I not have happiness?" Question yourself again and again. How can I get these (qualities)? There must be eagerness and a degree of concern and anxiety that is driving you forward.

After thinking and contemplating on this, someday, we will wake up and realize. We are so fortunate to have such people with direct knowledge (the lineage masters) and not roundabout knowledge. They are not talking about *Maya*, *Brahman*, *Atman*, *Paramatman*. These are just words that are totally deleted (ineffective in relation to direct knowledge). The last *prarabdha*, the future *prarabdha,* are just words. Real knowledge is within you, alone. In order to get the direct attention of the invisible listener, direct knowledge is given and attention is paid to that invisible listener, telling him, convincing him: "You are the source of happiness, you are the source of peace", not in the body-form. So, in this way, the identification with the body-form is gradually reduced, day by day. You have a lot of attachment to the body - even though we are 'spiritualists', there is a lot of attachment, love, affection for the body - that must dissolve. When it is dissolved, then you will come to know Reality. It is a known fact, open fact, open truth, Ultimate Truth, Final Truth.

Slowly, silently, and permanently, the illusory thoughts are supposed to dissolve, until they eventually vanish. It's a cleaning process, like when your laptop is crowded with unwanted files that you must delete because of a virus. This process is an anti-virus software that can control and guard, keep watch, and keep you alert. Every day, it is necessary to sweep away the dust and keep your house clean. Likewise, you have got to clean 'this house' every day, with meditation, *bhajan*, and knowledge, and then, everything will become very easy.

Devotion, extreme devotion, exceptional devotion, exceptional involvement is required. Nisargadatta Maharaj used to say, "Casual spirituality will not help you. Casual spirituality will not help you find complete peace". You see, everything is within you, but you are unaware, and instead, you go searching here and there. You go finding here and there. You have forgotten the "Finder". The Finder is the source of this world. But that Finder is invisible, anonymous and cannot be defined by words. Liberation is possible, but you must have strong faith and courage. There will be difficulties. When you are living a human life, many difficulties are bound to be there. But despite the difficulties, you must have complete faith - perfect foundations, strong foundations.

This direct knowledge is very simple knowledge, uncomplicated. There is no need to go here and there and read tons of books. That will only make you more and more confused. By all means, read books, but don't become addicted to the words. People are asking, "What is the meaning of this word? Some say it like this, some say it like that, etc.", when what is most important is understanding what the teachers are trying to convey - the principle. What is the principle? When you are reading a story, find out what the principle of the story is! If you are reading entire books of knowledge, find out what they are trying to convey?

You are not in words. You are not in books. You are not to be found in books. You are your own teacher. You are your own guide, the architect of your own life. So, see your Selfless Self! How? With the "Master Key", the magic key that has been given to you. It is a magic key, a secret key. The Master has given this *Naam Mantra* to you. It is not to be disclosed to anybody. This is strictly forbidden because if you disclose it - its value will diminish. The Masters are very strict on this subject!

Ultimately, we have a lot of attachment and affection for the body. This attachment needs to dissolve. Then only, will you be fearless! Every being is fearful. Why? Because the Spirit wants to survive through the body only. Spirit does not know itself. The Spirit, called *Atman*, *Brahman*, is not aware of its existence. When the Spirit came across/clicked with the body, it just accepted, "I am this body". And through this body, it derived happiness and peace. Put simply, Spirit is fond of the body. It likes the body. Through the body, it achieves survival.

So, there is a lot of attachment to the body because the Spirit likes it. I give it the name "Spirit" because we must use some words. What does Spirit mean? It is just a name that is given, like *Brahman*, *Atman*, *Paramatman*, God, Master. You can give any name to "That" through which your actions are made possible! You are nodding your head, looking at me, tasting various foods. You see the entire world, experience the thoughts, witness your thoughts. You are that invisible Spirit that is completely unaware of its existence. It is completely unaware of its own existence. Existence is only noticed through the body. The existence of the Spirit is only noticed through the body. The body that is made up of flesh, blood and bones is only a medium.

The body produces a family because of the Spirit. You have to know this secret that is your secret, and not God's, or *Brahman*, *Atman*, *Paramataman*'s secret. Know your secret, without the body-form. Know thyself and keep quiet! Don't struggle with all the words. This is not a debate. So many people are asking questions, saying this thing or that thing. The entire world is an illusion. We are talking about the "unborn child". The child we are talking about all the time is unborn. Nothing has happened. Nothing is going to happen. Nothing is happening! Therefore, the basic thing to know and absorb is that you were not a body, you are not a body, and, you are not going to remain a body. The body is your external part, external clothing - like this. [Maharaj tugs at his shirt.]

You have to convince yourself in various ways, and after convincing yourself, you will reach a conclusion and conviction. Convincing leads to conviction. Convincing leads to the conviction: "Yes! All this wandering, here and there, when all along, I was the destination". You are Ultimate Truth. You are Final Truth. Nisargadatta Maharaj used to say "Read, read, but don't drown yourself in reading". Therefore, bookish knowledge, literal knowledge may offer a little happiness for a certain period of time, but it is only spiritual entertainment, momentary entertainment.

One should see the Seer, but this cannot be seen because the Seer is invisible, anonymous, unidentified. Spiritual knowledge is your spiritual eyes. When 'I' disappears, there is nobody there - no "I", no "you" - nothing! Completely empty, you will be unconcerned with the world. No experience, no experiencer, no witness, no duality - nothing is there. No duality, no individuality also, no duality, no individuality. This is rare knowledge. When everything disappears, there you are! When you realize there is no-thing, it means you are every-thing! "Nothingness" is not annihilation or nihilism. It is beyond all concepts.

You will come to know this for yourself, after self-involvement. All that I am saying now, you will come to know directly, later on. When I first went to Nisargadatta Maharaj I was not able to understand what he was saying. It was like a foreign language to me because my mental and spiritual capacities were very low. He was using a very direct approach. But he kept saying, "Listen to me, listen to me". And now since that truth has been exposed, it is very easy. (In time, the understanding came naturally.)

Q: What age were you when you met Nisargadatta Maharaj?

Maharaj: I was around 21 years old in 1962. What often happens is that circumstances force you to go to Ultimate Truth. If you are comfortable you will not go, but if some difficulties arise, you will embrace them. When you are a child you may say, "there is a ghost!" and so you embrace your Mom. You say "Oh! I'm scared of this ghost!" and you hug your Mom because in your eyes she is the ultimate, your protector.

It is the same with the relationship between the Master and the devotee. The Master is a mother, the Master is a father. The Master is everything. The Master is God. Nisargadatta Maharaj used to say: "If I am fortunate, difficulties will come to me", and he really did have a lot of difficulties in his life, many difficulties. But he did not run away in fear. Some people who are doing meditation say, "Oh! Why are these problems coming to me when I'm meditating?" His relations who know he is doing meditation and *bhajans* also say: "if your practice is working, you would not be suffering physically, or whatever". They make the mistake of trying to interrelate their body-based knowledge with spiritual knowledge. This is not the way!

The foundation must be very strong. If it is strong then it will lead to conviction: Except this - nothing is there. So don't let anybody divert you from this constructive knowledge. Do not be distracted!

Q: Be careful of the company you keep.

Maharaj: Therefore, Nisargadatta Maharaj used to tell his devotees and disciples, not to mix with the type of people who will disturb and distract you from your principle. If the mind is weak, then it will get distracted, so he advised them to be careful. Once he said, "Don't be so cheap that you let the world pocket you". Yes, he often gave very good advice. You must have self-respect.

He was very, very practical. It was all due to him that I received my education. I was so small. I am a miracle! It happens. I am a miracle, really! I know my past. What I am today is all because of him. Dramatic changes have taken place in my life because of Nisargadatta Maharaj. And now, I am trying to share the same knowledge with everyone. But how many will accept it? I am trying, I'm making continuous efforts. It's up to you to assess and decide where you stand. Ask yourself: "Where do I stand?" You may accept it, or not. It is my duty to open the secret. The cave filled with jewels is open for you. Take your fill! Take from it as much as your capacity holds. It is free of charge.

Q: Take it all, not just a little!"

Before breaking up, Maharaj wanted to stress the importance of the practice:

"But again, I repeat that, at the initial stage, you have to undergo this discipline strictly because meditation is essential to digest the knowledge. To give you an example, say, I am suffering from a cold. The doctor gives me an antibiotic. Then there are side effects. To treat the side effects the doctor prescribes an anti-acid medicine to dissolve the acidity. Similarly, this knowledge is just like an antibiotic that needs meditation, so that the knowledge can be absorbed. Meditation is the anti-acid. I am convincing you in different ways, using varied language, to erase the many lasting impressions that you have gathered from so many illusory thoughts. To dissolve and remove these thoughts, you have to undergo this discipline strictly, until it becomes automatic for you."

Listening to Maharaj's discourses is fructifying. As time goes by, we are beginning to feel more at ease in his Presence, and we can even joke with him. We are getting into the rhythm of ashram life and making great strides in our meditation. We have started earnestly learning the *bhajans*. After all our initial protestations, we find we are even enjoying them! Now when I am singing, I feel as if I am attending a party in the sky, a celestial celebration, just vibrating in the light as light, with complete forgetfulness of the body-mind!

Evening – We attend the *bhajans*. This evening, the ageless lady keeps smiling at me as we sing together, when suddenly, a fit of hysteria descends! The two of us cannot stop laughing. I try to contain it, but cannot do so! Then, I try even harder to halt the spontaneous flow of laughter, especially after two male, Indian devotees, turned around and threw daggers at me. But all my attempts are futile. Maharaj says that singing the *bhajans* is a tonic that lifts the Spirit. So true! They also help us to absorb the knowledge. I especially love the evening *bhajans*! They are so inspiring and elevating! As we sing, they take us higher and higher, until we feel we are going to burst!

The next day – Dr Satishji Avhad, (*Gurubandhu*), a fellow disciple of Nisargadatta Maharaj, and close friend of Shri Ramakant, arrives at the ashram. He published the great book, *Master of Self-Realization*! After the *bhajans*, we approach Maharaj and bow at his feet. Shri Satishji is seated next to him. Suddenly, he takes hold of both my hands, looks me straight in the eyes, and says, "Mind gone!" It is a special, powerful moment. Precious! His energy is beautiful, soft, gentle and flowing!

Early November – This morning, as we are listening to Maharaj's discourse, something extraordinary happens! A few words come out of my mouth unexpectedly and spontaneously, saying: "I accept everything you say". Who spoke these utterances? It wasn't me speaking. At this moment, when time seemed to stop, I am as stunned listening to these words, as Charles and Maharaj are, whose stares are fixed on me. Then, after what felt like a long pause, in another dimension, Maharaj continues discoursing.

I knew, well not really "I knew", but there is a knowing that the "Invisible Presence" within had spoken. Listening to, and hearing the knowledge, has had the effect of penetrating the layers and touching the core of my being! It is truly amazing!

Later on, Charles tells me off, saying, I shouldn't say things like that. "You cannot accept everything blindly!", he exclaims. In my defence, I quickly reply, "I know that! But it wasn't blind acceptance and it wasn't me who was speaking either". I was not speaking, rather, it was the "Invisible Listener", "Spontaneous Presence" or whatever you want to call it, that spoke!

Many unexplainable things are happening here. We cannot use the rational mind to understand them, no matter how hard we try! I have never been a "Yes" type of seeker, who blindly accepts something without careful consideration, so my understanding here is that what occurred earlier is beyond the grasp of our little minds! Self-Realized Master, Ramakant Maharaj, is not a person, but the Ultimate, therefore, being in His Transcendental Presence works in mysterious ways that we simply cannot understand!

We have been at the ashram now for a couple of weeks. Today, Maharaj informs us that the apartment next to his is available for rent. And, if we are interested, we can move in immediately, adding that it will be more comfortable for us. He asks us again how long we plan to stay? We say keenly: "as long as possible"! Maharaj says: "I am very happy that you will stay. I can see you are both really listening to the knowledge, smiling, laughing and looking very contented. This means the knowledge is touching you, penetrating the layers".

"Absolutely", we reply! Then, Maharaj exclaims that usually when visitors come to see him, they sit in front of him like statues. He does not see any changes taking place. "They come as statues and they leave as statues", he says, shaking his head.

We have a six-month visa. There is no longer any question of us going elsewhere. This is everywhere! It is here, there and everywhere! We have found the gold we have been searching for, tirelessly! We recognize Maharaj's uniqueness, and we are convinced that his teachings are the highest, the most profound, yet at the same time, the simplest and most direct, we have ever encountered, in our long and often torturous journey!

We move into the apartment. Amazingly, we are now Maharaj's neighbours! *Quelle chance!* What a privilege! In the early morning, before the *Kakad Arati*, the first *bhajans* of the day, we exchange a few words with Maharaj over the wall, as we drink our morning coffee. Once settled in, Maharaj comes round to our flat, and we visit him in his flat. When we sometimes go to his home in the evening, we usually find Anvita transcribing or translating Maharaj's teachings. She is always absorbed in absorbing Ultimate Truth!

It is pure grace to be so physically close to Maharaj, even though we know he is not the form. Living in an apartment with a cooker and several bathrooms makes life easier. We can cook for ourselves and thus take better care of our bodily needs.

When the mobile market sellers appear outside our flat, we usually meet Anvita who is also buying her fruit and vegetables. We always stay clear of the softer fruits that are usually covered with flies! Sometimes the seller overcharges us simply because we are westerners. On these occasions, Anvita usually steps in, demanding the seller reduce the price. It is only a matter of a few rupees difference in most cases, but Anvita adheres to the principle of fairness and equality for all, and she is adamant that no one cheats us! Sometimes the seller shouts back at Anvita's interventions, but she retaliates with the same, if not greater, force. Occasionally, when Maharaj hears the commotion, he would come out and partake in the illusory drama! We are amused at how much energy is expended. We do not really care. We are tired and just want our papayas!

The next day, after the morning *bhajans*, we go out for some exercise. We bump into Maharaj, who is also taking a walk around the patio, outside the ashram. This is his recreational, keep-fit period. We stop to chat with him briefly. There is a great feeling of camaraderie between us. He is so warm and unassuming, and yet majestic, simultaneously!

10th November – This morning, immediately after the *bhajans*, Maharaj says to me, "You have the eye of knowledge!"

Maharaj always asserted that he is nothing but his Master's puppet, who is only able to give discourses because his Master, Nisargadatta, speaks through him! As we are about to leave, he spontaneously announces: "Nisargadatta says that she, (pointing to me), has to do the book, (of RM's teachings). "Oh!" was my only response. "So, start recording all the Talks and then type them out!", he commanded.

12th November – No sooner had we started to record the Talks, than Maharaj tells me to come to his home at 10 am, to type them out. Our *seva*/service to the Master has begun!

This morning when I appear at 10 am, Anvita tells me to go upstairs to Maharaj's room where he has his computer. As I enter, I notice Maharaj is wearing just a towel around his waist. He is in the middle of performing ablutions and washing clothes. I feel a little uneasy and embarrassed, but Maharaj who is not the body is oblivious to everything. When I ask him nervously, if it is a convenient time, he tells me to sit down at the computer and carry on with the work!

After just over an hour, I tell him I am leaving to prepare for the 11.30 am session. I suggest that maybe I am intruding into his private space. He says "nonsense", and tells me to return at the same time tomorrow! (There is no escape!) He has no problems, of course. I am the one who feels a little awkward or embarrassed! "Who is feeling awkward?" I ask myself.

Later that day – An animated Charles feels compelled to tell Maharaj about our progress: "Maharaj, we are making progress in leaps and bounds. In fact, we both feel we have taken off, (without the "we"), and are flying. The way you teach

Maharaj is fantastic, and so easy to understand. The knowledge is definitely going in, even through this thick skull of mine", he jokes, (tapping his head with his knuckles). He went on to tell him that, there is nothing on the internet about him, and that we feel compelled to tell the world about him. We have to tell everyone! We feel we have no choice in the matter. Since we, ourselves, are benefitting so much, then we see it as our duty to spread the "Good News". Maharaj listens attentively, claps his hands once, then exclaims, "I am very happy".

The next day – While I get busy transcribing the Talks, Charles embarks on setting up a Website for Maharaj, (www.ramakantmaharaj.net), as well as a Facebook page. We can see the excitement in Maharaj's eyes, when later on in the day, we inform him that many people from all over the world will come to see him, as they will definitely want to hear his rare and amazing discourses, as well as receive the *Naam Mantra*. The website is coming together. Not long after uploading it, Charles begins to receive mail from interested seekers.

Since meeting Maharaj, we realize it is our destiny to be the propagators of his teachings! We reflect:

"Oh, Maharaj! Oh, Beloved! Hearing the knowledge, the secret of our eternal reality and absorbing it, has bonded us to you. We are now linked for eternity. We are committed to you. How can we not wish to serve you, when you have drawn us deeper towards you with your infinite love, peace and compassion! Your happy servants are filled with gratitude. We already feel we will never be able to repay our dear Master! We are infected by the divine touch of the Guru and have surrendered. We understand that our wish to serve Maharaj was ignited by being in the Presence of the Ultimate, that he is! We know we are not serving a person but the impersonal Absolute!"

Today's Talk:

"**Q**: Presence and awareness. Whose Presence and whose awareness? As a child, you grow up, you are aware and gradually, hopefully, awaken in this world, to come awake in the world. How would you describe Presence?

Maharaj: How do you see the entire world? Do you see the child, the man, the woman, the world? It is the reflection, projection of your Presence, your Spontaneous Presence. There is no individuality. Presence is everywhere, very vast. We use the word "Presence", but this word is also an illusion. We use it just to illustrate something. We must use so many words for understanding purposes. You say, "awareness", "consciousness", "beingness". These are the words to guide you. They are just pointing, directing and messaging your unidentified identity. Reality is without words! There is no existence, there is no Presence. We are (trying to) talking about Presence, so these are kind of egoistic thoughts, intellectual or logical thoughts. There is no logic, no intellect, no mind, no ego, nothing is there, absolutely nothing. But out of nothing, you see everything.

When nothing dissolves, absorbs, there you are: where there is no awareness, no consciousness, no Presence. So what do you see out of your

Presence? It is a Spontaneous Presence that cannot be defined by any words. There is no individuality, but for our discussions, we are using many words, to grow in conviction, so as to know that the invisible listener's own identity is just like the sky. The sky does not know/have any feelings, no mind, no ego. If at all you wish to compare yourself to something, compare yourself to the sky. You are just like the sky. You see this sky, you see the sea. It is the seer's reflections. If the seer is not present, how can you even say the word "sky"? So, your identity is beyond that, beyond, beyond that.

[Silence]

Q: About awakening... When and who is awakening?

Maharaj: There is nobody awakening. There is no question, no consideration of the body-form. There is no awakening, no consciousness, no beyond consciousness, no before consciousness. These are the words we use, simply for our understanding, for conviction. But we are nothing to do with this world, and we have nothing to do with individuality. You can visualize your Presence through the body only. Nothing existed prior to body-based knowledge. You did not know the question, "Who am I?". Because of this body-form, we have forgotten our identity. Therefore, all these explanations, all these words we are using, are needed to awaken the attention of the invisible listener, the spontaneous listener within you, that has no shape. As long as we still have a lot of bodily attachments, love and affection, we will not be able to know ourselves in a real sense.

Q: You said everything comes from nothing and absorbs back into nothing?

Maharaj: Of course, you can see yourself.

Q: So what is nothing?

Maharaj: "Nothing" cannot be defined. Nothing is nothing. It cannot be defined. What is "no knowledge"? It is no knowledge. The child that is not born, we are talking about the unborn child – nothing, not born – nothing.

Q: But there is still something after the dissolution? There is something in the nothing?

Maharaj: No! Nothing! No something, no dissolution – all these words. Again we are talking through our body-mind information.

Q: Yes, but you did say that there is still something... when everything disappears and there is nothing, there is a little?

Maharaj: "There you are" – just for conviction. We have to use some words.

Q: And "there you are" is Spontaneous Presence?

Maharaj: Yes, because without your Spontaneous Presence you cannot see the world. It is invisible anonymous, unidentified. We are using some words to convince you, but I am asking everybody not to analyze the words, but, instead focus on what they are trying to convey. I tell everybody, again and again, not to take what I'm saying literally.

Q: Nisargadatta Maharaj talks about when you are a small child before you identify with the body and the name, you know, like a baby. He talks quite a lot about that – the "pre-I Am" state, before identification with the body.

Maharaj: What he is saying is to try and convince your Presence, from different angles and dimensions. Again, don't take the meanings literally, instead, take what they want to convey.

Q: Before pre-I am, before the body at all - full stop. So this is more than "I am".

Maharaj: It is your own anticipation. What's there before "I am"? All this anticipation is related to the body-form. There are no words. All the words end there. No language, no words. Even "existence" is anonymous or cannot be defined in words. All the questions are raised because of the body-form.

[Long Silence]

Q: The answers are in silence.

Maharaj: Silence is the answer to all questions.

"Sitting in the Guru's Presence is like bathing in the sunshine, and then, that sunlight becomes the disciple's inner light of Self-knowledge. It feels very sacred. We are at one – atonement!"

End of November – Anvita has been helping me find suitable clothing, like kurtas or tunic tops with leggings and loose trousers. I know I will never manage to wear a sari, even though the ladies look so elegant in them, as it would take too long to work out the puzzle of reams of material and wear it properly! We have little time as it stands.

Now I fit in better with the others, thanks to Anvita choosing the right outfits! Charles, too, is freshly attired, wearing a simple white dhoti and pajama pants. Maharaj comments on how smart he looks, saying: "Now you are dressed like a Master!" Maharaj notices everything, no matter how minute!

Today Anvita is wearing an elegant white sari with gold borders. She is looking radiant. Anvita's gentle Presence is full of grace. She does not walk, but glides across the room, like an angel. Her devotion and service to Maharaj are exemplary. It is so touching to see her bowing at Maharaj's feet. She is a beautiful being emanating warmth and kindness, never failing to display great humility.

We are learning so much here from the Guru. (Unfortunately, the "Guru" has been given a bad name in our day and age, not least, because of the many recent scandals surrounding some of them.) By learning obedience, the mind deactivates, the thoughts are put into abeyance and the ego is starved. These are the benefits that come from associating with an authentic Guru!

As the Guru instructs and the disciple obeys, the devotion to the Guru grows and deepens. If the seeker is laid back and casual about finding Truth, the process may be a slow one. But, if the seeker is serious, earnest, driven, one-pointed and hungry to know the Truth, the relationship will develop at speed, propelling liberation. If we follow the Guru's instructions and do everything we are told to do, eventually, the ego which has created the illusion of separation will break down, resulting in a merging and oneness with the Guru. And through that process, the purest love begins to grow, deepen and emerge in the disciple.

We feel a strong bond with Maharaj, our Guru! We know he is not a person but, at the same time, we feel our relationship with him is extremely personal and intimate. What is happening here is the classic "*Guru bhakti*", the love for the Guru that we have read about, and which I have longed to experience! Now that it is happening, it is indeed indescribably powerful and beautiful! We treasure the special nature of this "relationship in oneness", based on unconditional love. It is a paradox to say that this strong bond between the Guru and the disciple is deeply "personal", when the Guru is "impersonal". But, that is the way our association with Maharaj is unfolding, which has been experienced similarly, by countless others throughout history.

The deepening of this bond, or inner attunement with Maharaj, is making me more courageous in his Presence. Nowadays when we line up to bow at Maharaj's feet, I touch all of his toes, albeit still very, very gently! However, in time, I know it is a certainty, that I will place both hands firmly on his Holy Feet.

Program days or Celebrations at the ashram are frequent, either celebrating a birth (*Jayanti*) or death (*Punyatithi*) anniversary of one of the Masters, or the beginning of *Shravan*, a holy month, or the biggest festival of the year, *Guru*

Purnima, as well as other more social events, such as *Diwali*, ("New Year" in India).

2nd December – Today during the morning *Dasbodh* reading I hear a voice within say, "Grace is going through you".

Program Day – Today we celebrate Shri Siddharameshwar's "Death Anniversary". On these special days, attention to detail is of prime importance, eg, the way the devotees hang the garlands with such precision, over the pictures of the Masters. They must be exactly centred. Where and how everything is placed needs to be perfect! Numerous plates of *prasad* offerings are always displayed in front of the altar: fruit, freshly baked sweet and savoury dishes, are lovingly positioned before the Masters.

On these special occasions, the devotees decorate the outside entrance of the ashram with chalked, floral designs. The mixture of scents emanating from the jasmine flowers and the sandalwood incense is overpowering. The atmosphere on these special days is electric, with the male singers putting their all into belting out the *bhajans*. They sing a couple of lines first, followed by the women, singing the next two lines. The ashram is beautifully decorated with an abundance of offerings.

The ladies have been busy since yesterday, preparing enough food to feed everyone. The energy is very elevating, though, at the same time, it is a long day which starts at the usual time of 6.30 am, and does not usually finish till after 8 pm. On such days, there are endless rounds of singing "*Jai Guru's*". Each time we think the program has finished, another round of "*Jai Guru's*" follows.

Wonderful as the Program was, with the cymbals banging and the drums beating all day, we are happy to retreat into our quiet space, at last! We don't know where Maharaj gets his energy from… well we do…. but he seems to never tire! Even after the long day's Program, devotees would go to his home, and spend an hour or more, with Maharaj! His door is always open, apart from a quiet time between 3-5 pm, when no devotees, absolutely no one, is permitted to disturb him. During this time, Maharaj usually climbs the stairs to the top floor, and then onto the rooftop, to sit on his chair that is strategically placed under the sky, where he sits, as if, communing, in oneness with the sky!

The day after – During today's meditation, Siddharameshwar appears dressed in full regalia. He is very tall, gigantic and majestic. I am standing in front of him. It is like an initiation ceremony. He says, "You, too will become a giant".

Another day – Morning *bhajans*. Today as we are singing the morning *bhajans*, Maharaj walks past me. He exclaims, "such devotion in the voice!" After we finish singing, Maharaj instructs me to start practising the *bhajan*, *Chidananda*. Knowing it is not an easy tune to learn, I say, "I will try"!

Chidananda is a beautiful composition by the great philosopher and Self-Realized Master, Shankara, (often referred to as the *Adi Guru*, meaning the "first Guru"). The verses contain the whole essence of Advaita, using the classic method of "*neti neti*" – "not this, not this", to discard everything that is an illusion.

Today Maharaj begins his Talk, narrating the story behind *Chidananda*:

"**Maharaj**: Shankaracharya was told that his mother had died when he was 8 or 9 years old, so, he asked all the people in his village for help: "Please help me"! He had to take the body to the funeral place. At that time, there was a lot of hatred towards saintly people. Finding himself helpless, he had to cut up the body of his mother into manageable pieces, so he could take it to the funeral grounds. There is "no mother, no sister, no brother, no father...", *Chidananda Sivoham Sivoham.* He lived the words he composed, and found the extraordinary strength within him to carry out his duty.

The song is exceptional, with very high meaning. It is the summary of our philosophy: "There is nothing: no sister, no brother, no Master, no disciple, nothing. No witness, no experience, no experiencer".

The Ultimate Truth is in you, but your attachments are not allowing you to be close to your Selfless Self. It's not impossible to be free of all attachments.

[Maharaj plays a recording of the song *Chidananda* on his mobile phone]

Maharaj: It reaches the innermost part of the body deep, deep within!

Q: Beautiful!

Maharaj: Practise it, Ann! After listening to all this spirituality, there should be a melting process. Only then, will there be complete peace. When the ego, intellect and mind melt completely, then love and affection towards Selfless Self arise - spiritual love, spontaneous love! There is no hatred, no duality, just complete calm and quiet. There is no jealousy either because of the realization: "I am everywhere". The bodies are different, but the Spirit is one. Oneness has no brother, no sister, no Master, no God. These are all body-based relations. When you came across with the body, all these relations formed - God, *Brahman*, *Atman*, Master, brother, sister, mother. All these relations are body-related. Your Presence is an exceptional Presence, where words cannot reach. Be calm! Be quiet! Forget everything you have been told! At the last stage, when you are leaving the body - at that time, exceptional happiness will appear within you, which cannot be explained by any words. Just complete calm and peace, absorbing totally, totally, totally.

What I am saying, is that the Spirit within you has tremendous power, but you are ignoring that. Therefore, we are reminding you and directing your attention, to your inner power, so you can come out from all this ignorance!

All the saintly people faced a lot of difficulties, but they had constructed good knowledge, perfection. Achieve that perfection! Don't ignore it! Don't take it casually! Do your job, do your duties, no problem. The body is there, so you must look after its survival! But you have to know yourself in a real sense. All that you know and do, all that is connected to the body-form is not Ultimate Truth because the body has a time limit. This process is not impossible but complete humbleness is required, otherwise, you may say proudly, "Oh, yes! I am somebody!" No! You are nobody! "My Presence is everywhere. My Presence is in each and every being." The bodies are different. Every being acts, but the actions that are taking place happen only because of the Spirit.

Slowly, silently and permanently, calmly and quietly, total silence will emerge. There will be a dramatic change in perspective, like: "I am everywhere, just like the sky!", without the ego or the mind. You can use the mind, the ego and intellect, as and when required, but don't become a victim or their slave. They are co-relations: the thoughts come in the mind, the intellect instructs: "Do this!" and then the ego says, "Yes!"

Q: They all work together.

Maharaj: The mind, ego and intellect are interconnected, just for knowledge. Use these instruments, as and when needed, and then, forget them! Ok."

When Maharaj assigns one a task or project, he always expects it to be done yesterday! I had just started practising *Chidananda* when Maharaj asked me to sing it to him. I had been trying to learn it by singing along to a recording of it, to grasp the melody. That did not go down well with Maharaj, who told me to dispense with the recording, and "just sing it!"

I want to please the Master, and so, I try hard, but it still isn't happening. I try again, but I cannot sing it! Anvita who is always supportive in these kinds of situations, which seem like unrealistic expectations from the Master - counsels Maharaj to give me more time to practice. But, impatient as ever, he seems frustrated when I tell him I need more time, and walks away.

Every other day after that, when Maharaj enquired after "*Chidananda?*", Charles would start laughing quietly, as I was put on the spot, time and again! My reply was always the same: "No! Maharaj, I'm sorry, but it is too difficult". Finally, to my great relief, he let it go! I felt the pressure leaving me at last! Phew! But this brief moment was quickly overtaken by a strong feeling that I had let Maharaj down! We had already learned that adhering to the Guru's commands without fail, is so vital to the process of chipping away the ego! When the Guru gives us an order, we must obey, just like in the army! Here in "Nashik Army Ashram", we are spiritual soldiers who need to follow the rules and discipline of our commander! Why? So that we can be knocked into shape and remoulded!

This evening, Charles and I speak again about the importance of the Guru-disciple relationship. Sadly, so much negative publicity surrounding Gurus of all traditions have given Gurus a bad name. It is regretful because obedience and obeisance to the Guru fast-tracks the demolition process of the ego, (this continues to be our experience), thus promoting humility, love and oneness. Unfortunately, in the west, the concept of devotion to a Guru is an alien one, anathema, that arouses suspicion and smells of cultish brainwashing!

Since being with Maharaj, we know and appreciate the benefits of "doing as we are told". In this Navnath Sampradaya Lineage, the Guru-disciple relationship is central, as is the transmission of the *Naam Mantra* from Master to disciple. Many contemporary spiritual teachers can only speak from the limits of their knowledge, and not beyond. Without self-transcendence, the power behind the words is not transmitted. Here in the ashram, we are fortunate to be in the Guru's Presence. We are guided by one who has gone beyond knowledge, and therefore, by one who knows all the pitfalls along the way. We need a light to guide us, otherwise, it is very easy to lose ourselves in the dark, or, as Siddharameshwar Maharaj says, "mistake your imagination for *Brahman*!"

Daily Talk:

"**Q**: You said, "Spirit doesn't know its own identity".

Maharaj: Correct.

Q: But then you said also, that when it hears stories about itself, it's happy, so I was trying to understand.

Maharaj: We're in the body-form. In the body-form, there are some feelings of happiness and peace. There are all these needs for happiness, peace, a tension-free life, like that, but basically, you were not the body, you are not the body, you are not going to remain the body. The Spirit does not know its own identity - the Ultimate State. Since you are holding the body, you want to eat food and have some entertainment. This is a material body, so, the material body requires everything. Prior to the material body, there were no requirements. Nothing was needed! So, during the material body's lifespan, we need some things that will bring us peace because we have none. We are under the pressures of constant tension.

Small things create conflicts and confusion, which, in turn, drive the tension. To overcome this, you must know your Self in a real sense, like this: "Though I am holding the body, I am unconcerned with the body-based knowledge because the food-body is not my identity. It is limited, so I am unconcerned. I do not have any time limit! Prior to the body-based knowledge, my existence was there, but without any form. It was formless".

We do not know what type of existence it was. That is beyond our imagination! Spiritual science says so many things, when, as a matter of fact, prior to our manifestation we did not know anything! When the Spirit clicked with the body, all our needs appeared. As the demands started, so, we started looking for happiness, peace, a tension-free and fearless life. All these needs are connected to the dream, but at the moment of conviction, namely, on realizing that "I am not the body, I am not going to remain the body, I was not the body", at that time, everything will vanish. It's an open fact.

These are simple, simple teachings, but you have to absorb them. Because of your long association with the body-form, you have a lot of attachment to the body, and all those body-related relations, such as, "my brother, my sister, my wife, my son, my daughter, my relative, my God". Everybody has a different God, but no one is seeing, or looking with their eyes wide open, with the eye of knowledge. Don't have blind faith. Find out: "Who am I? Why this life? What is good? What is bad? Happiness/unhappiness"? There is no duality! You have only absorbed concepts to date! Find the secret of your existence without concepts, without complications. This is straight knowledge, direct knowledge!

The basic thing is that the body is not your identity because the body is transient, perishable. Even if you try to survive for longer, employing various doctors and medicines, they will still not manage to postpone your life indefinitely, and stop you from dying. A small child grows up to be a young lady, then an old lady. Sooner or later, she will leave the body. Question yourself, use Self-enquiry: "I am unborn because the body is not my identity, so, where is the question of death and birth?" It's an open fact, but you are not accepting that fact because of your love and affection for the body. To have this conviction, you have to undergo certain disciplines – then, slowly, silently, permanently, the entire truth will be absorbed. And then, "Eureka!"

Throughout your life, you make yourself dependent on others – the husband, wife, family, employer, etc., yet you are totally independent. You are vast, limitless like the sky. The sky does not know its own identity. There are no feelings. Does the sky have a brother, sister, Master? We are not accepting the facts, the reality, because of our identification with the body-form. The pressures arising from the love and affection we have for the food-body keep our attachments going. So many thoughts were accepted, so many illusory thoughts were accepted blindly. Don't depend on anyone's thoughts! Believe in yourself! You are not having faith within you. You do not know you have tremendous power. You are always expecting somebody's help: "Please take care of me!" Why? Stand on your own feet!

This is a process of regenerating your power. Power is there within you, but it's unknown to you. You are unaware – and even if you are aware, you are not giving enough cognizance to it, therefore, you are underestimating yourself. Be strong, have courage! Why courage? Because there should not be any type of fear when it's time to leave the body. That is most important. It is very easy to talk about spirituality, but you must Self-enquire! I am directing people, not to do this or that thing, carry out rituals, follow tradition, etc, but to keep asking, "Who am I?" You have to start with yourself. You are the starting point because everything starts with you, and everything ends with you! You are the end point!

Teaching is very easy. Anyone can talk about *Brahman*, *Atman*, *Paramatman*, God, if you read many books. The question is, has your reading made you fearless? To what extent has that knowledge been absorbed within you? What is the effect of all this knowledge, if it does not leave you unconcerned with the world, calm and quiet? When you awaken from the dream, there will be patience, no hatred, no struggle. Why have struggle? Why hatred? Who is the enemy? There's no enemy. You are fighting with the air! Who is bad? Who is good? Find out!

After enlightenment, when you know yourself in a real sense, you will be completely transformed. Then the feeling will arise: "I am everywhere. My Presence, Spontaneous Presence, Invisible Presence is everywhere, in every being". We will no longer look at "others" with indiscriminate eyes, thinking, "Who is good and who is bad!" because we will know that the same Spirit is here, the same Spirit is there, the same Spirit is everywhere - neither good nor bad.

Q: In *I Am That,* I seem to remember Nisargadatta Maharaj saying something about there being no good and no bad. People were very shocked because they had never even thought about that.

Maharaj: Yes. Good and bad are related to the body-based knowledge.

Q: They were absolutely shocked. With all the wars, all the troubles in the world, all the murders and that kind of stuff...

Maharaj: Because we perceive, measure ourselves in the body form, therefore, we see good and bad. You were never a body, and you will not remain a body, that is the Ultimate Truth. There's no birth and death. These are all concepts. No birth, no death, no bondage, no salvation.

Q: No wars, no heaven.

Maharaj: Yes, nothing was there. As I told you, everything comes out of nothing, and it will be absorbed, merged back into nothing. It's an open fact. Along with the body, the memory disappears. But we are under the impressions/pressures of this body, so much so, that even though we know the reality, we are not accepting it. To dissolve the body-based knowledge, you have to undergo this process. The first lesson is meditation. Out of meditation the pressures of the ego, intellect, mind and all the illusory concepts will dissolve, disappear, slowly, silently, permanently. Then everything will open up because your existence is spontaneous. You will not be a part of any kind of notion, such as, "I will take birth in America, England" or something like that. You can't do these things. Everything happens spontaneously.

So, embrace the reality, not the body-form. You must have strong faith, strong dedication. Even if some so-called God appears before you, you should not give it much cognizance because to say, God, your Presence must be there first. "If my Presence is not there, how can I say God?" So that appearance, that image of

God, that figure is a reflection of your Presence, the reflection of your Spontaneous Presence.

Q: Because Presence is a prerequisite. You have to be there first?

Maharaj: Just like in a dream, you see God, the world and everything.

Q: Where is this God?

Maharaj: To say, God, to say something, your Presence is needed. If your Presence is not there, how can you see the gods and the goddesses? Behind everything, lies your Spontaneous Invisible Presence. We call that *Brahman*, *Atman*, *Paramatman*, God, Master, any word you wish! Therefore, Nisargadatta Maharaj said, "Except your Selfless Self there is no God, no *Brahman*, no *Atman*, no *Paramatman*, no Master".

Reality is beyond the imagination, beyond the intellect: Final Truth, Ultimate Truth, Exceptional Truth, you may use any word. Language, words are only a medium.

Q: For communication.

Maharaj: We have given birth to the words, created an alphabet and given them meanings. Therefore, literal knowledge is not sufficient.

Q: A few words.

Maharaj: Contained in all these words, some indications give messages. We have invented the alphabet and given meaning to the words. See, this Spirit is in the body-form for the communication of thoughts. We are using some words for conversation.

So, the principle of spirituality is that one must know oneself in a real sense: "I am totally unborn". Then only, will you become fearless. Why should I fear? There is no coming, and no going. Does the sky come and go? Welcome the sky, welcome the sky. We are constructing all the walls, the divisions, these walls, those walls, yet the sky is there. And when the walls collapse, does the sky go anywhere?"

Convince yourself in this way. The Master Key has been given to you, now you have to operate it. This is the Listener's Truth. This is the Listener's Truth, the invisible, anonymous, listener. Who sees through these eyes? Listens through these ears? Tastes with this tongue? Spirit makes all these organs active. If the Spirit is not there, you cannot see through these eyes, you cannot smell, taste. Ok."

In the evening, we discuss Maharaj's method of teaching and its simplicity, which leave little room for the mind. We loved the last Talk, so fresh and logical, powerful and efficient! His emphasis on the *Naam Mantra* and the cleaning process is another win-win, that works perfectly in tandem with the discourses. We notice that now we can absorb the knowledge more, because the *Naam* is clearing out all the clutter and baggage we were carrying around, that was in the way! We also love his emphasis on language and those frequent cautionary notes, such as, "don't take my words literally", and "there was no language prior to beingness".

He is completely intolerant of concepts. This suits us, as so much time can be lost on intellectual discussion and debate. He often reiterates: "This is not a debate. You are to accept what the Master says, not dissect it!" The teachings are strict. It is like walking a tightrope! If we falter and allow the concepts to enter, Maharaj acts as a safety net and catches us! He quickly and easily reinstates us back into the stateless state of "prior to beingness" – asking where this, or that, particular concept was then! He is a wonderful teacher, as he never lets us get away with anything.

We are both having many experiences during meditation. The ones that Charles has are usually very spacey and light-filled. Frequently, he sees himself getting smaller and smaller until he disappears completely. And then, all that remains is the expansion of space. Sometimes, he says, he can see a light that expands into infinity.

In contrast, my experiences at this time, appear more earthy, and continue to occur under the guidance of Shri Bhausaheb Maharaj: I am receiving clear instructions and teachings directly from Shri Bhausaheb. Yesterday, he commanded me to: "Kneel down, make amends and pray." I did as I was told. Then today, he said, forcefully: "Give me your happiness!" Wow! Steady! Wait a minute! My immediate thought was: "I will gladly give you my unhappiness, pain and suffering, but I'm not so sure about giving you my happiness"! At times, I had felt that my lot in life was unfairly weighted on the side of unhappiness, and not much on the other. Therefore, in "my life's dream", there is some resistance. I am not going to give up the little amount of happiness I have experienced and enjoyed!

As this thought passed by, a sudden flash of light illuminated, to remind me that happiness and unhappiness are both illusory layers, that must dissolve. They are concepts! I immediately follow his command and begin to surrender my precious layers of worldly happiness and memories! It is funny that in this illusory world, we continuously seek to "make memories", yet here, we seek to "unmake" them!

During the morning *bhajans*, we usually line up to kneel at Maharaj's feet, one at a time. When I am kneeling at his feet, I feel as if Maharaj is transmitting and pouring energy into me, like overfilled buckets of grace, which has the effect of making me lose all sense of time. I can almost feel and see a shaft of light entering into this being. I can't describe it, but I know something miraculous is happening.

After the *bhajans*, Charles chastises me again: "When you kneel at Maharaj's feet, you are taking too long! I could see the ladies standing behind you becoming impatient, waiting for you to get up. They were not too happy and were making faces". I protested, saying that I was unaware that it was too long, (really unaware of anything!), but I will definitely try and make it shorter next time. Tomorrow, when I kneel at Maharaj's feet I will remember what Charles has told me!

The next day – With the best of intentions, I try to keep the kneeling short. "Was that better?" I ask Charles, during lunch? "No! it was worse", he grunted! "You took even longer than before". Lol! I told him it was not deliberate, not my doing, that I am not in control over what is happening! He is not convinced and not too pleased, but thankfully, does not labour the point. Whatever is happening is out of "my" control and beyond understanding. Charles is too concerned about what others are thinking just now, instead of letting the spontaneous process unfold.

The practice is taking me deeper and deeper. The *Naam Mantra* is doing its job, emptying "me" of all the clutter, and removing the layers that are obscuring my true nature. Eventually, during the meditation, I see myself looking at an image of myself, deep, deep underground, stripped of everything, and on solid foundations. I understand this symbol to mean that my Reality can now begin to emerge because the old, illusory house I used to live in, is no longer. It had started to crumble, and now, it has been totally demolished.

These days, when Bhausaheb Maharaj appears, he speaks to me in a softer, more loving tone, often smiling, letting me know he is pleased with the progress. I thank him for his guidance and once more, express sincere sorrow, for anything untoward that this illusory doer has done - which I can remember - as well as anything else, I cannot remember. The slate is clean again, now ready to start afresh.

Charles is also undergoing a major spring clean. "Maharaj is right," he says. "The *Naam Mantra* is a spiritual broom that sweeps everything away". We are both feeling much lighter, as if we have finally put down two heavy suitcases, after a long, long, exhausting journey. These days, we are also feeling very happy all the time for no reason, for simply being. We just are, spontaneously!

Maharaj uses skilful tactics to chisel the stubborn ego and keep it in check. Today we went round to his house, as usual, only this time, Maharaj is watching TV. I try to get his attention, but fail. Then Charles tries, but there is no response. What can be so engrossing? When we look at the TV, we notice pictures of cartoon characters! Again, we try to speak with him. He smiles at us momentarily, then continues watching the cartoons. Finally, we get the message loud and clear: we are no more important than a cartoon program because everything is an illusion! Maharaj's refusal to speak to us on this occasion, dented the ego effectively!

Charles has arranged several Skype sessions with seekers from the States. Maharaj freely gives of his time, always saying he has a duty to share the knowledge. He is very happy to make contact with new devotees from different countries. He speaks with the "foreigners" (as he calls us), at around 8 pm each night, for at least half an hour, before his evening meal. We always eat earlier.

25th December - Daily Talk:

"**Q**: How to handle family relationships and problems?

Maharaj: As usual, normally! Family relations need not be a blockage or hurdle to spirituality. Be normal! When did you first come across the family? When the body appeared, the world and the family appeared. So do your normal duties. There's no problem! No problems! All these saints had a family life, (pointing to the Masters), most of them were married, had children, did their business. Ranjit Maharaj was employed in a shop doing his duties until age 73, Nisargadatta Maharaj had his own shop for many years, Siddharameshwar Maharaj was also employed some years back, and then he left that job, and Bhausaheb Maharaj as well. They had a family, children, but that aspect of their life did not cause any disturbance.

Spirituality is on a level of its own. Spirituality means just to know oneself in a real sense. Repeatedly, I am telling you that you are unaware of your identity.

You are unaware of your truth, Ultimate Truth, because you are giving more priority to the body. Through the Master, you are being reminded of your forgotten identity. He is inviting the attention of the Ultimate within you, without the body-based knowledge. The body has its own limit, its own time limit. The body is not ultimate, it is the Spirit that is important. If the Spirit goes away, the body dies. There is death, a dead body! What is the value of this body? In this event, what is the relationship with your Mom? Who is the mother? Who is the father? Who is brother? Who is sister? Who is God? Who is Master? Who are friends? Who is wife, son? All relations are related to this body only. It is an open fact. After death, what relations will there be? There are no relations, no family life. So all these relations come out of this body-based knowledge only. The body is a food-body. As long as you supply food to the body, it will live. The moment you stop supplying food to the body, the Spirit leaves. It's an open fact.

Q: Maybe a conflict can arise between the teachings and the family, if the family don't agree with the teachings?

Maharaj: When did you come across the family? The family is a concept like everything else. Spirituality has nothing to do with family problems. *Chidananda Sivoham Sivoham*: no mother, no father, sister, no brother, no friend, no death, no Master, no disciple, nothing, nothing. Out of nothing, the entire world has emerged and is projected. This world is a spontaneous reflection. Your Spontaneous Presence is behind everything. Without your Presence, you cannot see, you cannot talk, you can't do anything. So, just know oneself in a real sense. Just know oneself in a real sense. We know ourselves in the body-form with the mind, ego and intellect. This is a dream world.

Q: So, you would say not to worry about the family, but know yourself in a real sense?

Maharaj: Why worry about the family? You can do your job, no problem....

Q: But sometimes there is a disturbance. Even close family members can make it tough.

Maharaj: Because there is so much affection for the body, so much affection, love. Spirituality doesn't say ignore your family life. They, (the Masters), have not run away from their family duties. The family is not a hurdle, not an obstacle, not a blockage.

Therefore, with meditation, the purification stage will start. Purification means that all the concepts will dissolve, slowly, silently and permanently. At the beginning stage, you may experience an imbalance, some confusion or conflicts. Forget about spirituality! Prior to beingness, you did not know anything about the world, the family or God. All your needs and demands are orientated through the body-based knowledge only. When there is no body, there is no family, no need of a wife or husband, no child, no father, no Master, no disciple, no God. At the moment when the Spirit clicked with the body, your story started with, "I want happiness, peace". These are all concepts.... Who wants peace? "I want peace", you want peace of mind. These are only the concepts...

Q: My mother used to say, "all I want is peace".

Maharaj: When did you encounter peace? You are yourself disturbing the peace. Peace is there, it is you who disturbs the peace!

Q: When doing work in the world, I get absorbed in it. I forget the Self and then I get upset. How do I stay...?

Maharaj: This is mental level talk. At the moment when you realize that the entire world is an illusion, you will see that the upsets and depressions are arising on the mental level. Because things that we are expecting did not go according to expectations, it causes disturbances. Those things which do not turn out according to your expectations disturb you: wife, son, daughter, father, anybody.

There is some circle of expectations. If you act within the circle, you are seen as a nice person. If you go beyond the circle, then, "oh, he's not a nice person". You have created this circle. If your parents say, "you are a good boy", you say "oh! I am a good boy", but if your parents say "you are a bad boy", you feel bad. This is all mental level talk. There is no bad and no good. This is all beginner's stage talk.

Reality is supposed to be absorbed totally within you, with the melting process. So, complete involvement, complete devotion is supposed to be there, and then there won't be any problems. Prior to 100 years, did you have any problems? And after leaving the body, will your problems still be there? Problems originated at the moment when the Spirit clicked with the body.

Q: Yesterday you said the Spirit doesn't know itself. What can I do to help the Spirit know itself?

Maharaj: Don't make any efforts, your spontaneous existence is there. Spirit is only a word I am using, in order to know yourself, so don't take what I'm trying to say, literally. It's what I want to convey that is most important. It's your story, the listener's story. The discourses will help you.

The questioner is the answer to all questions. The questioner is the answer to all questions. You are ignoring the Questioner: You are not separate from your own identity. Because of the body, you say, this is *Brahman*, this is *Atman*, this is Spirit. All these words were created for discussion purposes only, just to invite the attention of the invisible, anonymous Spirit - that "I" without saying it, out of which the entire world is projected. Your Presence exists prior to everything. Prior to everything, there is your Presence - anonymous Presence, invisible Presence, unidentified identity. It cannot be defined. We are trying to impress the reality, the listener's reality. The listener is not in any form. If you were to compare yourself, compare your identity to something, compare it to the sky. The sky is not aware of its own existence, the sky does not know it exists.

This is very simple knowledge. Don't stress your brain! Don't stress your memory! What memories? Who am I? Who am I not? When all the thinking processes stop, there you are, in the thoughtless state. Depression, confusion, unstable mind, mind, ego, intellect - these are the subtle parts of the body you have embraced. You have got to come out of it all with the conviction: "I was not a body, I am not a body, I am not going to remain a body". Then the question of death and birth will never arise.

Counsel yourself: "I am unborn". It's an open fact that you are unborn. We are measuring ourselves in the body-form, therefore, it is difficult. All the time, we are considering ourselves to be the body-form. Because you are underestimating yourself, you end up begging, "Oh! please do something, Oh! please help me". It is your ego that is creating problems. Your ego is sticking in, goading you, saying, "I am somebody"! Humbleness is required. Knowledge with ego is meaningless.

A complete melting is required. All these saints were very humble, very, very humble. They were not discriminating, saying, "I am a great Master". So, the ego is a blockage, a hurdle that is standing in the way of your reality. You have knowledge, but it is tainted with ego. The subtle ego is there - "I am somebody". Humbleness is not there. With practice, everything will be easy. It will not be difficult.

First, respect yourself, and then respect others. Respect yourself, then respect others. To respect yourself doesn't mean respecting the body or your status. The truth is "I am nothing", so, why should there be any ego? All the saints are very pious, very calm and quiet, with no irritation, no disturbance, no conflict. That is the spontaneous reaction that will appear inside you, when you see yourself in a real sense. Complete patience will reign at all times, whether someone is angry at you, or not. Nisargadatta Maharaj used to say, "If anybody says good things, I am not happy. If anybody says bad things, I am not unhappy". The concepts of happiness-unhappiness are body-related. But, it will take some time. We are like computers that store everything, therefore, there is bound to be some physical ego, mental ego. Ok."

His Talk today is appropriate for Christmas time. Again, later on in the day, we share, how impressed we are with the pragmatic nature of the teachings. The lineage masters are householders – most of them are married with families. They do not live like hermits in caves, but work and support their families. What struck us most of all in today's Talk was what he said about family problems having nothing to do with spirituality!

Monday – More email requests to Skype with Maharaj are coming in. We try to tell the Master which countries the seekers are from, but the concept of "countries" does not mean anything to him. So, we buy a map of the world and pin it to a wall in his room. Charles gives Maharaj a short geography lesson, but we don't think

Maharaj is at all interested, in listening to the illusory names of all these illusory countries! Lol. It is all just space where manmade names have been assigned!

30ᵗʰ December – We decide it is a good idea to interview Maharaj, and then post it on *YouTube*, for all to see. We prepare some basic questions, really an "Introduction to Maharaj", and a little about the time he spent with Nisargadatta. We ask Maharaj about the idea? He agrees to do it the next day. When I suggest to Maharaj that he could maybe think about what he might say in the interview, he nearly bites my head off, saying: "I don't think!" Ooops!… sorry….

Charles is hoping I will do the interview, but there is no way I feel that I can. He is better at speaking in public than I am. Naturally, Charles is a little nervous at the prospect. To tell the truth, I would have been petrified! It isn't just anyone he is going to interview, it is Maharaj!

31ˢᵗ December – Charles interviews Maharaj:

"**Q**: I would like to introduce Ramakant Maharaj, a direct disciple of Nisargadatta Maharaj: I am very pleased to meet you. Maharaj, can you tell me a little bit about your background, childhood, and the early years of your life?

Maharaj: In the early years, I was in my native place where I completed my education. Then I came to Mumbai/Bombay where I carried out some small service. Then I went to live with some relatives, and through them, I met Nisargadatta Maharaj. After some months, I took the *Naam Mantra* with Nisargadatta in 1962.

Nisargadatta Maharaj gave me the *Naam Mantra*, the Guru Mantra. After that, I visited Nisargadatta Maharaj and listened to his lectures. Meditation is most important, according to Nisargadatta Maharaj. He stressed the importance of meditation, every day.

Q: So, you were with Nisargadatta Maharaj for nearly 20 years?

Maharaj: About 19 years, from 1962 to 1981.

Q: What was it like for you as a disciple of Nisargadatta Maharaj? How did it feel for you to be with him?

Maharaj: His speeches and lectures were very touching, exceptional, though, at that time, I was not mature enough to understand what he was saying. He used to say "listen to me, listen to me", and gradually the understanding came…. Every morning he gave lectures, and in the evening, between 6.30 to 7.30. We listened to them and then sang the *bhajans*.

Q: You're now teaching here in the ashram in Nashik. Are your teachings the same as your Master's, Nisargadatta Maharaj, or slightly different?

Maharaj: The teachings are the same, but the words are different. The principle is the same: "Except your Self, there is no God no *Brahman*, no *Atman*, no

Paramatman. This is the principle of spirituality. I am delivering the same thing to the devotees, the Ultimate Truth, using different words.

Q: You are part of a very strong lineage here. Can you speak about the lineage and the Masters?

Maharaj: The head of the Navnath Sampradaya Lineage is Dattatreya. His disciple was Raghunath Maharaj who was followed by his disciple Kadsiddheswhar Maharaj: (There were five Kadsiddheshwars!) And then 300 years later, in Pulapur, there was Guru Lingajangam Maharaj, followed by Bhausaheb Maharaj, Siddharameshwar, Nisargadatta, Ranjit Maharaj and so on.

Q: Maharaj, can I ask you about the role of the Guru?

Maharaj: The Guru's importance is that "He", (the Guru is beyond "he" or "she") is inviting the attention of the invisible silent listener, your true nature, which has been obscured and buried by illusory concepts. The Guru is a guide who removes the darkness of ignorance by shining a light. The Guru has walked the path before, so He knows all the pitfalls. He convinces the disciple that Reality is within, that the source of knowledge is within. Everything is within! The Guru convinces the disciple: "The seeker is he who is in search of himself."

Q: Can I ask you what you mean by Self-Realization? Sometimes you say it is easy to attain, and at other times, you say it is difficult.

Maharaj: Just to know oneself in a real sense. We know ourselves in the body-form. It's not your identity. Your identity is an unidentified, invisible, anonymous identity. The world is the projection of your Spontaneous Presence. You are ultimate truth. You are unborn. Devotees/seekers are people who are looking for happiness, peace of mind, a tension-free life, and a fearless life. This will happen, after you know yourself in a real sense. You are unborn, but you think you are born, and you are going to die. That concept is an illusory thought. This enlightening knowledge will help you realize the Ultimate Truth, the Final Truth.

Q: You often say that book knowledge is dry and of little use. Why is it not helpful?

Maharaj: "*Brahman*", "*Atman*", "*Paramatman*" - these are the polished words we use, the theory, but these words do not help us. Self-enquiry is necessary to find out if you are happy, fearless, tension-free and at peace. And if the answer is, "No! then it means the knowledge you have collected has remained, nothing more than literal knowledge. We have to undergo a process to uncover the power, the energy, the Spirit's driving force. Everything is within you. You have been underestimating yourself and, therefore, you need to go deeper and deeper to see yourself in a real sense. You're not in the body form. You were not born. You have to convince yourself and confirm the truth for yourself. The conviction, "I am not the body" has got to be there!

Q: There are a couple of books such as *I Am That* by Nisargadatta and *Master of Self-Realization* by Siddharameshwar Maharaj. What makes these books different?

Maharaj: Siddharameshwar Maharaj and Nisargadatta Maharaj conveyed the same message: "Except your Selfless Self there is no God, no *Brahman*, no *Atman*, no *Paramatman*". All the saints, all the so-called Masters in their different discourses gave one message, that nothing exists, except Selfless Self. Therefore, you must know yourself in a real sense.

You have to absorb this knowledge. What is said in *I am That*, and all these books, are guidelines that direct the reader's attention to his reality, to the knowledge that he is Ultimate Truth, Final Truth. All these spiritual books give the same message: God does not exist outside of you because in order to say "God", your Spontaneous Invisible Presence is required!

Q: If I were to try and compare your teachings and the lineage to another tradition, what might be the closest, or is this tradition unique?

Maharaj: In this lineage, we use some scientific methods. We give the Guru Mantra to work directly on the very sensitive Spirit. After reciting that Mantra, the realization process will take place spontaneously. Your Inner Master will wake up with all this knowledge, spontaneous knowledge. You already have it, but you don't know that you do, because you are not aware. Because you are unaware of your identity, we have this process of reciting the Mantra.

Q: Shankaracharya. Do his teachings lead to ...?

Maharaj: The same teachings. They are the same. Shankaracharya says: "To say, 'I' is an illusion, to say, 'you' is an illusion, to say, '*Brahman*' is an illusion. The entire world is an illusion". The same message is given by all the spiritual masters.

Q: Thank you for your time, Maharaj! I am sure many people will be interested to know that you are teaching here in Nashik.

Maharaj: Self-enquiry, Self-knowledge, Self-Realization. These are the set stages. Everyone's reading so many books, talking about *Brahman*, *Atman*, *Paramatman*, God. It is very easy to talk about the concepts. But one should question oneself, "What am I getting out of this knowledge?" Am I completely free from fear, the fear of death? Do I have complete peace? Do I have complete happiness, without any material cause? One should question oneself. If the answer is "No", then your knowledge is only literal knowledge.

Be practical! Everything is in you, but we are searching, here and there. We are ignoring the searcher, we are ignoring the finder. You have tremendous power, but you are unaware of that power. You are underestimating yourself, saying, "I am a man", or "I am a woman". That is not your identity, that identity is going to dissolve.

The body has a time limit, but you are everywhere, omnipresent, just like the sky. We are bound by a lifetime of body-based knowledge, food-body knowledge, therefore we are trying to find out where we can find happiness, where we can find complete peace. "Complete" and "happiness" are only words, all of them are illusory!

Just stop, and think for a moment! How was I prior to beingness? There was no God. There was no *Brahman* or *Atman*, these are just words. God, *Brahman*, *Atman* are body-related concepts, illusory concepts. We have to come out of all the illusion and uncover reality. What is reality? The Master hammers reality into the listener, the invisible, anonymous listener. What is the result of that? Once you know yourself in a real sense, you will be out of fear. When you know that you are unborn, all that deeply ingrained fear of death will vanish. There is no birth and death. No birth, no death. Questions about heaven and hell will never arise. The purpose of spirituality is to know yourself in a real sense and erase all the illusions. OK."

Charles finished asking the questions after 11 minutes, or so. Although Maharaj answered them, we could see that he was sitting there enduring the questions, while in the process of "firing up on all cylinders"! He could hardly wait to share the knowledge. As soon as Charles had finished thanking him, Maharaj spontaneously dived into teaching mode. He probably thought… no, not thought… but was happy, not to have to answer any more body-based questions! There was no stopping him, once he had started. He was in full flow!

When we play back the video recording, we are amazed to see at the bottom of the wooden ashram door, near to where Maharaj is sitting, a face appearing, which looks like Nisargadatta Maharaj! It is a little miracle that happens after 1 minute 25 seconds, the exact moment when Charles asks him if he was with

Nisargadatta for 20 years, and Maharaj replies "for 19 years". We upload it to YouTube, calling it "The Interview", like the famous one with Princess Diana!

Reflections: The more we learn about this lineage, the more we are amazed! We feel so privileged to be a part of it, even though we know, as Maharaj has told us many times, that the Lineage is also a concept! Forewarned is forearmed, so, we are not going to fall into another trap of developing a spiritual identity/ego! However, we recognize the effectiveness of the army camp or commando training we are undergoing. It is perfect, and, as Maharaj says, "It is the shortest cut to Self-Realization"! In Appendix 11 of *I Am That* Maurice Frydman writes: "The teaching of Nath Sampradaya offers the seeker the royal road to liberation, a road in which all the four by-lanes of *bhakti, jnana, kharma* and *dhyana* seem to unite" (ie devotion, knowledge, work/service and meditation). The path shown by the Nath is the best of all, and leads directly to liberation".

The method and practice offered to us are like a perfect cocktail, consisting of Knowledge, Mantra, *Bhajans* and Devotion. We are taking the medicine as prescribed – all of it, not just the sweet part, but the bitter and sometimes acidic medicine, too. Maharaj often describes the medicine humorously, saying: "Knowledge is just like antibiotics. To absorb the knowledge, meditation is needed. Meditation is the anti-acid and *bhajan* is the tonic, the B-complex!"

31ˢᵗ December – Where are we at now on this last day of 2013? The knowledge is being absorbed, the Mantra is very productively doing its job of hammering the ego. The *bhajans* keep us flying, while our devotion is deepening!

2014

New Year – It is the beginning of the new year according to our western calendar. This year we are celebrating it uniquely. So happy to be with Maharaj! What are our wishes? The desire to be established in Ultimate Reality, serve Maharaj, and spread the Teachings.

January – We are starting to miss western food, I mean, really miss it, especially the sweet things. Treats are in short supply here. The only fun foods we have encountered so far are dry biscuits called "Parle-G", reminiscent of a bygone era! However, today our longing for a treat was appeased!

An important group of medics arrive at the ashram. They have travelled from Beed, about 400 km from Mumbai. Generally speaking, doctors in India are treated like saints! We immediately notice Anvita carrying to the kitchen, a mouth-watering, luxurious cake with cream and fruit for the occasion.

The group of doctors are avid students of Nisargadatta Maharaj. They saw our Facebook (FB) page which we called "NisargadattaRamakant", to draw people in. They gather around Maharaj excitedly, asking him numerous questions. Then they ask us how we discovered Maharaj, as we live in the UK? We explain a little about how it all transpired!

Maharaj gives a long Talk:

"**Maharaj:** Everything comes out of nothing. Your Presence was there prior to consciousness. Consciousness came afterwards. In order for you to say, "consciousness", your Presence has to be there first. The Presence is anonymous Presence, invisible Presence. Even your "I" is not present there. To say "I", your Presence is required. Without using the body you cannot say "I". Therefore, naming or calling something using words came afterwards. Prior to these words, your Presence was there. I am speaking to that Presence, that invisible anonymous Presence, that has been ignored, buried and forgotten about.

You are anonymous, because "you are", without knowledge. The mind came after. The moment the Spirit clicked with the body, the entire world was projected out. Prior to that, there was your spontaneous, invisible existence. I am talking to That! Forget about reason and meaning. It is not awareness. When you say "awareness", it implies that there's something there, a form. There is nothing there. You are formless. These are all words. Your Presence is an indescribable Presence that is beyond words. We have created the words, and have given meaning to the words, but what I am trying to convey here is beyond the words. We use words like "mind", "awareness", "consciousness", etc. These are just reference words: this is A, this is B, C and so on.

Siddharameshwar Maharaj and Saint Tukaram both convey the same thing: "When there was no world, there was nothing". At that time, your invisible Presence was there. Your silent, anonymous, invisible Presence existed before the word "God". You have given birth to God. Who is God? Because you are measuring yourself in the body-form, you are completely unaware of your importance, your godliness. You have immense power, exceptional power, but it is hidden from you because of the body-form.

Understand that you are separate from the body and the world. You have separated yourself from your source. We are thinking, using terms that are limited to the circle, the confines of body-based knowledge. Every question, everything is body-based knowledge. It is an open fact that you are not a body, you are not going to remain a body, and you were not a body. Forget about spirituality! The body is not your identity, nor is it the reality. Some day or other, the body will stop functioning. Eventually, something is bound to go wrong with the body-form. That conviction is most important.

Once reality is known, you should not be tempted to go elsewhere. This is Ultimate Truth. You are Ultimate Truth. It is your reality. Why keep saying, "Where is *Brahman*? Where is *Brahman*? Where is *Brahman*? You are Ultimate Truth, Final Truth.

Use discrimination, and come out of the trap of body-based knowledge! You are the source of happiness and peace. Try to understand the process. As soon as you see yourself: "I am", you see the world. Then the words follow: "This is mine", "this is yours", when in fact, nothing is mine and nothing is yours because there is no separation, and no "I" or "you". Whatever comes out of this body-form will not last. Use discrimination, *Viveka*! *Viveka*! Always use discrimination! It is not difficult.

Continue with your responsibilities and duties. There are no restrictions. Some people come here after abandoning their parents. Why are you leaving your parents? Do your duty! Take care of them, look after them. Spirituality should not disturb your family life. Get to know yourself in a real sense. What is the fate of the world? The moment the body disappears everything disappears. [Maharaj claps] The body disappears and with it, all the knowledge you have gathered. It is very simple! Don't swim in the sea of bookish knowledge, literal knowledge. It is what the books wish to convey that is most important.

Your Presence is devoid of imagination and concepts. It is similar to the state of deep sleep when you are not aware of yourself. That is Reality. Don't stress your brain, don't stress your mind. Everything is within you because the Masterly Essence is already within you. But you are not giving any importance to that. You have been looking out, instead of in, and therefore you have forgotten all about your inner Master.

You may have some book knowledge and common-sense knowledge. Books promise many things such as: "This knowledge will give you peace, happiness, even power", but they do not bring you to the full stop, the destination, complete rest! (Thus, the haphazard wanderings of the aspirant continue!)

Everything is within you. Be simple, be calm. Everything comes out of nothing, then nothing absorbs into nothing. Everything comes out of nothing. Everything is absorbed within nothing which is everything. Think on this! "I" became an "I" who started saying, "yes, yes, yes" to everything... and then that "I" returned to nothing". Nisargadatta Maharaj says, "everything comes out of nothing and is absorbed in nothing". You are to teach yourself in this way!

I am talking about the listener, the silent, invisible, anonymous listener, not the body-form. It is your story, the listener's story. We have given shape to the listener. "I am somebody, something". You are nobody because you are everybody.

You are nobody! You are nothing because you are everything. Because you identify with "I am somebody", you are placing yourself, confining yourself within a circle or square. You are limiting yourself. Your identity is beyond any square, circle or boundary. You are formless and limitless, therefore, you are everybody.

You are prior to everything. Your Spontaneous Presence is prior to everything. What is this so-called peace of mind that you are searching for? The "mind" just means the flow of thoughts. The seer is within. Who sees? You are the witness that is witnessing everything. You are not the mind.

Go deep and deep and deep! Where everything ends, there you are. Where everything ends, there you are. You do not have a form or shape. There is no awareness, no unawareness, no consciousness. The term "consciousness" is always related to the body-form. "Consciousness" and "awareness" are simply terms that are related to the body-form, to some form. Prior to consciousness, there is your spontaneous invisible Presence, nothing more!

It is simple if you follow the directives of a Master. Dry discussions alone will not help you to know yourself. At the initial stage, a guide is needed, a Master is required. You may go and see any Master, that's up to you. But when you do find a Master, you must use discrimination, and make sure that he is a true, authentic Master. Then you must have strong faith, complete trust.

There is a story about Nisargadatta Maharaj. There was a great saint in the Himalayas who, with foresight, could see that Nisargadatta was the only person to whom he could transfer his powers. So, he sent one of his disciples to ask Nisargadatta Maharaj if he would take on his powers.

Nisargadatta Maharaj refused. He was very strong, saying, "I am not a widow. Though my Master no longer exists in the body-form, "I am not a widow". He had complete faith and trust. There can be no compromise where faith and trust are concerned. Even if God appears before you, you will remain resolute and say, "No, no, no, no!" That firm stance leads to reality. What I am saying is also an illusion, but this kind of total and absolute Conviction leads to reality.

A philosopher used to come to Maharaj nearly every day. One day, he said, "Maharaj, I know what you are saying, but the truth is still not established within me". He was a great philosopher and politician, who also had a good command of spirituality. But after 5 or 6 months, he said: "I can understand the knowledge, but it is still not established within me." At this point, he asked Maharaj for the *Naam Mantra*, to establish the Truth within him.

You have to forget about body-based knowledge and literal knowledge. It is not the Ultimate Truth. Unless you forget about it all, the unidentified power, the Ultimate Truth, will not be uncovered. Serious meditation is needed in the beginning. Casual meditation will not work!

Initially, when the Master is hammering you with: "You are *Brahman*, you are *Brahman*", you will not accept it. Why? Because you are surrounded by the illusory world and you don't want to come out of it, and leave that big story behind! Forget about spirituality! Wake up to the fact that your body is not going to remain. Confront this fact that someday you must leave the body.

At the early stage, meditation is most important. Meditation is a cleaning process. When you have a cut or wound, you let the doctor apply an antiseptic to it. Similarly, let meditation clean your wounds of illusion!

Q: When I go in the direction of "I am", when I get established in that "I am"...

Maharaj: Why go anywhere? There is no going or coming. "I am" is *Atma*. You are already there! Why are you going towards the establishment of "I am"? You are that "I am"! Why go and make some deliberate efforts, telling yourself, "I have to go into "I Am" and get established in "I Am"?

Q: He says no going, no coming.

Q: Absolutely.....

Maharaj: Therefore, meditation is required – it is the medicine. After a period of meditation, there will be exceptional calmness. Have courage! Everything is within you, open, self-revealing. What you have learned and absorbed, will be established through meditation. When planting some seeds, prior to that, you must clean the ground, just like you clean your wounds before applying ointment to them. The field will be cleared totally. You will be cleansed and washed by the light. Find out who you are so that your suffering will end. This will prepare you for when it is your time to leave the body. If you are prepared, you will not suffer from confusion or distress. Therefore, meditation is the first step, through which everything will be made clear. And then, the Knowledge will open up to you. You are Knowledge.

Q: In Marathi. When I am-ness.....

Maharaj: When you come to know the Reality, why do you wish to remain in "I am-ness"?

Q: This is a direct method!

Maharaj: Be as it is! Very simple. Don't do anything. Forget it! There is no deed, no doer because you are everywhere. So don't make any deliberate efforts. What we have discussed so far, just remember and absorb it. That is enough. Don't put in any effort! Did we make any deliberate efforts to come here? Did we make any kind of effort to enter this abode? After our life here in India, will we take birth in another place? Did you pass any examinations to get here? No! Everything happens spontaneously!

Don't do, don't try to remain in "I am-ness". It is okay, but it is nothing but a child's game. You are no longer a child. How long are you going to keep saying, "this is the base, this is the base, this is the base"?

You need to have conviction, a firm stance. Strong foundations are most important. Then there won't be any temptation to keep searching, to go elsewhere. Everyone is living casually. Sometimes, we have to visit our family members. When you do, don't let your guard down. Shri Siddharameshwar talked about this. Do your duties, but at the same time, be convinced that you are nothing to do with this world. Remind yourself and say, "I am nothing to do with this world".

You are completely free. You are a free bird. You can fly using your wings, you can fly with your wings. Have some courage! Many saints were illiterate, so why should it be difficult for you? You went to college. You are educated!

There was a lady with an asthmatic problem. She said that at 4 o'clock precisely, her pain started. She was attached to this concept. She saw a doctor who prescribed pain killers, then another doctor and another. Nothing worked! At 4 o'clock, she would glance at the clock and her pain would start up again! We are like that. We are victims of our own psychology.

Therefore, be your own master. You have a good base. With all your knowledge, you will not find anything impossible. Take your own medicine. There is nothing wrong with you, except for a lack of courage and confidence. You have imagined things from others, borrowed from others, accepted from others. It is all an illusion! If someone says something is wrong, you immediately accept it. It is the nature of Spirit to be sensitive. Convince yourself that you are Ultimate Reality. Convince yourself with the reality, in the same way, you allowed others before, to convince you with all their illusory concepts! Find out for yourself and finally accept this!

One devotee asked his Master what *Brahman* is like? The Master replied, it is just like an onion. After removing each, and every skin, nothing will remain. Convince yourself in this way. You have good knowledge, no problem, but it is not pragmatic. It is not lived. That is the problem."

Later on, we continue the discussion at Maharaj's home where Anvita has been hard at work, as usual, preparing the food for everyone. The questions are flowing. One of them asks: "Are you realized, Maharaj?", followed by, "how do we know if someone is realized?" Spontaneously, I reply, "The devotee knows!", at which point, Maharaj turns his head around and looks straight through me, or so it felt. "Find out if you are realized. That is the most important question!"

Frequently, the group speaks in Marathi. We ask them if they can translate what is said into English, as we are recording the Talks for English-speaking seekers? They did it for a while, but then, overcome with excitement, slip back into their native language. After a few days, the group leaves.

10th January – Evening *bhajans*. Feeling so happy. Feel like throwing my hands in the air and singing at the top of my voice. Shouting and dancing like a dervish, but I need to restrain myself in the ashram.

Mid-January – One of the earliest visitors to the ashram is an elderly seeker from the States. Maharaj is very fond of him. He eagerly listens to Maharaj's discourses while admitting to being very fixed in his ways. He often tells Maharaj that he is too old to change, even if he wants to change. Despite Maharaj telling him repeatedly, that every concept he came up with is an illusion and has nothing to do with his Reality, he still refuses to budge. We wonder why he has bothered to come if he is happy with the status quo. Maybe he wants to have his cake and eat it! Or, maybe, he hopes that the *Naam Mantra* might be a magic wand that will change everything and liberate him, without any effort on his part! Whatever his motives are, there is a lot of humour in the exchanges, as well as much affection and warmth.

After he leaves, Maharaj says the same thing that he often says about some visitors to the ashram, namely: "Maybe it isn't his destiny".

The more time we spend with Maharaj, just being around him, listening to his discourses, etc, the closer we feel we are being drawn and pulled in towards him. Not we, but that one Essence that we all share is merging into Him.

Maharaj gives an excellent Talk. He uses the phrase, "The Melting Process is Marching towards Oneness". This has been our experience: Melting on hearing the Highest Knowledge! We transcribe it, and send it to "*Speaking Tree*", a popular, online site on spirituality, which subsequently attracted many seekers to Maharaj. Here is the discourse:

Maharaj: "Watch and wait! The melting process has started. So many experiences will happen that will make you strong. Don't think, or try to identify what is Ultimate Reality, and what is not. Is this it, or is that it? Forget about the words "ultimate" or "not ultimate". Remove these words. Your Spontaneous Presence is ultimate, your spontaneous and invisible Presence is ultimate and beyond that. Upon your Spontaneous Presence, experiences have appeared.

Whatever you are experiencing during this dissolving process, is happening correctly, as it should. But you've not to question what is happening, or not. It is the melting process marching towards oneness. Some types of layers of experiences are happening during this melting process that is dissolving you. In the ultimate stage, the witnesser, the witness and the witnessing will all be completely dissolved. You will not witness anything. This happens - it is the outcome of the meditation.

I emphasize meditation because so many thoughts were impressed upon us, from childhood till today. Therefore, the melting process will take some time, and that is why meditation is required. "Strong dedication" is the perfect term - you must have strong dedication towards your Self, dedication to the Master, who has shown you that unidentified identity. Why do you require a Master? It is only because of Him that we have the Teachings! Without Nisargadatta, I would not be able to talk, not one single word. I would still be going to some God temple or other, looking for happiness and peace. But now we have some strong foundations. What he, (Nisargadatta) says is: "except your Selfless Self, nothing is there". When I see my Self nothing is there. What do you want me to convey? Except yourself, there is no God, no *Atman*, *Brahman*.

Then it will be open. The door of Knowledge will be completely open. So, this dedication, this conviction, what Nisargadatta says is perfect.

There is the popular story of a beggar boy whose uncle tells him one day: "You are not a beggar, you are really a millionaire". The boy doesn't believe him, and says, "You are making a fool out of me. You are a liar. That's impossible!" So, the uncle takes him to the bank and shows him the account, with all the money in his name. Only then, after having all the evidence in front of him, is he convinced and accepts it. Likewise, the Master says: 'You are *Brahman*, *Atman*.' Why are you not believing it, saying: 'No, you are joking'? How can you be convinced? For you to have conviction, you need this process of meditation. The effect of the meditation is that all the illusory layers will dissolve. All the illusory layers will dissolve. Then you will come across your Perfection – "Oh! I Am That!" The spontaneous perfection. (He gestures with amazement). The Master is perfect, therefore, your devotion to the Master grows because He has shown you your Ultimate Truth.

We are not talking about blind faith here. It is not blind faith. We are indebted to the Master because without Him, we would not have been able to "catch" Reality. You realize that, if you had not met a Master, you would likely still be going round in circles, going here and there, (seeking/reading etc), checking out this, and that, type of knowledge, that type of person, guru, this master, that master. Except for your Self, nothing is there. Be strong! (Maharaj gestures with a clenched fist). How to accept it, how to absorb it? Slowly, silently, permanently!"

When a group of people are gathered together for *Satsang* with Maharaj, there is unique energy, an intimate and joyful atmosphere, like sitting around a campfire listening to a wise old "Indian chief". Here, the roasted marshmallows we are consuming is Truth, and its fragrance is the play of words, humour and laughter that transform us into enthusiastic, innocent children!

End of January – "Now you are at the last stage", says Maharaj to us both. The words of the Guru are always true. All that he has taught us so far, has been absorbed. In only a few months, under the guidance of Maharaj, we have gone through the process of Self-Enquiry and Self-Knowledge, leaping forward, without any attachments to the past. Now we are at Stage 3 – Self-Realization! We have truly been on an express train: the "direct line to Self-knowledge". Charles created an image of a train with Maharaj's face on the front, to depict the quote, "Get on the direct line to Self-knowledge. It will take you Home!" This post amused Maharaj no end!

We are feeling very, very blessed! We realize how fortunate we are to have received the *Naam Mantra*, which has removed all the rotten deadwood, that had been stopping the inner fire from blazing!

Maharaj frequently says that experiences are not Ultimate Truth, but he also states, as he did in his recent Talk, "so many experiences will happen that will make you strong". We have been blessed with many beautiful and encouraging experiences. And while we know that these are not the Ultimate Truth, we also understand that they deepen our conviction. They are signposts that encourage and reassure us, that we are inching closer and closer to Ultimate Truth! Also, these experiences are not fleeting, many of them are direct experiences of Truth that heighten and intensify our conviction. Our experiences are reminders of our nature, deepening the Self-Knowledge along the way. Their impact endures. So, while experiences are not Ultimate Truth, they do, as Maharaj says, make us strong!

Recently, during my meditation, various images arose, including that of a lion. These appearances remind one that everything happens spontaneously! Similarly, when we hear, see, or feel the touch of the Master, these experiences deepen our devotion and love for Him. They draw us closer to Him, and, therefore, draw us closer to Ultimate Truth.

We are not getting hooked on experiences, but we both know they are escalating and strengthening our conviction! The way we see it is that while the experiences are all illusions, the knock-on effect they have, of reinforcing the conviction, is real!

We are so grateful to Maharaj for being willing to initiate westerners. Nisargadatta initiated very few, as he considered us to be mere "spiritual tourists". For Maharaj, however, receiving the *Naam Mantra* proved to be a landmark moment, a catalyst that changed his life forever. It helped him so greatly, that he naturally wished the same for everyone else! He wanted to share it with as many sincere seekers as possible, irrespective of whether they were Indian or not! He did not give it to everyone, though. We witnessed him refusing it to one gentleman, who kept appearing at the ashram, asking for the *Naam*. Knowing that he would exploit the sacred *Naam*, Maharaj rejected his every request, even when the man resorted to begging.

Annual Pilgrimage – Maharaj is getting ready to go on the traditional annual pilgrimage with a group of Indian devotees. They will visit various locations of the Masters such as Gurulingajangam Maharaj's shrine in Nimbargi, Bhausaheb Maharaj's at Umadi, and Inchegiri where he taught. Then onto Pathri, the birth place of Siddharmaeshwar and Bagewadi, where he taught, as well as Bijapur where Siddharameshwar did intense *samadhi*. Then there is also Nimbal where Gurudev Ranade lived, and Kanure, Shri Ganapatrao's place. There were other sites, too, such as the caves of Shri Samarth, where the sacred *Dasbodh* was orally transmitted.

Maharaj invites us to go with him, but we decline, as we do not wish to risk our health. Also, we heard that it would be a rough, demanding pilgrimage, where we would be sleeping on the stone ground. Now that our bodies are ageing, we are very cautious and really do not feel it is the right thing to do! On top of that, we have a lot of work to do, transcribing talks, admin, as well as serious meditation.

We tell Maharaj, that it is best if we do not go this year... maybe next year! He is fine with our response. Before leaving, he tells us to look after his home, and entrusts us with the keys, telling us to make ourselves comfortable, and use his home whenever we wish! It is easier to use Maharaj's big computer screen for work, instead of our smaller laptops.

When Maharaj is about to depart, a group of devotees gather around him to say goodbye. We stand next to the Indian devotees. A couple of them have been suspicious of us since our arrival. They do not think we are as devoted as them because – despite Maharaj's teachings of oneness - they still view us as westerners! One of them tells me to kneel on the ground and bow at Maharaj's feet. "Why are you not bowing?" he asks. It feels like he is challenging me. I start to bow, but Maharaj stops me, saying, "No, no, not on the ground", which was quite dirty. The devotee insists, so, I try to bow again. Maharaj stops me for a second time. Eventually, I just bow at Maharaj's feet, and the devotee walks away. Whether he was satisfied or not, I cannot say and, it does not matter!

Now we have the whole ashram to ourselves! Our meditation intensifies, and with it, the falling away of more and more conceptual baggage. One "Aha" moment during meditation concerned the concept of a "door", which I had read about in one of the Nisargadatta books, a long time ago. It had something to do with standing at the door, the portal to Reality. It was only today I realized that this door concept had become another barrier, that I was not even aware of! I had been carrying, what felt like a heavy solid wooden door (lol) all this time!

First of all, in the meditation, I see an image of a door. Then the image vanishes, and with it comes the realization that there is no door. As soon as this happens, I see Nisargadatta gesturing to me with his hand to "come in"! He says:

"Enter, enter!" It is another wonderful meditation. Thank you dear Nisargadatta Maharaj!

In the absence of devotees around us in the ashram, we freely and spontaneously bow to the Masters, as often as we can, without care! Filled with joy and without inhibition, we lie on the floor, humbly prostrating to them, praising them, thanking them for everything, for all their sacrifices, for finding us. Our shared laughter frequently explodes across the ashram like volcanic eruptions.

Shri Bhausaheb spent years in the forest in meditation, trying to create a simple practice that would lead to liberation. During this time, he even tied his pigtail to a water wheel, so that if he dozed off, he would wake up immediately! Such was his devotion, determination and selfless desire for others to awaken! He strove to find a way of knowing Reality directly. He used to say that we only know our true nature through words, indirectly, therefore, he put together a practice to remedy this. The scientifically proven *Naam Mantra* worked well. But he realized that more was needed. He enrolled the help of Guru Ranade, an eminent philosopher, to select appropriate *bhajans* with the highest meanings, to further aid the dissolution process of the ego. These beautiful, powerful Masters tried to simplify a practice, that would encapsulate the highest teachings, and offer the shortest cut to Self-Realization. We are indebted to them!

These Masters are amazing, with each one refining and advancing the Teachings. We did some research on the Lineage, and found out more about the Inchegiri Navnath Sampradaya.

The origin of the Navanath Sampradaya Lineage goes back over a thousand years, to Dattatreya. One branch of the Navnath Lineage, (Nine Masters), eventually became the Inchegiri Navnath Sampradaya, founded by Shri Bhausaheb Maharaj. This is the direct line that leads to Shri Ramakant Maharaj.

This Lineage is relatively unknown, as the Masters were all very humble. They did not give themselves much importance, but they were all dedicated to spreading the Knowledge and the Teachings. Shri Bhausaheb Maharaj, Shri Siddharameshwar Maharaj, Shri Nisargadatta Maharaj and his co-disciple, Shri Ranjit Maharaj were ordinary people.

Oneness of knowledge and devotion, (*jnana* and *bhakti*), is key in the Lineage teachings. Devotion is the Mother of Knowledge. Only by intense devotion to the Guru, and worshipping Him with full faith, will the knowledge of Self-Realization be revealed. In the end, there is total unity between knowledge and devotion.

The Lineage is a Guru-centred one, where the Master makes Masters out of disciples. The Guru initiates the disciple with the Guru Mantra (*Naam Mantra*), the Master Key. The Mantra, the Guru and the Initiation are inseparable. Faith in, and complete acceptance of the Guru, and Guru Mantra are essential. The Masters of this Lineage have all recited the same Mantra. By taking the Sacred Naam, one is receiving the help and power from the Masters of this Lineage. Ultimately, one becomes One with the Master, *Sadguru*. Ramakant Maharaj says, "Reciting the Guru Mantra leads to true Self-Knowledge, and is the only truly effective way to return to the Original State".

Siddharameshwar Maharaj, himself, gave all credit to Bhausaheb Maharaj. Nisargadatta Maharaj did the same with Siddharameshwar Maharaj. Similarly, Ramakant Maharaj gave all credit to his Master, Nisargadatta Maharaj. There is a very strong connection right through the whole Lineage, "I am just a skeleton, a puppet of my Master", says Ramakant Maharaj.

"In our Lineage, we give 'Direct Knowledge' to your 'Invisible Presence', not to the body-form", says the Master. "This Knowledge is Spontaneous Knowledge. It is not bookish knowledge, it is Spontaneous Knowledge. The words are different, the style of speaking may be different, but the principle is the same. There is nothing except Selfless Self". This Knowledge is Rare Knowledge, as the Masters do not simply talk about Reality, but will show the Reality in oneself, in the disciple. This Direct Knowledge coming as it does, from this long line of sparkling Masters, is further empowered by the sacred *Naam Mantra*.

The teachings are solid and strong, with the whole Lineage behind them. They are pure and extremely powerful. The Masters share all the secrets. Nothing is kept hidden. It is Open Truth that has always been shared freely, without any expectations. There is to be no commercial abuse of the Knowledge that is one's inherent property - Truth. Bhausaheb Maharaj said, "In our Lineage, you are not to take any monies from devotees. Any association with money will spoil the *Naam Mantra*. The Sampradaya does not demand anything".

Bhausaheb Maharaj (1843-1914), was initiated by Shri Raghunathpriya Maharaj. His *Sadguru* was Shri Gurulingajangam Maharaj whom he loved deeply. He was known as the saint of Umadi and was a householder. Bhausaheb Maharaj had many disciples, including Shri Siddharameshwar Maharaj, Shri Gurudev Ranade, and Shri Amburao Maharaj, to mention but a few. His way is known as the "Ant's Way", using meditation, dispassion and renunciation.

His main emphasis was through the medium of meditation, rather than knowledge. This was because many of the disciples came from rural communities and were illiterate. Bhausaheb Maharaj endured great hardships, as he strove to find Reality. He stood in the forest for eighteen years without rest, meditating for twelve hours at a time. Stressing the importance of remembering the Divine Name, he would say, "Take it to your bones. Always do fierce repetition of the Divine Name in the mind with meditation".

Siddharameshwar Maharaj (1888-1936), was born in Pathri, Sholapur. When Bhausaheb Maharaj saw Siddharameshwar Maharaj for the first time, he announced, "This man is greatly blessed", and gave him Initiation on that very same day.

He was in the company of his Master for seven years. After his Master's passing, he was so determined to attain Self-Realization, he was prepared to sacrifice his life for it. He started intense meditation, coupled with penance. It is said that he reached such extraordinary heights while meditating, that he emitted a beautiful nectar-like fragrance, which perfumed the air all around him.

Siddharameshwar Maharaj, like many other Masters of this lineage, worked and had a family. Being a householder was not to be seen as an obstacle, but instead, as an opportunity for selflessness and detachment.

Through his practice, it was becoming clear to him, that meditation was only the beginning stage, in the process of reaching the Final Reality. And so, he advanced the teachings, moving from the "Ant's Way", to the "Bird's Way". Reality can be reached through discrimination and dispassion, "Illusory" means that one does not have to throw it away. One just has to realize its deceptive form, and then bring it into action in everyday life. Otherwise, even if the knowledge of the Self is understood intellectually, it will never be totally imprinted in one's heart and mind.

It would not become active. His spirituality, like his Master's before him, was pragmatic.

Two years later, his beloved Master, Bhausaheb Maharaj, blessed him with a vision and communicated, "Now you have reached the Final Reality. There is nothing left for you to do".

He started teaching, using simple language to communicate knowledge and devotion. It is said that he initiated many people from all walks of life. The figure is not known exactly, but it is believed that dozens were realized through this extraordinary Master! These include Ganapatrao Maharaj, Bainath Maharaj, Nisargadatta Maharaj, Ranjit Maharaj, Muppin Kaadsiddheshwar Maharaj, Balkrishna Maharaj.

He kept his teachings practical, using examples from daily life. The method of Self-enquiry, discrimination and dispassion was encouraged.

To prevent the Knowledge from staying dry and hollow, Siddharameshwar Maharaj stressed the importance of devotion and honouring one's Master. The book, *Master of Self-Realization*, containing his teachings, is a spiritual classic.

Nisargadatta Maharaj (1897-1981), was devoted to his Master, Shri Siddharameshwar Maharaj. He was very fortunate to have met him, only about three years before his Master's passing, at age forty-eight. Remarkably, a few years later, he, himself, attained Self-Realization.

Maharaj advanced the teachings yet again, with his sometimes snappy, yet always piercing Direct Knowledge. His remarkable teachings awakened many seekers. The famous book, *I Am That*, published in 1973, with the clarion call of, "The seeker is he who is in search of himself", brought a flurry of western visitors.

Speaking on the *Naam Mantra*, Nisargadatta Maharaj said: "The Mantra is very powerful and effective. My Guru gave me this Mantra and the result is all these visitors from all over the world. That shows you its power".

Ramakant Maharaj (born 1941-2018), was initiated in 1962, by his Master, Nisargadatta Maharaj, and evolved the teachings of the Lineage once more. His approach was ground-breaking, radical and absolute. He did not entertain concepts, quickly cutting through everything, including the "I Am" concept. He offered a shortcut to Self-Realization, presenting the Highest Teachings, in down-to-earth language. These Lineage Masters are passing on the highest knowledge, selflessly and openly. Dependency on the Master, and the Master's form, is strongly discouraged. Their sincere and noble wish is to transform the disciple into a Master. Therein lies the uniqueness of the Inchegiri Navnath Sampradaya.

Here we can see the stark contrast to those teachers in the west where the travelling circus of *Satsang* never ends! Maharaj often says: "Have *Satsang* with yourself!" That is the true meaning of *Satsang*.

Mid-February – We are dwelling in Truth and watering the seeds! There is so much serenity all around, within, everywhere! We both feel it strongly, as if we are being held and enveloped in peace. Once more, we share the recognition of our utterly good fortune to be here. We feel undeserving of the grace and blessings bestowed upon us! But who is undeserving? Only the remnants of who we once thought we were! There is no such thing as deserving or undeserving – grace touches all!

Devotion is somewhat alien in the west, yet it is essential. In this lineage, all the Masters were devoted to their Masters. Shri Nisargadatta was devoted to his Master, Shri Siddharameshwar, but that aspect seems to have been forgotten or submerged, deliberately, or not. When we read Shri Nisargadatta's spiritual classic, *I Am That*, we realized that knowledge, by itself alone, is insufficient. It is only through devotion, along with meditation, that the ego is hammered efficiently and effectively. Knowledge may cut off some of the ego's branches, but it will not uproot the ego. For that, we need a cleansing process that will demolish our fake egoic foundations, and allow for the knowledge to seep in and be absorbed. We also need to develop humility.

Being here in the ashram with Maharaj, has taught us that when we bow to the Master with our hearts, with our all, humility grows. And when we obey the Master, in that act of surrendering, the ego diminishes. It is a powerful and beautiful teaching! Inside and outside, we are enfolded in light and immense peace, bathed in the light of the sun, the sky, the universe.

17ᵗʰ February – Today we summon up the courage to take a rickshaw, or "tuk-tuk", as they call them - to the hustle and bustle of Nashik city centre. It was both amazing and scary, in the midst of the chaotic traffic, busyness and array of colours and smells! We buy a couple of papayas, which we have grown very fond of during our stay, as well as coconuts. Then we find a clothes shop, and splash out on a couple of smart outfits. We are driven to dress more respectfully for the Master who has reignited the fire within us! It is indeed true that if the seeker is ripe and hears the Truth from a true Master, the work is done - transmission then transformation! And who better than Shri Ramakant Maharaj, who spent timeless years with the great Nisargadatta! We keep our trip short, as the noise is overwhelming, in contrast to our hermit-like retreat, during the last few months.

Back at Maharaj's house, Charles is eager to put up another post on FB. He has noticed a few times, that whenever he posts a quote of Shri Ramakant on a Nisargadatta FB page, it would somehow mysteriously disappear, soon after. And not only that, he sometimes found a few comments such as: "Do we really need another Guru after Nisargadatta?" There is obvious resistance to Ramakant Maharaj and his Teachings. Recently, when Charles uploaded a discourse entitled "Beware 'I Am' is a concept", there were even more negative reactions. Many Nisargadatta followers have been practising a kind of "I Am" meditation, and here comes Ramakant who sets it aside. "Everything must be thrown out", says the Master, "because there is nothing prior to beingness: no words, no concepts, no language, no feelings, no senses, no nothing!"

Here is the wonderful discourse which clarifies a lot about the "I" and the "I am":

"**Q**: When people practice the "I Am" meditation, they don't seem to know how to cross over. In my case, I did not manage to go beyond it.

Maharaj: To say the word "I" is ego, an egoic act... Why are you trying to remain in, or, as "I"? It means you are taking on some sense of ego, saying, I am something, somebody else. Feeling the sense of "I am", or intending to remain as "I am", means you are separating yourself. It infers a doer that is trying to do something: with eyes closed, staying with "I am". This is duality. No effort is needed! You know that you exist. You know that you are. That is enough! Meditation on "I am" is meditation with the subtle ego. Your Presence is spontaneous, therefore, don't think, don't apply the intellect, don't feel. This way is unnecessary and is just an illusory concept. You are already in that; it is already within you.

Be as it is! Just be that Reality, without thinking. Don't pressure the brain! The feeling "I am" is spontaneous. You have turned it into a concept and a practice. You are trying to experience, "I am *Brahman, Atman*", and to do that, you are separating yourself from the source that you are.

Q: So there is duality, there is a split?

Maharaj: Yes, immediately! Why practice in this way, to stay with "I am"?. Why try at all? Why even have the intention of, say, "I want to stay as Charles. I am Charles. I am Charles". You already are Charles! You already are what you are! Your Spontaneous Presence, existence, is without shape. Don't try, just be! Because you already are! Who says you must stay as "I am"?

Q: I think the understanding is that if you stay with the sense of "I am" and meditate on that, then it will take you beyond. But I don't think many are managing to go beyond.

Maharaj: You see, your spontaneous existence manifested, so, apart from that, there is no other focus. This kind of practice brings the subtle ego. Don't make any effort! Don't take these spiritual pointers or directives literally. Try and understand what they are trying to convey. Meditation is a spontaneous action. It means concentrating on the concentrator, which means forgetting about your bodily identity.

You always remain as you are. You remain as Charles, without making any effort. Similarly, with meditation, you are already that invisible, anonymous identity, therefore, there is no need to add to that, or to try and stay, or remain, as that!

Q: So, when people sit down and meditate on the "I am"...

Maharaj: In the beginning, meditation just means you are concentrating... I told you what meditation means! You are concentrating and forgetting your bodily identity! When you are told you are *Brahman*, that you are Ultimate Truth, and you accept it, then spontaneously and completely, you forget about the body. And then, after some time, you will exclaim, "I am That!" I am that Ultimate Truth, through which I know myself in a real sense. It does not have any figure, shape or form. It is formless!

You cannot realize the Presence, by thinking, feeling or sensing through your bodily "I". Where was that "I" prior to beingness? You have dumped yourself in an illusory muddle. You have dumped yourself in it, by taking the words too literally. You've kept yourself in an illusory balloon!

You are in a bubble or a balloon and trying to concentrate hard to stay there. Now you need to burst the balloon. How do you burst it? Let's look at the chicken and egg for a moment! Inside the egg, the little chick pecks and pecks, using its beak, until it finally breaks out of the hard, confining shell. So, let us say that here, the beak stands for knowledge. You are confined. You are trapped in an illusory circle. Knowledge is given to you, so that you can break out of that circle of illusion, just like the baby chicken spontaneously breaks through the thick shell.

Q: So the beak represents knowledge, which is used to break through the hard shell of illusion?

Maharaj: Ultimate Truth is like that. What you call *Brahman, Atman, Paramatman..* its action is spontaneous. When the egg matures the breakthrough happens. You see, it is a very hard core, but despite this, the small chicken manages to break it. Similarly, all around us, there is a hard core of illusion. But, with the knowledge, with the Ultimate knowledge, Spiritual Truth will peck and peck, until it emerges from within. You are your own Master. Whatever you read or listen to, is helpful to some extent, but once you reach the final destination, you will no longer need the address. Be careful not to take the Masters' words literally. What they want to convey is what's important. You stuck with a concept and that concept has paralyzed you. You became stuck with the "I am" concept which you blew up like a balloon. You blew it out of all proportion.

Q: Maybe somewhat similar to misinterpreting Ramana Maharshi's guidance about asking, "Who am I?" And last night you said, "The answer is the questioner" which made people laugh. And yet many people are sitting for years, asking "Who am I?"

and not making progress.

Maharaj: Self-Enquiry is very important. First stage Self-Enquiry, second stage Self-knowledge, third stage Self-Realization. After obtaining extensive knowledge, reading endless books and listening to the Masters, you must ask yourself, "Where do I stand? Am I fearless?" If the answer is "No", it means that you are still holding a blank cheque despite your efforts. True knowledge should make you fearless.

This is simple knowledge that tells you: You are not the body, you were not the body, you are not going to remain the body. Through the body, you imagine and encounter many concepts. Prior to beingness, there were no concepts. After the so-called death of the body, all the concepts will disappear. Who will be saying or feeling, "I am", when the body dissolves?

Since the beginning of life, you have been saying "I, I, I"... Prior to beingness there was no "I", after the body dissolves – again, no "I". So why concentrate on the "I" at all?

Q: So, if the meditation on "I am" does not lead to Ultimate Reality then it's not very helpful to keep on doing it?

Maharaj: Why colour what you already are with a form? This is not meditation. Prior to beingness where is that "I"? As I told you, your invisible Presence is just like the sky. This is the reality. You are unaware of your identity. You do not know yourself. That unknown Spirit has been covered with illusory thoughts... mind, ego, intellect. We give the Mantra so that you can come out of this illusory field. What is the meaning of the Mantra? I am *Brahman*, *Brahman* I am, like "I am That, I am That". After concentrating on the Mantra, you will forget your identity and all about "I" or "I am"!

So, through meditation, you will become blind to everything, as if you are in a trance. But it is not exactly a trance, as you can witness a trance. The state is beyond a trance! After the conviction arises, there will be nothing to do. Your reactions will be spontaneous.

We will finish now. But let me tell you a story! A foreigner came to India and asked a guide, "Who made the Taj Mahal?" The guide said, "I don't know". He visited many places and asked the same question. The guide gave him the same answer each time: "I don't know the name of this person or that person". Eventually, the foreigner sees a dead body being carried along the street. Again he asks, "Who is that?" The guide says, "I don't know".

What he is saying is that he does not know the name of anything or anyone. Everything in its entirety is a dream, and therefore, the only possible answer is "I don't know". So, he says this, meaning he does not know the name of anything or anyone. Similarly, what can we say about the whole world except, "I don't know". I tell you this just for the purpose of understanding.

Q: Having read Nisargadatta Maharaj's books, I got the impression that the "I am" was the doorway, and like a tunnel, you had to go through it, like the chicken with the egg.

Maharaj: You need to undergo a process, through which you will arrive at the Final Truth...

Q: Sometimes I have attached myself to concepts. I told you that during a meditation, I realized I had been hanging onto one of Nisargadatta's concepts. He said, "Stay at the door, the door is open" But then, not realizing it, this door had become an obstacle, until it was pointed out to me during meditation.

Maharaj: There is no door at all, no walls, no barriers, no obstacles no hurdles. Everything is open!

Q: I removed the door and I was through...what I mean is the door was no longer there!

Maharaj: So you broke through the concepts. The Master has given you the key that shows you how to open the door. Ok!"

After hearing this powerful and liberating discourse, we name it, "'I Am' is a Concept. Beware!" It received a lot of negative responses, as Maharaj tugged away at what had become a stagnant, comfort blanket for many.

We suspect that the way the "I Am" meditation practice has evolved, and the importance it has been given, was not Nisargadatta Maharaj's intention. We also have a hunch that this came about because Nisargadatta was not willing to initiate westerners, with the *Naam Mantra*. He freely initiated the Indian devotees, but only initiated very few westerners! How does the *Naam Mantra* meditation differ? The *Naam Mantra* is not a word or words, but a powerful vibration.

End of February – I put together a "Method" and "Process" section for the website that will help inform and prepare visitors before their arrival at the ashram:

Method Guidelines

Shri Ramakant Maharaj, is part of the same lineage of Masters, as Shri Nisargadatta Maharaj, of the Inchegiri Navnath Sampradaya. The teachings are the same as his Master's, but differ by way of method and expression.

His method of teaching is also radical - again, like his Master before him - with a fresh approach in terms of delivery, and stance. It is uncompromisingly absolute.

Maharaj shares 'Direct Living Knowledge'. There are no long-winded explanations that take you round in circles. References to other sources are kept to a minimum. "There is no difference between the Master and you", he instructs, "you have just forgotten your true identity". The Teachings are simple. He hammers home the same Truth, again and again: "You are not the body. You were not the body. You will not remain the body." "The body is not your identity." "Your

Spontaneous Presence is anonymous, invisible, unidentified identity". "You are Ultimate Truth, Final Truth. You are the Final Destination", etc.

The Master's method needs some clarification, for visitors who are new to these teachings. His method aims to cut through the body-based knowledge and bodily identity, as quickly as possible, and get down to the business of Reality.

Ramakant Maharaj defines Presence as: "Spontaneous, Invisible, Anonymous, Unidentified Identity".

Guidelines

1. The Master teaches, using carefully selected, specific words, as in the above phrase, that have an undefinable quality: "invisible", "anonymous", "spontaneous", "unidentified". These words allude to that which is hidden, and come close to the "unknown", close to the "unrevealed", coming close to the "Reality", beyond all words. These words cannot easily be grasped by the "mind". Instead, they disarm the mind, and prevent the imagination from conjuring up any associated thoughts and concepts.

2. The Master "acts" as an exterminator of all your concepts, clearing them, bypassing them, and speaking directly to the denuded essence, That You Are. This nameless "Source" that you are has been given many names, such as the Ultimate, Ultimate Reality, Ultimate Truth, etc. The Master is speaking directly to the

"Invisible Listener", beyond words. This means that he is speaking to that, which ultimately cannot be named - the ineffable.

3. The Master's method of teaching is unique, in that he is not giving YOU instructions, instead, he is reawakening and regenerating your Inner Master. "I am addressing the Invisible Listener in you". HERE IT IS TO BE UNDERSTOOD THAT THE INVISIBLE SPEAKER AND THE INVISIBLE LISTENER ARE ONE AND THE SAME.

4. The Master's approach is direct. It is the shortest cut to Self-Realization. From beginning to end, he hammers the same message: "You are Ultimate Truth, Final Truth. You are nothing to do with this illusory world". He cuts through all 'body-based knowledge'. DON'T EXPECT HIM TO BE INTERESTED IN YOUR THOUGHTS, CONCEPTS, MEMORIES, EXPERIENCES. He teaches: "The entire world is an illusion, including the body. You are not the body, you were not the body, and you will not remain the body", therefore, engaging in any body-related knowledge and body-related spirituality is time-wasting.

5. Words are only indicators. DON'T TAKE THE MASTER'S WORDS LITERALLY. Focus on the meaning, the essence of the message, or using the Master's words, the "gist" of the message.

6. The Master's method means that he is always speaking to your Reality, your Ultimate Reality. He is not addressing you, as James, Ravi or Sita with all your bodily identifications. WHEN YOU ASK QUESTIONS, THE MASTER IS ADDRESSING THE

"INVISIBLE QUESTIONER". He will say, "ALL OF OUR QUESTIONS ARE BODY-BASED".

7. The Master teaches: "We created language. We created knowledge. Prior to Beingness/Consciousness, Nothing was there. You were unknown to you. There were NO WORDS. You did not even know the word 'KNOWLEDGE'. THIS IS A USEFUL POINTER TO HELP YOU PUT ASIDE ALL THE KNOWLEDGE THAT YOU HAVE GATHERED TO DATE.

8. "Nothing has happened. You are talking about the Unborn Child", he says. This message is another reminder for you: Try and resist the temptation to talk about "YOUR PERSONAL STORY", "YOUR KNOWLEDGE", including 'YOUR SPIRITUAL KNOWLEDGE'.

9. The Master is speaking to the 'Invisible Listener' in you. To maximise the flow from SOURCE to SOURCE, PREPARE YOURSELF! THIS MEANS BEING QUIET, OPEN AND RECEPTIVE. Put the mind, ego, intellect aside. Being, as it were, like a blank screen, will free up your attention and increase the chances of benefitting from the teachings. And if the ego doesn't like it and rises up, so be it. Let it be bashed, including the 'spiritual ego'.

10. When the Master talks about Knowledge, he is not talking about intellectual knowledge, literal knowledge, book knowledge, dry knowledge, experiential knowledge, or any other kind of knowledge that is second-hand. It has nothing to

do with information that has been sourced from outside of yourself and/or accumulated from books, via the body-form. True Knowledge/Self-Realization is non-intellectual. It is simply "KNOWING YOURSELF IN A REAL SENSE". Knowledge means "SELFLESS SELF KNOWLEDGE". This definition may assist you in NOT talking about your body-based "knowledge".

11. You will have questions that need to be asked in the beginning. ASK QUESTIONS AND CLEAR YOUR DOUBTS. You will find these dry up, the more the Master hammers your Reality into you. His method has the effect of silencing you. You will notice the emergence of Spontaneous Silence.

12. The Master is sharing RARE KNOWLEDGE, TRUE KNOWLEDGE, IRREFUTABLE KNOWLEDGE. Understand, therefore, that this Knowledge is not up for debate. Master advises you to AVOID DISCUSSIONS, ARGUMENTS, COUNTER-ARGUMENTS. It is helpful for you to know that this Knowledge is not coming from the realm of ideas. It is REALITY, YOUR REALITY. THAT YOU ARE! Ultimate Reality is speaking to Ultimate Reality.

13. The Master tells you to be calm and quiet. "Don't stress the brain! Your inner Master is listening, analyzing and recording, all that the Master is teaching." What this means is - there is a flow between the Master and you, that is spontaneously happening. Ultimate Truth is reaching and reawakening, the Ultimate Truth in you. DON'T TRY TO GRASP THE TEACHINGS. JUST BE!

If you follow the Master's instructions WITH TOTAL FAITH AND ACCEPTANCE, then slowly, silently and permanently, your "Spontaneous Presence" that is invisible, anonymous, unidentified identity, will merge with Selfless Self.

The Process

The following points are only guidelines:

Maharaj says: *"In reality, there is no process, no guidelines. There is no Master, no disciple, no outer or inner Master".*

The language that is used here, is for the purpose of understanding. Nor does the 'process' operate in a linear fashion:

"Do not take the words literally, as they are only indicators, like the flashes emitted from a lighthouse". Also: *"You are not to compare different Teachers, Masters, Gurus and different teachings. This is not a comparative study. It is Direct Knowledge."*

The process is one of making you a Master. As Shri Ramakant Maharaj's Master, Shri Nisargadatta Maharaj, before him, said: *"I am not making you disciples, I am making you Masters."*

The Master gives instructions and guidance. He asks the disciple, to follow these. He guides the disciple from illusion to Reality, from the Outer Master to the Inner Master. He does this by addressing the *"Silent Invisible Anonymous Unidentified Identity"*, which is our Reality, saying at the same time:

"The Invisible Speaker in ME and the Invisible Listener in YOU are One and the same".

Oneness is always there but has been hidden, covered by the 'ash' of illusory concepts.

1. Reawakening: Maharaj will say that there is no difference between the Master and the disciple, except that, the Master knows he is not the body, whereas the disciple does not know. He explains that Self-Realization simply means to know oneself in a "Real Sense":

"We know ourselves in the body-form, this is not our real identity".

The Master begins the process of convincing the disciple.

2. Direct Knowledge: We have forgotten our true identity. This is covered by the ashes of illusory concepts. The Master's Direct Knowledge reminds us of our true identity.

3. Self-Enquiry: Master tells you what you are not:

"You are not the body, you were not the body, you are not going to remain the body".

"You are not a man, nor a woman".

"The mind, ego and intellect are your babies", etc.

He asks you to find this out for yourself, through Self-Enquiry.

4. Meditation: The Master defines meditation as a 24-hour practice. Total self-involvement is needed:

"You are boiling, you are on fire to find out the Reality, to uncover the Source. Nothing will stop you from finding out, 'Who am I'?"

He says that meditation is an essential discipline in the early stages. It is the foundation of the whole process and practice.

This practice is also an illusion, but, *"We have to use one thorn to remove another thorn".*

Later on, the whole practice can be dropped.

5. Final Truth: The Master teaches that everything is within you. You are the Ultimate. There is nothing else, nothing beyond. He tells you what you are:

"Your Spontaneous Presence is a silent, anonymous, invisible, unidentified identity. You are unborn. There is no birth and no death for you, it is only the body that dissolves. The entire world is the Spontaneous Projection of your Spontaneous Presence".

He asks you to accept this Reality, your Reality.

6. Prior to Beingness: The Master reminds you: *"Your Presence was there prior to beingness. It will be there after beingness. It is there now, as the holder of the body".*

He explains that all our knowledge is body-based knowledge, which started after *"the Spirit clicked with the body".* Then came the impressions, conditioning, pressures and illusory concepts that we accepted. These kept us trapped in the circle of body-based knowledge.

7. Dissolving Body-knowledge: The next step is for us to get rid of all the illusions. The Master instructs us as to why this is necessary:

"Ultimate Reality will not emerge until all body-knowledge has been dissolved".

As we practice Self-Enquiry, the Master gives us a useful tool, the "Master Key", the Lineage *Naam Mantra*, which will help to *"erase the memories"*, and *"regenerate the inner Master"*. We recite the Mantra which means, *"I am Brahman, Brahman I am"*. At the same time, the Master continues the process of direct hammering, to further convince us:

"You are Brahman, You are Brahman, You are Brahman."

The singing of *bhajans* or devotional songs, replete with deep meaning is also included in the dissolution process. This makes the whole undertaking a living, flowing and happy one. While singing these, together, the meanings and vibrations uplift the Spirit, and we forget about the body.

8. Surrender and Acceptance: Momentum increases. You feel more and more driven to uncover the Source within, to find the Reality. Our trust in the Master, and ourselves, increase simultaneously. We accept his teachings without question. Conviction is established.

9. Absorption: The Knowledge deepens. We ask questions, receive answers, and any lingering doubts are cleared up. The Knowledge is being absorbed *slowly, silently, permanently.* As the little self is dissolving, and the veil begins to lift, the unadorned purity of Selfless Self shines forth. The Master cautions us:

"Always be alert! Don't let illusion back in! Keep doing the practice!"

10. Spontaneous Conviction: The Master tells us not to think about what is happening, and not to make any effort. *"Don't stress the brain! The conviction that you are not the body, will arise spontaneously. Then, you will <u>KNOW</u>, I Am That!"*

11. Merging: At this time, as well as at other times, the feeling of separation between the Master and disciple dissolves. Again: *"The invisible speaker in me, and the invisible listener in you, are one and the same"*. A merging, so to speak, into Oneness, takes place. As Maharaj says: *"The melting process is marching towards Oneness."*

12. Be With Selfless Self: At this stage, the Master actively prompts the Inner Master directly, saying: *"Talk to your Inner Master. Demand answers! Your Inner Master will respond and give you instructions. Your Masterly essence will guide you. Embrace Selfless Self"*.

Your Inner Master is reawakening: *"You are Ultimate Truth. You are Ultimate Reality. You are Final Reality"*.

There is nothing more. Words are now redundant. Knowledge has served its purpose. It has removed the illusion of ignorance. Likewise, the illusion of knowledge must also be dissolved: *"Total Knowledge is absorbed in* Oneness".

13. Be Within Selfless Self: The process from illusion to Reality has, as it were, ended.

"Be calm and quiet. Be happy. Enjoy the exceptional peace, exceptional silence. Be intoxicated with the nectar of Selfless Self".

14. Bowing to the Master:

Spontaneous gratitude arises, and devotion to the Master continues unabated. He has shown that the disciple is Ultimate Reality, Final Truth. Selfless Self is revealed. *Jai Guru*!

The Master asks you to listen carefully: *"This phrase contains the gist of all the teachings".* He repeats and emphasizes, again and again: *"Except your Selfless Self there is no God, no Brahman, no Atman, no Paramatman, no Master."*

Homage to Shri Ramakant Maharaj, Shri Nisargadatta Maharaj and all the Masters of this Lineage. We bow to Selfless Self. Jai SadGuru!

We uploaded this section, adding: "This page is an attempt to put into words and allude to that which is ultimately indescribable. It gives but a glimpse into the workings of the Guru-Disciple process".

Beginning of March – Preparing for Maharaj and Anvita's return. We clean and tidy their home. Maharaj phones to let us know the time of his arrival. As he approaches the house, we walk towards him and bow. We are so pleased to see him again. Once settled, he takes a look at Charles' quotes on FB. Maharaj approves!

He likes them, because he says, they are bird-sized quotes, not big lengthy ones. "Little birds cannot digest well, therefore, these bytes are perfect for digestion! Long paragraphs are too hard to digest!" he comments. He also likes the way Charles applies his creativity to the pictures accompanying the quotes, which are very delicately, cleverly and appropriately done.

Later on that day, Maharaj spontaneously announces that we have a past connection, a spiritual bond, and that we are very close to him! We are very happy to hear this! We tell Maharaj that we sent an article to *Guru's Feet* about how we discovered him. *Guru's Feet* is a popular spiritual site. We posted the article in the hope of drawing many seekers to Maharaj. He is very happy to hear this, and then shares some amazing new information with us. He informs us that in 1979, when Nisargadatta visited a disciple called "Babusav Jagtap", at his home in Nashik, he made an announcement:

"Treat this day, 25th January, as a Festival Day. In the future, some great and wonderful things are going to happen in this corner of Nashik. Build an ashram here! One day it will become a very busy ashram with visitors from around the globe".

"Wow! We did not know that Maharaj! Thank you for telling us!" The current ashram in Nashik Road was built in 2002. An Annual Program is held on 25th January, following the wishes of Nisargadatta Maharaj. The area is now called "Jagtap Mala", in honour of this disciple and his Master.

The next day – Martin, an eager visitor from Europe, arrives at the ashram hoping to receive the *Naam Mantra*.

"**Q**: It is very important for me to get initiation from you, Maharaj, and get the *Naam Mantra*.

Maharaj: Do you have any Guru/Master?

Q: I have! My Guru is Nisargadatta Maharaj: And you are his disciple, and for me, it is the only way to get initiation into this lineage. And this is why I have come to meet you."

Maharaj has no problem with this request. He has initiated in the name of Nisargadatta Maharaj and Siddharameshwar Maharaj, too, before. Martin wishes to know if he will still receive the blessings from Nisargadatta, even though he has left the body. He continues:

"**Q**: Is it appropriate that I should be initiated by you, when my Guru is Nisargadatta Maharaj? Is that a problem?

Maharaj: No problem. Everything is the same.

Q: Exactly - Is it a problem that he is not in the body?

Maharaj: You see, there is no individuality. Is there a difference between the sky here, and the sky elsewhere? No! Is the sky divided into an Indian sky, European sky and an American sky? No! Are they different? No! Are there any conflicts between the sky in India, and the sky in America? Not at all. Nisargadatta Maharaj, Ranjit Maharaj, myself, yourself are not individuals, are not separate. It is only the bodies that are different.

Because you think you are separate, you think that Nisargadatta Maharaj is separate, Ranjit Maharaj is separate, Siddharameshwar Maharaj is separate. The bodies are separate, but there is no separation in Ultimate Truth. There is no issue!

Q: So there is no difference between a living Master, and a Master who is not in the body?

Maharaj: Of course not!

Q: Also, what about the intensity of the contact with the Master? If one is very certain and 100% devoted, is the contact with the Master, who has left the body, sufficient, just as good?

Maharaj: There is no difference!

Q2. I think what you are trying to find out is, if the Master is not alive, is that the same as if you have a living Master? And it is in the same lineage too...

Maharaj: Yes correct - it's the same!

Q: So I need not have any doubts, everything is ok?

Maharaj: None at all! Everything is ok!"

Afternoon – We call the next discourse, "Simple Teachings". Charles asks the following question:

"Q: The simplicity of the teachings is remarkable because it is not - though we use words - it is not verbal at all. It is on a different level.... One of the great difficulties, a big stumbling block, is the fact that we do use words.

Maharaj: If you have a background, then you can understand the language, but don't get caught up in the words. Here we use simple language, a simple approach, a direct approach with few references. It is only sometimes that I use references in story form, to help the understanding... just as indicators.

Q: Not too literal.

Maharaj: Because one thing is there, (one question everyone must ask), people have spirituality at home, people are reading so many books, listening to various Masters. But then, you must find out, and ask: "Why am I reading all these things? What will I get out of reading? What will I get out of listening to the various Masters, and visiting sacred places?" You must know the purpose. Why are you doing these things? The answer will usually be, to find peace, happiness, a fearless and tension-free life. But who wants this? Who wants a fearless life? Who wants peace? Who wants a simple life? Who wants happiness? Keep questioning! And then, after Self-Enquiry, the enquirer comes to the self-centre. Exceptional silence will be there. The "enquirer" disappears.

The first thing you should ask is: "How is that 'I'?" It is anonymous and unidentified. The second thing is for you to look at all your needs – for happiness and peace, etc, and ask the question: "Were these needed prior to beingness?" No! "Will they be needed after the body expires?" No! It is only because you are holding the body, that we have needs. This means that all this knowledge is body-based knowledge, body-related knowledge.

In short, because of the body, you started believing yourself to be somebody – a man or woman, *Brahman*, *Atman* or God. All these names are mere concepts, that had no existence previously. This means that your spontaneous, invisible, existence has been given the names *Brahman*, *Atman*, *Paramatman*, God.

This is the way of Self-Enquiry. Practice it until the enquirer becomes silent. You have been thinking, using your body-based reality. To change perspective, we recommend meditation, taking the Mantra, reciting the Mantra, sitting for meditation and absorbing the knowledge. Why? Because the last day, the last moment, should be a happy moment. There should not be any illusion or fear in the mind, when the body is separating from the Spirit. Don't entertain the thought of "I am dying". By then, preferably before then, you should know, that you are unborn. With this conviction, you will enjoy the sweetness of a happy mood, a happy moment before leaving the body.

After conviction, you will have no further need of reading books, meditation, etc. These are the steps, the indications that lead you to Self-Realization. You are totally different from this world because the entire world is your spontaneous projection. Without your existence, without your Presence, you can't see the world.

So, you are prior to the world, prior to the universe, prior to everything. To say *Brahman*, *Atman*, *Paramatman*, God, universe, sky etc, your Presence is required. Your Presence is a Spontaneous Presence, that does not have any limitations, or any circle around it. This is simple knowledge! You have been going round and round and round. Why? Self-Enquiry leads to Self-Knowledge, and Self-knowledge leads to Self-Realization.

After knowing the Reality, you will not be so wrapped up in desires and feelings, for money, power or sex. Who wants power, when no one, and nothing, exists? Who wants money? You can't take your money with you, when you leave the body. What about sex? It will give you momentary happiness, not permanent happiness. These are the needs, not Ultimate Truth

After conviction, Ultimate Truth will be established and you will know: "I am nothing to do with this illusory world. The entire world is an illusion, including this body". When your needs subside, you will be carrying out your duties in a relaxed, casual manner, knowing you are acting in a drama, acting very nicely in a drama. You will be aware of yourself roleplaying, either as a man or a woman, but at the same time, knowing that it is not your identity. After conviction, there will be quietness and calmness.

All the questions, so many questions, that everyone asks, are body-based questions, coming from the illusion of being a separate person, a somebody. You say, "I'm somebody" and "he is somebody else", and then, because of the perceived duality and conflict, criticism arises. Conflicts, confusion, doubts, these are all body-related. Prior to beingness, there were no doubts, no knower, no knowledge.

This is very, very simple knowledge. Arguments and counter-arguments are not necessary because this is not a debate. What is true? What is false? There is no true or false. Everything is true and everything is false. That is called Ultimate Truth. Nothing is happening because you are unborn!

Most seekers enjoy comparative studies, posing as a somebody, and learning from that stance, accumulating knowledge, to stimulate the mind. They read books, compare the teachings, and then they think they have knowledge. It happens all the time. But true seekers are serious. They are seriously involved in Self-discovery. They go to the root, the base. The root is your Selfless Self. We could go on talking for hours together, years together. This won't help you! Meditate and find the truth within you! That will help you!

After the Talk, in which Maharaj mentioned "Spontaneous Presence" and "Spontaneous Existence" a few times, I asked him if he could expand on these terms, (with the forthcoming book in mind). But he had no wish to do so, saying, "what I have said is enough!" He doesn't want anyone to try and analyze or work out the meanings intellectually. The words are only vehicles, and behind them is the energy he wishes to convey, arising from the invisible speaker, and transmitted to the invisible listener.

We tell Maharaj about a few people who wish to Skype with him. One is a Catholic nun. We arrange for her to speak with him this evening. We both say at the same time, "this will be an interesting one!" Maharaj's main message to her is: "There is nothing to be found in churches because everything is within us. Don't look for truth in a church, or from bishops or superiors. Realize that everything is in you! It is ok to visit a church, and sit and meditate, or pray there. There is no harm in doing what you are doing, as long as you know that nothing exists out there! There is nothing higher than you, more superior, or greater than you!"

She was definitely ready to hear the knowledge, as she did not resist Maharaj's words. She understood and got it straight away! She felt very happy and free at the end of the Skype call!

March – I have been spending the last couple of days in bed. I may have caught a bug or something, so the body needs to rest. There is also a feeling of exhaustion, maybe the effects of the regimental, commando training! In this army camp, a "day-off" remains a fantasy! I feel the need to catch up with sleep. Maharaj comes to check on me a couple of times. Semi-asleep, I hear him climbing the stairs, asking Charles, how I am doing? He is always so caring! He asks Charles to make sure he tells me that Maharaj says, "take complete rest".

Shri Bhausaheb returns. Last night he appeared as a huge giant and was floating above me for a timeless moment, as I lay on the bed. He was wearing a gilded blue cloak that struck a chord in me. Suddenly, I feel I need to get a picture of him dressed in blue, urgently! (If I was his disciple in a bygone age, perhaps he was wearing this particular blue cloak that I saw in my vision!).

Two days later – During meditation, Bhausaheb Maharaj places a crown on my head, saying, "This is your rightful inheritance". I ask to speak with Maharaj at home later. In the afternoon, I go and see Maharaj. Anvita is also there. I tell them about the meditation, and what happened with Shri Bhausaheb. Anvita says, "You have to tell everyone!"

"Yes!" says Maharaj. "But not yet. Later!" He explains that the crown is the Master's crown and that Bhausaheb has confirmed something to him.

The next day – Maharaj sometimes shares snippets of his own story, describing his life as miraculous. Not only did he reach the pinnacle of spirituality, but he did so, despite suffering from poverty, hardship and humiliation as a youngster, as well as numerous difficulties later on. His stories are inspiring! If he managed to reach the peak of the mountain, then we all can! "Nothing is impossible", he would say, as long as there is a longing to know the Truth, alongside a big dose of humility. And Maharaj is the embodiment of humility!

We can both relate to his journey in terms of worldly, career/ambition and status struggles. We have always felt like two fish out of the water, while trying to stay faithful to the dictum, "Know thyself".

Mid-March – A couple of visitors who had been at the ashram for just one week, ask Maharaj if they can put together a book on his teachings. They also ask Maharaj for his blessings, as they want to start teaching.

Their questions fire up Maharaj, who responds with a firmness we have not seen for some time:

Maharaj: "Don't write books unless you are one with the knowledge! This is very important. The knowledge, the writer and the reader must be one, otherwise, the knowledge is empty of power, and nothing but more words to stimulate the reader's mind! You have only been here a week, and you think you can write books!

Nisargadatta enjoyed writing poetry. And even though the poems were about his Master, Siddharameshwar, he was told to stop indulging in that exercise, as "he" was enjoying it too much! Nisargadatta, being the perfect disciple, did not argue back, or complain about his Master criticizing him. No! He obeyed and stopped writing poetry immediately. It is the same principle as teaching. Don't teach unless you have gone beyond knowledge!"

The visitors are annoyed. Instead of respecting the Master's answers and remaining silent, they retaliate: "Why are you criticizing us?", the husband demanded. "How do you know we are not one with the knowledge? We think we are ready! So, you will not give us your blessing?" Maharaj says, "No!" Their egos arre fighting back! The couple decide to leave because they do not get what they want!

Criticism is only seen as such if the ego is still there. Otherwise, there would only be indifference, no reaction at all! If the Guru says, "don't do this", and the disciple ignores the Guru's command - because he wants to obey the ego's command instead - then, obviously, the Guru-disciple relationship is not working.

It is simple! Obedience and service to the Guru chip away at the ego forcefully, until it caves in! Another important aspect is acceptance in all of this. It is simple! When the Guru teaches or instructs, all the disciple has to do is accept it! Shri Ramakant used to say, "My Master told me: "You are Final Truth", therefore, I am Final Truth! – end of story! No further questions are needed, no debate, just humble acceptance".

End of March – Maharaj is not able to give any more Talks as has lost his voice. Time is precious, so, I put together a series of questions for Maharaj to answer, which I think will be helpful to readers. The next day, Maharaj hands the sheets of paper back to me with the answers. I send him some more questions, and he is happy to write down the answers again.

April – The landlord arrives unannounced, to check on his apartment. He is furious that we have moved some things around. In a fit of anger, he points to the door, saying something in Marathi. Charles tells him to calm down, that we do not understand a word he is saying. Next, he knocks on Maharaj's door!

Maharaj arrives, and tells us that the landlord wants us to leave, because we have touched and moved some of his things. We explain that as we are now living there, we were just making it more comfortable. "This is ridiculous", says Charles, shaking his head and beginning to lose it. An Indian drama is a heated one! Maharaj, calm as ever, tells us to sit down and have a cup of chai. "We will talk later!" he says. He told us before that when he worked in the bank, this was the way he used to treat some of his irate customers…first of all, calm them down with a cup of chai! If this was a test, we failed miserably, as we took it all for real!

However, the issue was resolved that same night, and we stayed on! Afterwards, Maharaj came back round to the flat, bringing with him a beautifully framed picture of Nisargadatta Maharaj, which had been gifted to him by Nisargadatta himself. He loaned it to us. His gesture was timely, so caring, and effective, instantly making us forget everything about the recent illusory exchange!

We will be leaving at the beginning of May, which will bring our five and a half-month stay to an end. Last night, we talked about how lucky we are to have stayed more or less healthy throughout, despite the changes to our diet, the climate, etc. Today, however, Charles is not feeling so well. It is his turn to take to bed.

I cross the road to the ashram, to tell Maharaj that Charles will not be coming to the *bhajans*. The timing is fortuitous! It is grace! Someone is talking to Maharaj. I bow at Maharaj's feet, and as I get up, Maharaj slaps me on the back, and says, to my sheer delight: "This is Shri Balwant Maharaj, the grandson of Siddharameshwar Maharaj". I am blown away. Immediately, I prostrate at his feet, and, lo and behold, he transforms into Siddharameshwar Maharaj! I am elated, speechless! What a beautiful being, with a shining, beatific smile!

Maharaj speaks with him in Marathi, mentioning that we are crazy about Shri Siddharameshwar, that it was his promptings, along with Nisargadatta's, that brought us to Ramakant Maharaj! A little dazed, I explain to Maharaj about Charles, before leaving. When I tell Charles what had just happened, he asks me if Shri Balwant is going to be there later on? I tell him that I don't know. Afterwards, we find out that Shri Balwant had left. Darn it! He missed him!

End of April – Charles is feeling better. We only have one week left with Maharaj! What an adventure it has been! We both feel "free as birds", to use Maharaj's expression. I feel that I am "dancing on bubbles". We are immensely happy. When we talk about the transformation in us both, we often say that we already had the cake, and Maharaj put the icing on top. Or, to put it another way, the *Naam Mantra* cleared out the clutter, so that the knowledge could be absorbed. Then, knowing and being merged into one! That said, we don't spend too much time trying to decipher it all. Who wants to know anyway? What we do know is that our devotion to Maharaj is eternal!

A few devotees of Ramana Maharshi are visiting tomorrow. They see no contradiction between Ramana's and Maharaj's teachings, and they are, of course, right! They would like to receive the *Naam Mantra*, to rid themselves of any remaining body-based knowledge.

During *Satsang*, Maharaj talks about the great saints, pointing to the pictures on the wall, and appropriately, today, he also speaks of Ramana Maharshi, in the same breath. Maharaj initiates the group of three. After a couple of days, with a lightness in their step, they return to Tiruvannamalai.

Charles is receiving many emails from a variety of seekers. Some of them seem despondent, after following a particular tradition or practice, for a long time, yet failing to see much progress. The emails are from Buddhists, as well as from several people who are practising *Vipassana* or TM meditation. Once, during *Satsang*, when a visitor asked Maharaj, "Who is eligible to receive the *Naam Mantra*?", he replied: "Everyone, if they are sincere". And when he was asked if one needed to, "join the Inchegiri Navnath Sampradaya" if one took the *Naam Mantra*, he would say: "The Sampradaya, like everything else, is a concept"! He also greatly emphasized that, the knowledge shared by the Masters of this Lineage, does not belong to the lineage. This knowledge is "Universal Knowledge"! He was cautioning everyone, not to take on another illusory identity, such as becoming a lineage member. (Where was the Lineage prior to beingness!) And not to be possessive of it either! After all, everything is an illusion, including the Lineage!

To quote Maharaj, "Once you have arrived at the destination, throw the address away". In other words, knowledge is a vehicle or medium, that takes the "Invisible Listener" to Self-Realization. Once it has served its purpose, we are to throw it away. Or, putting it another way, he often says: "There are two thorns. The first thorn is the thorn of illusion or ignorance. The second thorn is that of knowledge. Both thorns are illusory. We use the secondary thorn to extract the primary thorn. Once the "medication" has been applied, we throw both thorns away!"

We ended up staying with Maharaj for as long as possible. Though the "Commando-training" was tough, ie, 3 times a day for *bhajans* and Talks, we know it was necessary – like being in a Rehab Centre to detox. We are here to detox from all the illusions! Maharaj and his teachings, coupled with the meditation practice, emptied us of the false, and established us in the Ultimate Truth, filling our empty vessels with peace and happiness.

Last day at the ashram – After five and a half months with Maharaj, we understand the high significance of the Guru-disciple relationship, as it unfolded for us, in a beautiful and wondrous lineage, that seeks to make Masters. Nisargadatta Maharaj said again and again: "I am not making you disciples, I am making you Masters!" Many Gurus or teachers are searching for followers to emulate them, and make them - consciously or unconsciously - dependent on them. They do not empower seekers to realize their inner Master, and/or enable them to stand on their own feet. This is what Maharaj has been doing for us, tirelessly. He never puts himself above us, or anyone else! He always reminds us - that, like every other thing that does not exist - neither does the Guru and the disciple. After all, there are no exceptions to the rule: Nothingness is always the baseline! Where was the Guru? Where was the disciple, prior to beingness?

The Guru is, as has been said many times, the mirror in which you can see your Self. The Guru is a catalyst and a transmitter, bringing you into the space where there is nothing, the space in which the authentic Guru abides, the Stateless State. But it takes two to tango, and the Guru never imposes or coerces anyone. He cannot force a disciple to do anything.

Here is where the importance of obeying the Guru's commands enters: As we know, there is only One Reality. There are not two: the Guru and the disciple. The process of removing the layers of illusion, under the guidance of the Guru, along with devotion to the Guru, bring about the merging of the illusory two! Bowing, serving, surrendering to the Guru, all help to dispel the notion of separateness, thus enabling the yoga, or union with the Guru. This, in turn, leads to union with, (and the realization of), our true nature.

The Lineage teaches the importance of devotion after Self-Realization. We understand it perfectly, because while we know that there is no individual Guru, and no individual disciple, we cannot forget, that the process from illusion to reality, was made possible by the Guru. We know that the "mystical", yet pragmatic association or dynamics, between the Guru and the disciple, is the catalyst. And without that, without Him, enlightenment may have taken many more years, or possibly lifetimes! We both know that our devotion to Maharaj will continue unabated. That said, we also know that this devotion is ultimately, to Selfless Self, that one Essence that we all share!

Maharaj tells us he is very happy with us! We can't thank him enough for everything he has given and shown. That is wordless! "The Master who shows you, God in you, is indeed a rare Master", said Swami Vivekananda.

Maharaj books a taxi for us which will pick us up early in the morning. He looks after his devotees well, with nothing ever being too menial, or small for him. After the *bhajans*, Maharaj invites us to his home. Sweet Anvita serves up our usual tiffin – rice and dahl, only, this time, there are pakoras too! What a treat! (He also gifts us two packets of raisins for the journey.) Maharaj tells us to keep the practice going. He promises to Skype with us, as soon as we return home. He looks at me sternly and reminds me about the book. "How can I forget Maharaj!"

"You have the understanding! Use your own words to convey the meaning. Make the book attractive and easy to read. It is for beginners and advanced devotees", says Maharaj.

I emphasize again, that it will take some time. "There is no time", he responds. I have a feeling that as soon as we return home, the pressure to complete the book will start building!

We do not sleep much on our last night, as we know we will be leaving at 4 am to catch our flight back to the UK. Around midnight, we look at one another and say: "We did it!" We know there is no "we" and no "doers"! These are just words. We knew what was conveyed. We survived the commando training and left behind our egos!

When devotees depart from the ashram, and they ask Maharaj if they can leave a donation, Maharaj always replies with: "Yes! Leave behind your ego, mind and intellect! That is the best donation!"

The next day – We are on our flight home, both feeling very empty, light and pure. We found the treasure, the casket of jewels! We filled ourselves with them, and then, ran off!

We feel we are not just flying on a plane, but flying without bodies! The air hostess asks us if we would like a glass of wine. We both say "No, thanks", without giving it a thought. Normally, we would enjoy a glass on holiday, but we are not on holiday, but endless "holy days". Who needs alcohol, when you are already inebriated with Reality's clear vision!

We love Maharaj and pledge to serve him, till the end of our days! We try to describe our current state. The best I can say is that there is emptiness, an emptiness that is full of happiness. There is an inner joy that remains undisturbed. We love the Teachings, the nectar plant which has been truly planted within, emitting an indescribable perfume!

After commando training, one may be shipped out to war. But for us, the war has ended. It is peacetime! Eternal peace! I remind Charles: "Remember I always said to you that we needed a Guru?" He laughs, and says, he was just thinking the same thing: "I knew you would throw that back in my face!", he says, "and I'm glad you kept pestering me. You were right". We laugh together like children.

It is wonderful to meet the Guru, and also incredibly beautiful, to be able to share the experience with a close partner! We are feeling so blessed and thankful.

Our devotion to Maharaj will continue forever because, without him, we would not be liberated from our little selves! Now (we) will continue to remain humble, quiet and established in our true nature.

May – Back in the UK. There is a feeling of having been away for years, light years, never mind, months, along with a sense that we have not just been in India, but on another planet! Lol.

Jet-lagged, we need to take "complete rest"! (Maharaj's "Indianisms" have stuck with us!) We are happy to be back home, safe and well! Our journey into the unknown is indescribable! Now that we are home, we will be able to reflect, and absorb it all.

No sooner had we retired to bed, than Maharaj was on the phone, checking to see if we had arrived safely. How kind and "thoughtlessly thoughtful"! He tells us he will Skype us the next morning!

We have a spontaneous workload awaiting us: lots of emails asking about Shri Ramakant, with questions for the Master to answer. Also, numerous recordings will need to be transcribed first, before any progress can be made with the book.

The next morning – Maharaj Skypes us, asking for news! We have none, as we have just been sleeping! Perhaps he is checking up on us, making sure we have not strayed! But no! He knows we belong to Him!

Maharaj briefly mentions the book. He only insists on two requirements regarding the book: the title which is going to be *"Selfless Self"*, and for some of the text to be printed, using capital, bold letters, to slow the readers down and hammer them adequately. To protect the text and prevent future alterations, he requests that the copyright be registered in the name of "Ann Shaw". I assure Maharaj that it will all be done!

We tell him again that we are so grateful for everything! He smiles and then reminds us to continue with the meditation. "We will have a revision of Reality once a week!", he says, before waving us goodbye.

June – Since returning home from Nashik, a new pattern to our days has emerged spontaneously. We retire to bed at 8-9 pm and rise at 2 am. Now our routine is meditation, working on transcribing the recorded talks, admin, spreading the good news, walking, eating, more work, meditation, eating, walking and bed. Charles' energy has definitely been regenerated. When he wakes up in the early hours, he runs downstairs with fresh purpose, renewed determination and an insatiable appetite! Doubtlessly, he is on a serious mission. He is building the website for Maharaj and also attending to the countless email requests, from those who are seeking an opportunity to Skype with Maharaj.

We both continue to have many amazing experiences during our meditation. Enjoyable as these are, we know Maharaj will listen to them attentively, before rejecting them, as he always does! (All experiences are illusions.) He will remind us again, that they are not Ultimate Truth, but progressive landmarks! Sometimes spontaneous happenings arise, like messages coming through, or communications taking place outside of meditation.

Today, on my birthday, 24th June, I was quietly sitting on a bench in the garden, when at 6.15 pm, there was one such happening. I heard a voice which said, "You are Selfless Self". These words were accompanied by a pink light. The message and the light seemed to be coming, happening from both inside and outside. I whispered, "Thank you", and bowed.

Later on that evening, we Skype with Maharaj. This time, after sharing what occurred earlier, Maharaj responds differently: "This is Ultimate Truth! It is exceptional, and very rare for this to happen, in such a short time! Then he went on to say to us both: "You have a very important job to do! You have to enlighten all the devotees in the world!" Charles smiles and says: "That's a big job, Maharaj", and we all burst out laughing.

When we are not singing the *bhajans*, we have them playing in the background, as constant reminders. When we hear them, we are immediately transported back to the ashram. It is exactly what Maharaj says, "Spirit enjoys the *bhajans*!" They give happiness and fuel the knowledge. When we are singing or listening to the *bhajans*, thinking stops!

What is life like for us now that we are back in the UK and separated from Maharaj? There is no separation! We are closer than close! We hear Maharaj's voice. His quotes pop into our heads. His singing, his energy, all that is Maharaj, permeates around the space. We call on him before falling asleep, and he appears! I often joke with Charles, saying: "There's now 3 in our marriage!"

Transcribing the talks and listening to Maharaj's sweet voice, immediately takes us back to the ashram. His way is so direct and refreshing! Today I was listening to a Talk… a visitor "on fire", is burning to ask a question. With high intensity and desperation in her voice, she asks: "Maharaj, I want to know the Truth! Please tell me the Truth!" Maharaj replies, simply, powerfully and unequivocally: "You are the Truth!" Maharaj dissolves her longing for Truth in an instant, and with that, the visitor explodes into uncontrollable laughter!

We discuss the Teachings again. We find them superb, while, at the same time, we are aware that perhaps, the "ordinary Joe", may well find them, simply preposterous! Most of us wish to get rid of our pain and suffering, but we do not wish to relinquish the happiness we think we have! In general, we hold onto our experiences, treasuring them, reliving them and wishing we could have more of the same. We reject ugliness and embrace beauty, yet beauty is as much of an illusion, as ugliness; happiness is as much of an illusion, as unhappiness.

In this world of duality, while the values most people have built their lives around are okay for worldly life, they are ultimately to be perceived as illusory, because they are manmade and transient. We recognize this knowledge is a tough call, when most of us just wish to replace suffering and unhappiness, with endless, happy times!

Our understanding is now clear. We understood the philosophy of Advaita or Non-duality before, but now it has become pragmatic. It is lived! The process involves the negation of all the illusions. Once this has occurred, there is a change, or shift in perspective, after which everything is seen afresh, including the reflection of the world, which is part of that one Reality!

12th July – Guru Purnima. On this special day, we decide to meditate throughout the whole day, to praise and give thanks to Maharaj. During the meditation, I become aware of my body shaking and vibrating. Then I sense that "I" am touching something very sacred and holy. Feeling moved and tearful, I bow and surrender to this holy ground of being. I surrender consciously. I know, and feel, that there is no separation, between Maharaj and myself. I am in Maharaj, and Maharaj is in me.

There is oneness. Later on, the symbol of a ring appears, floating in a fluid-like, oily, peaceful darkness.

In the evening, with some excitement, Charles tells me that during his meditation, he received a visit from Shri Nisargadatta, who said: "You like to dance! (It wasn't a question but an exclamation!) Well, one day, you will truly dance!" It has been a beautiful, magical day!

20th July – Since *Guru Purnima*, more than a week ago now, there has been a feeling of lightness, tingling and sparkling energy moving around the body and head. There is a sense, too, of an opening in the stomach region or solar plexus. Today after reciting the *Naam Mantra*, complete stillness and quiet descended. There is also a feeling of an opening up, deep within the centre of my being. Then came a message: "One day the power will be transferred to you". It was not the mind because there was no activity, and there was a delay, before realizing what had just been communicated. I bowed and gave thanks.

Day after – We Skype with Maharaj today. It is always lovely to see him! I know that Maharaj, as Guru, is the impersonal Absolute, yet, at the same time, I feel the "relationship" between us is intensely personal and evolving like a deepening love affair! Perhaps the ring that recently appeared during meditation is symbolic of our forthcoming union!

Today Maharaj is coughing more than usual, with the same hacking cough we noticed back in 2013 when we first met. We ask him not to talk, and maybe postpone the Skype session, but he refuses point-blank. I share yesterday's experience. Maharaj says it is exceptional and shows that the knowledge is being absorbed. He smiles warmly at us, finishing with his usual encouraging words, "I am very happy with your progress. Go ahead! Go ahead!"

Before the call ends, Maharaj narrates the popular story of the musk deer in search of a scent, not realizing the scent is coming from within. Seekers are like that, searching for truth outside of themselves, until they realize it is within them! At this point, we turn the computer screen around to face the window, so that Maharaj can see several deer, resting outside our little Highland cottage! "Oh!" Maharaj exclaims, with great delight, surprise and childlike wonder!

This evening, Charles and I are talking about surrender, and how handing oneself over to Maharaj in totality is imperative. You can't just say, "I will surrender this or that part" - normally the easy ones - while holding back the rest. Spontaneously, we said a prayer: "Maharaj we surrender all of ourselves to you with complete faith and humility. We are your servants now and forever".

The next day – Maharaj Skypes us. We are not expecting to hear from him. The call is very brief. He says only three words to us: "You have surrendered!" before waving us goodbye. We are taken aback!

23rd July – Maharaj often uses the analogy of a bucket of water and the sea, to describe the process of dissolving the ego and merging with Selfless Self. If, for example, one pours a bucket of water into the sea, then it becomes one with the sea. It is an impossibility to remove that bucket, even if you wanted to do so! Last night, I dreamt I was the expansive sea. I was in the sea, and of the sea. At first, the waves were a little bit jaggy, crystal-like, which I interpreted to represent edges of ego that need to dissolve, before there can be a full and even flow. And then, when I woke up, a familiar image appeared which made me smile: "I am dancing on bubbles".

End of July – Today we travel to a nearby town for shopping. What happens there is a good example of how easy one's mood can change, if one is caught off-guard. We are both very contented, walking along the street singing, "*Jai Guru, Jai Guru, Jai Guru, Jai",* when Charles stops at a "hole-in-the-wall", to check his bank balance. When he notices a large amount of money has been deducted from his account, for an unauthorised transaction, the "*Jai Guru's"* suddenly stop, and his mood turns to anger!

"What happened to the "*Jai Guru's*", I ask? And he tells me! This unexpected worldly affair throws him off-course, momentarily.

"Forget it! You can sort it out later! Drop it now, don't dwell on it!" I say. He does just that, and we continue where we left off, singing, "*Jai Guru, Jai Guru.*"

5ᵗʰ August – Since our return, we have carried on with the meditation practice, and have had many experiences. We try to follow the important days that are celebrated in the ashram. Today is Siddarameshwar's birthday. We have powerful meditations and strongly feel the Presence of Siddharameshwar Maharaj. As we tap into his energy, we both feel we are going deeper. An image of a red-hot furnace spontaneously arises within me!

6ᵗʰ August – Skype with Maharaj. Something different happens today. It is an example of the workings of transcendental knowledge. As Maharaj is teaching, I undergo a kind of trancelike experience of him pouring nectar, a golden substance into me. I see, red-hot fire under a pile of ashes. There is shovelling taking place, transmuting. A golden fire appears. The words "forge" and "alchemy" surface. Then there is a vision of molten lava, and hot embers glowing. I am like an empty vessel and Maharaj is pouring fire, filling the emptiness with red hot energy and power. The fire is like liquid gold, nectar! I am transfixed for around 40 minutes. Silently within, I say, "Thank you, thank you. You are so lovely. You are love!"

Afterwards, I realize that I had absorbed all that Maharaj was teaching, even though, I could not remember any of his words! I interpreted the fire as a burning away of leftover impurities. Everything must be completely cleaned out! This tied in with a favourite teaching, one of Maharaj's important and frequently used reminders: "Ultimate Truth will not emerge until all the body-based knowledge has been removed".

8th August – Meditation is indeed cleaning everything. The process of absorption is happening. As I move closer to Selfless Self, this "I" is dissolving and decreasing, more and more, while Selfless Self is increasing. Selfless Self is absorbing the "I", devouring and consuming it like the bucket of water and the sea! The "I" illusion is dissolving, melting, merging with Selfless Self. I can see myself embracing Selfless Self, and there are glimpses of being held in a kind of *samadhi*-like state, the way I am prior to beingness.

I reflect on what Maharaj teaches on devotion. He says: "devotion means involvement and absorption". When we are told we are not the body form, that we are Ultimate Truth, *Atman*, *Brahman*, that that is our unidentified identity, we are to accept it totally. We are to absorb it all. Absorption is devotion because, through it, the process of conviction takes place which eventually leads to Spontaneous Conviction!

14ᵗʰ August – Maharaj guides us to ask our inner Master/Selfless Self to speak. Today I did just that. No sooner had I begun the meditation than I heard sounds, a voice that was neither male, nor female, communicating the following: "This is for you!" With these words, there appeared a container, like a large jug overflowing with a white liquid substance. I bow and give thanks.

26ᵗʰ August – These nights I have been kept awake. I am not complaining. Last night, I was awake for a few hours again, feeling very close to Maharaj, and the whole lineage. I just felt compelled to bow. I want to bow, bow, bow constantly, endlessly.

Earlier today, we had a session with Maharaj and I told him about lying awake in a state of bliss, smiling with spontaneous happiness. He said: "This is the fragrance of Selfless Self. Go deeper, deeper".

Increasingly, I am realizing what the melting process means. Yesterday I felt as if all the layers had been removed. What remained? Whatever I try and say in words will not be accurate, but I will try. I glimpsed the ground of being and out of that base, substratum, earth, I saw shoots sprouting upwards through the ground. I surrender my beingness to Selfless Self!

27ᵗʰ August – In the split second between sleep and waking, I see Maharaj: He is 10 feet tall, resembling the image of Bhausaheb I saw earlier in the year. He appears as a giant because "He" is dimensionless. At first, I thought He was standing on a high ledge or platform! I look at him in awe; he is transfixed!

Later on in the day, Charles shares his dream of Maharaj. He tells me that he saw me with Maharaj and that I had merged with him. He describes seeing Maharaj in *samadhi* and sees the two of us together as one! Amazing! I also share my experience of those "spontaneous shoots appearing". Charles says it reminds him of the cosmic egg post that he put up on FB recently: "Spiritual knowledge pecks and pecks, until it breaks through".

We are both awestruck at all the developments. It is like being captivated by an intensely fascinating movie, only, this is not a movie, it is the burgeoning of living knowledge, our reality, which is being shared and transmitted to us, by our very dear and great Master!

31ˢᵗ August – During my daytime meditation, again, the space appears as deep blue indigo, like a sheet of blue that is sometimes encircled by a golden aura. The blue space is coming closer and getting wider. When that power that is my essence is approaching, it is, as if, simultaneously, I am dissolving into the vastness and enveloped by it, little by little. I embrace it all and bow to the greatness, my greatness. Just as I am surrendering to it, the mind decides to pay a visit, lol. The moment vanishes!

During the afternoon meditation, Maharaj's face appears in the centre of this dark blue energy. His face is not clear, it is vibrational.

September – Most of the Talks have now been transcribed. I am trying to systematically gather the material, break it down, and, as far as possible, group the teachings. I will structure the book, according to the 3 stages Maharaj teaches, namely, Self-Enquiry, Self-Knowledge and Self-Realization. He instructs me to keep the book simple, while at the same time, making it suitable for both beginners, and advanced seekers.

As soon as I start putting the book together, I become aware of a guiding power taking over the task. The energy seems auditory, like "hearing and listening" to guidance. I pay attention, listen, and slowly move forward, as per instructions. I become more aware that I am not writing or compiling *Selfless Self*, it is being written by itself! As the book spontaneously comes together, I have no doubt that it is divinely guided!

November-December – As the prompts continue, and the chapters are arranged accordingly. For example, to "remove that line", or "this paragraph needs more added to it", etc. I continue to be guided, listening carefully and making the necessary changes, following the prompts of my invisible guide!

2015

January – We are both feeling very happy – empty and full, at the same time. Every now and then, we are overwhelmed by simultaneous feelings, of incredible disbelief and awe, at the self-transformation! As we go deeper in meditation, and the experiences keep happening, along with numerous "Aha" moments, once again, we talk about how fortunate we are, and how we will never be able to repay Maharaj for everything! We love him, not simply because we are so happy and grateful for all that he has shown, and given to us, but because he is pure love, beautiful and well, just, intensely lovable!

We reflect on our timeless relationship with our Guru. This special relationship is difficult to describe. It is magical, mystical, miraculous, precious. This process enables the unconditional love and protection of the "Mother" or divine feminine principle, to "love us to death". The layers have been removed, resulting in a return to childhood innocence. Finally, the root of the ego is removed, and one's true nature is revealed!

We have implemented the practice into our lives and live it. Maharaj is with us all the time. He is the boss, our only boss! We work for him only. His energy is around, within, all the time, as we walk, talk, eat, sleep. Nothing distracts us from Maharaj. We honour him by serving him, spreading the teachings and assisting other seekers. We live and breathe him. And, extraordinarily, we both have the blessed experience, of still feeling Maharaj's hand on our heads, from Initiation day!

February – We Skype with Maharaj. Charles is up to mischief today! He announces to Maharaj in a serious tone, that he has a problem. Maharaj does not like the sound of that! With an equally serious expression and raised voice, Maharaj queries, "Problem?" "Yes", Charles replies. "The problem is that we are TOO happy!" Maharaj's serious expression changes, instantly. Breaking into a huge smile, he says, "very nice". We laugh together like children enjoying a silly, little game!

When Anvita appears, Maharaj speaks with her in Marathi, telling her about Charles' problem! She smiles and laughs. Then, Maharaj and Anvita repeat what they have often said to us, about how we have sacrificed, and continue to sacrifice, so much time, and work for him. We tell them again that there is no sacrifice involved. The spiritual path has always been our life, and our service to Maharaj is our life's work! Nothing can be more important than that!

"There is no sacrifice here", reiterates Charles, "and meeting you, Maharaj, is truly the culmination of our journey for the two of us". They both listened and smiled.

10ᵗʰ February – There is even more confirmation now that the Masters are guiding the book, *Selfless Self*. During the last few days, the computer screen has been lighting up brightly by itself. Sometimes the letters of the text start moving around. It is as if the book is alive with *Sadguru's* power! Today, the screen and the area around it, turned pink, as if there was auric energy vibrating, in and around, the computer. To check my sanity, and ensure that I wasn't hallucinating, I tell Charles and ask him for a reality check. Have a look! "Do you see it?" Yes! He can see it, too! I am not just imagining it! He says it is amazing, miraculous!

I continue working on the book for a few more hours. After that, I stop, to get ready to go out for our afternoon walk, when suddenly, I notice a very bright light around the screen, expanding throughout the room. Assuming it is the light bulb, I leave my desk to switch it off. It is only then, as I put my fingers on the light switch, that I realize the light was not even on! Who says miracles don't happen!

March – The book is finished. *Jai Guru*! We Skype with Maharaj to let him know we will soon send him a copy. Maharaj is very happy!

Charles is the first one to read it. He asks me not to disturb him until he finishes it. He takes the manuscript to another room and closes the door. I make a cup of tea and sit down, fully relaxed, now that the work is finished. Suddenly, I hear Charles clapping his hands. That's a good sign, I thought… then I hear him laughing – another good sign!

A few hours later, he emerges, saying: "I don't know how you did it, but this is brilliant!"

I am happy to hear his response and reply: "I did not do anything. It wrote itself! It was written by Selfless Self, for Selfless Self. The Masters made it happen, spontaneously, using this vehicle!"

Now that the book is finished, we decide to go out, for a longer than usual walk, to celebrate. Soon after, the walk becomes a skip. We are holding hands, skipping along the path and joyfully singing, "*Jai Guru, Jai Guru, Jai Guru Jai*", all the way!

The next day, Charles gets busy contacting various book printers for estimates. We pay for 200 copies to be printed, and announce on the website, that Maharaj's book will be available shortly. We did not realize the book would be so expensive to post to the States – more in postage costs, than the book itself! Never mind… we are learning. And this is our *seva* or service to our Beloved Master!

April – *Selfless Self* is finally published! After Maharaj reads it, he Skypes with us. He is very happy. His exact words are: "This book is a miracle", and then, he looks at me, smiles and says, "Now I will call you, St. Ann!"

The only objection he has, is to the "Foreword", which we had asked someone to write. Maharaj does not approve. He instructs us to remove it, at once! We do so, immediately, and without question.

Alan Jacobs, "President of the Ramana Maharshi Foundation, UK" writes a glowing, 5-star review of *Selfless Self*. He says that there is no difference between the teachings in this book, and the teachings of Ramana Maharshi.

Within weeks, we receive various communications from readers, who tell us they can "feel the power, the energy in the book, just by holding it", even before they start reading it.

We are learning about book distribution the hard way, manually wrapping up the books, and posting one copy at a time, to seekers around the world. We pay for the printing, postage and other costs as a service to Maharaj. Charles jokes with Maharaj. He phones, saying: "I am calling from *Selfless Self* Headquarters, UK". Maharaj, pretending to feel threatened, replies, "No! The headquarters are here in Nashik!" They both have a good laugh!

More emails arrive with questions for Maharaj, as well as several enquiries about visiting him. When? How? etc. Charles attends to all the admin work with great devotion, competence and encouragement. He responds enthusiastically, to the many questions messaged to him on the Facebook page. He is the first point of contact for seekers, helping them every step of the way, with travel arrangements, hotels, and ensuring their safe arrival in Nashik!

End of April – One day, Maharaj and Anvita Skype with us. Maharaj says, "Anvita has something she wishes to ask". Then, Maharaj gets up from his chair, and tells Anvita to take his place. We are both overwhelmed by her humility and touched by her words. She says, in her sweet and innocent voice: "I would like to have permission to translate the book *Selfless Self*!"

We both say, "Of course, of course, Anvita, but there is no need to ask. The book belongs to Maharaj! We feel honoured!"

She thanks us. Then Maharaj says, "Do not tell anyone about it for the time being!"

After the call ended, we both felt blessed and happy, that Anvita is going to translate the book into Marathi. But we feel there was no need to ask!

May/June – As the word begins to spread about Nisargadatta's disciple, Shri Ramakant, Charles organizes Skype groups on Saturdays, for the American devotees. Among them are Jay, Sandy, John, Walter and Sonny. And on Sundays Europeans gather, including Sebastian, Paban, Jeen, Antonio, and Chaya.

Seekers are delighted to have the opportunity to see Maharaj online, and ask him questions, or even just to hear him speak – well most of them! Today, one seeker, a doctor based in the UK, appeared online. He was fully intent on attacking Gurus in general, and Maharaj, in particular. The Guru is there to answer questions and remove doubts, he is certainly not there, to be at the receiving end, of insulting questions such as: "Who do you think you are, telling me this?" which is what happened this afternoon! We were mortified.

The seeker was full of aggression and had no respect for Maharaj. He was basically a Guru basher! We cut him off Skype, as quickly as possible, though not soon enough!

When Charles apologized, Maharaj dismissed it, saying, "These things happen! Forget it!" Humility is crucial on the spiritual path. The caller was certainly lacking in that department. Because we feel so close to Maharaj and are very protective of him, we experienced a deep wound! Of course, Maharaj felt nothing!

We are baffled! Maybe we are naïve, but we cannot understand how anyone can treat Maharaj in this way. Usually, sincere seekers are instantly touched, just by seeing him! Seeing the radiance and pure love flowing through the Master is silencing!

Maharaj is always very happy to reach out to new faces, in different countries. His accent and "Indianisms", take some getting used to. So, when people don't understand, Charles clarifies for them.

Maharaj asks them when they are coming to Nashik? They all wish to travel, but cannot instantly drop everything. Sometimes, Maharaj's excitement translates into impatience, even though he knows and encourages everyone, to work, look after their responsibilities, and tend to their duties. They cannot just abandon everything at the drop of a hat!

Charles keeps Maharaj informed of the details of who is arriving in Nashik, and when! He advises the visitors to stay for a minimum of one week, though preferably two, and encourages those who can do so, to stay for as long as possible. Maharaj does not appreciate visitors who appear at the ashram, "to grab the *Naam*

Mantra", so to speak. He wants them to listen to his Talks first. Only then, will they be initiated.

Maharaj encourages Charles to scrutinize the emails from seekers first, and ask them questions, to ascertain whether they are serious or not. He is only interested in sincere seekers, not time wasters, who will indiscriminately act on a whim, only to go hopping from one Guru to another afterwards!

Today, Maharaj emails Charles, telling him he is not pleased with one particular visitor. Again, he emphasizes the importance of making sure that those who come are spiritually mature and serious. Charles is now scrutinizing them thoroughly!

End of June – Dhiraj, a devotee, makes contact with us, telling us of his intention to translate the book, *Selfless Self*, into Marathi! We find ourselves in a difficult position, knowing that Anvita is translating it already! Feeling somewhat compromised, we tell him that he cannot do so. We do not give him permission, and put this in writing. He is not pleased! It is unfortunate that he does not know the reasons for our refusal as we are not at liberty to say! He probably imagines the worst, that our egos have grown possessive of the book, or something like that!

4th July – Hamid, a musician from Chicago gets in touch with Charles again. They have developed a close friendship. Hamid affectionately calls Charles, "Charles Baba". Today he is eager to share his experience. He tells Charles that when the book arrived at his home and he held it in his hands, he could feel its tremendous power. At that moment, tears started rolling down his cheeks. He is very happy, knowing that this book, is the book to end all books! We pass on his comments to Maharaj, who is enjoying the positive feedback!

Mid-July – We decide to record the first 10 chapters of *Selfless Self* and upload them to the website. Charles reads one chapter, then I read the next. We find that recording these chapters helps us to absorb the Teachings even more!

August – Maharaj sends us a message on Skype, saying he wishes to speak with us. These days, when he writes to us, he addresses us, as: "Dear Devotee Charles and St. Ann", lol. When we Skype with Maharaj, Charles jokes with him. Today he asks Maharaj, "Why is she called "St. Ann", and I am simply, "Devotee Charles?" We laugh together!

    Maharaj says, "It is a great fact that both of you have done an exceptional job. It's just like Maurice Frydman who met *Sadguru* Shri Nisargadatta Maharaj, and totally melted with the exceptional, spiritual knowledge. You both have totally melted. Maurice firmly decided to circulate this knowledge all over the world. Similarly, both of you have done the same job. This happens according to the wish of our *Sadguru*! May you both live a very long life to spread the knowledge".

    We say, "Thank you Maharaj. *Jai Guru*!"

September – As further book orders come in from around the world, Charles posts them out diligently. He takes his role seriously because he knows the book's importance and potential. It has the power to end the search and change countless lives forever!

Late September – I am inspired to publish a pocket-sized book of Maharaj's spontaneous quotations. The idea behind this is for readers to use the quotes as a tool, that will keep the mind in check! When the mind comes back in to disturb the peace, then one can open this little book and read Maharaj's wonderful quotes! This will promptly bring him back to his centre, to Selfless Self. These quotes are so fresh and powerful, that they have the power to act as reminders of one's true identity, at all times. Maharaj often taught: "Be With You!" It strikes me as a great title for this project! Here are some of our favourite quotations:

"You have read all the books, but have you read the Reader?"

"Your files are corrupted. You need to install the anti-virus software of meditation to delete the program of illusion. Meditation is the only way to reboot your hard drive. The Master Key, the *Naam Mantra*, will open the door to Reality."

"You have been thrown into the ocean of this illusory world. Now you have to swim out of this illusory ocean."

"Your hard drive is choked. Be as you were before the add-ons. Self-knowledge means absorbing the knowledge, 'I am not the body'."

"Why keep travelling when you are the destination?"

"You are worried about death because you think you are somebody. You are unborn."

"Be with You and listen from the All. Read your book, it is the final edition."

"Make sure the knowledge you have is real and practical, otherwise you will be shaking and trembling on your deathbed."

"You are the architect of your own life. Stop running here, and running there, because you do not know the Runner."

"It is a great shame, a calamity, to accept that which you are not, and to keep on crying in the dream."

"This life is a long dream, a long movie. You are the producer, director and the star."

"I have presented you with the golden plate of Reality. There is no need to go begging ever again. You are the Final Destination."

"I am trying to remove you from the vicious circle of illusion. But again, you want to jump back into the ditch. Stop! Stop your clowning around!"

"I am the garbage man. Give me all your concepts that you have collected since childhood."

"When you no longer require happiness, you have reached the destination."

"Spiritual knowledge is also the great illusion. It is only there to remove the first illusion."

"You are the worshipped, the worshipper and the worship."

"Why ask for blessings? Put your hand on your head and bless yourself."

October – The number of westerners travelling to see Maharaj has been rising for months. Walter and Jan are travelling from the States, Dimitri from Australia and Ansan and Mona from Korea, as well as numerous devotees from different parts of India, who wish to spend time with this rare *Jnani*. Maharaj is in his element when he teaches, and the way he does is genius, in its simplicity and efficacy. He tells some of the devotees attending the *Satsangs*: to "send the recordings to Ann and Charles". The material will no doubt provide the content for the next book. When we listen to the Talks, we are instantly transported back to the ashram, and seated beside Maharaj.

December – Maharaj develops pneumonia. He is taken to the hospital and told to rest. We hear from the ashram that he has lost his voice. It is too late to inform some of those visitors who are in transit. Those who are already there are more than disappointed that they can no longer hear him speak!

2016

January – Maharaj is still very poorly. We see a recent photo of him with a group of visitors. Poor Maharaj! It looks like the illness has taken its toll. The body has aged a great deal! We feel for Maharaj, as well as the visitors, who have travelled thousands of miles to see him! Some of them were there for one week or ten days during Maharaj's illness. All of them, however, received the *Naam Mantra*! Maharaj made sure of that!

We hear that the book Dr Dhiraj was working on, comprising of some of Maharaj's earlier discourses and *Abhangas*, (devotional poems), has recently been published in Marathi. It is entitled *Atamanatma Vivek*.

February – Maharaj's health is improving. His wish is to spread these teachings all over the world. What better way than to work on translations of *Selfless Self*? A few of his devotees have already begun translating the book into French, Spanish, Dutch, Korean, and other languages. Maharaj instructs me to retain the copyright for these translations, too.

Mid-February – Ansan, a devotee from South Korea, has kindly been working on compiling and organizing the *bhajans*, to make it easier for western devotees to follow. We thank him for his *seva* and Charles uploads them to the website.

April – Spontaneously, we begin meditating and contemplating death. We each take turns and lie on the floor, with our arms crossed over our chests, and stay there for a few moments. We take pictures of each other in this death pose, and put them on the wall as reminders of the body's time limit. While on the floor, we contemplate the process of the Spirit separating itself from the body.

We also visit a nearby cemetery that acts as another reminder of the body's brief sojourn! Maharaj used to recommend spending some time in a cemetery.

July – A few months back, our friend, Krishna, suggested to us that we send a copy of *Selfless Self* to the *Mountain Path* magazine for review. We had posted a copy to Christopher Quilkey, the Editor of the *Mountain Path* Magazine. Today, we discover the review in the summer edition! We are very happy to see it and Skype with Maharaj to tell him the news. He is delighted!

In the past, Maharaj described how events tend to repeat themselves: what happened with his Master, is now happening again. History is repeating itself! One example of this was the arrival of the foreigners to Nisargadatta's ashram. And now, we have come, as well as others! Then, there was *I Am That*, and now there is *Selfless Self*. Seeing his book reviewed now, also reminded him of Jean Dunn, when she submitted an article about Nisargadatta Maharaj to the *Mountain Path*. The impact of the article brought many more devotees to Nisargadatta. We tell Maharaj that he better prepare for a fresh influx of seekers', travelling to see him in Nashik! Maharaj smiles. He is always happy to share the knowledge, enable seekers to wake up from the dream, and put an end to their suffering!

Here is what Christopher Quilkey wrote:

Mountain Path Review – July 2016

SELFLESS SELF Talks with Shri Ramakant Maharaj edited by Ann Shaw.

"Ramakant Maharaj (RM) is a direct disciple of Sri Nisargadatta Maharaj (NM). He was born in 1941; is married with two sons; and qualified as a lawyer and worked in the banking industry. He spent 19 years closely associated with NM from whom he received *Naam Mantra* in 1962. For the past decade and more he has been guiding students from his ashram in Nasik, Maharashtra. He belongs to the Inchegiri Navnath Sampradaya. Fortunately for those who do not speak Marathi, he speaks English and has evolved the teachings of the Lineage to meet the ever-changing circumstances of modern life in India and abroad. He cuts through all concepts including the 'I Am' concept and strongly discourages dependency on the master or his form. He points to our 'Invisible Presence' by giving 'Direct Knowledge'. RM says: "It is my duty to share this Knowledge, the same Knowledge that my Master shared with me."

The book format is different both in dimension and presentation. It is meant to encourage reflection. It is not meant to be read cover to cover but rather to be picked up and absorbed in section by section. The layout with its use of bold capital centred statements means that the reader is alerted to important statements which cannot be ignored. The book is long and dense. The book is divided into three parts: Self-Enquiry, Self-Knowledge and Self-Realization. The book is not so much a presentation of concepts as a manual addressed to the 'Invisible Listener' in us. The Inchegiri Navnath Sampradaya is known for its practicality and this book is no different.

The teaching of RM is concrete and radical. He hammers the same point over and over again with subtle variations: The body form is material and all knowledge is material knowledge. He constantly directs our attention to the illusion of our identity with the body-form. "When You Become One With Selfless Self, Your Identity Is Forgotten, Your Identity Then Poses As Your Master. It Takes The Shape Of Your Master." "You Are The Cause And Consequence Of Your Entire World." "Try To Know Your Identity. Try To Know Your Unidentified Identity. The Knower Will Disappear While Trying To Know Ultimate Truth. The Knower Will Disappear. No Knowledge, No Knower."

This book may appear to be just another recitation of the familiar party line of Advaita but what differentiates it is the obvious sincerity and one-pointed focus and power of the teaching. RM does not tire in pointing out the fallacy of our false identification with that which has no existence in its own right. We are reminded of Sri Ramana's who consistently taught self-enquiry to all who entered his Presence. Truth does not grow stale. It is ever fresh. To state it, again and again, does not show a lack of imagination but indicates a powerful and unceasing conviction that reinforces the essential from whatever angle one takes.

At first, one may feel intimated by the size, scope and seeming repetition of the book but with patience one can see its value. The book aims to bring the reader back again and again to the central point: Who is the knower?

RM reminds one of NM whose fierce uncompromising commitment to the truth quelled the superficial questions and arguments of the curious. This book too is not for the casually inquisitive or faint-hearted. One has to breathe this book not think it. There is more happening in the dialogues than words can say. After reading through this book I have come to the conclusion that to be in the Presence of RM is to enter another dimension of understanding."

August – We intuit that Maharaj is feeling the cold more these days, so, we are inspired to buy him some items of clothing, to keep him warm. Instantly, we see a lovely woollen cream-coloured sweater/cardigan. "Maharaj will like that", says Charles. Then, we find a maroon coloured woollen hat and scarf to match. We wrap the gifts up for Maharaj, alongside a silk scarf for Anvita, and box the items. We enclose a letter to Maharaj, once more using the opportunity to express our infinite gratitude, and our wish to be with him again.

After Maharaj and Anvita receive the gifts, we receive a big "Thank you" call! Initially, they give us a row, saying, we should not have gone to any trouble. Maharaj does not like accepting gifts, accepting anything, in fact. We tell him that it happened spontaneously. We just want him to keep warm. He smiles.

Mid-August – Before leaving for the States, Maharaj Skypes with us. He tells me to write another book on his Teachings. His directives for this book are more detailed and specific, than the ones he gave for *Selfless Self*. This time, Maharaj has chosen the title, *Who Am I?* He wants me to write it in a very straightforward way, (keeping references and confusing Indian terminology, to the minimum). It is his wish that this simple, powerful knowledge reach many more seekers, far and wide.

"I want you to write this book in a popular style, for westerners, in particular. You know the culture. You know better. Use modern language with references to today's fast lifestyle, a society that is consumed by the internet and mobile phone culture! Frame the knowledge in a contemporary way, so that the ordinary person, will be able to understand it! Make it light and fun!", he stipulates.

It sounds like a tall order with many requirements. I respond, spontaneously and humorously, using one of Maharaj's hip quotes:

"So, basically, Maharaj, you want me to spread the word, and tell the readers to "Insert the program of Selfless Self because it runs faster than Google!" Maharaj laughs and says, "You know better!"

"I will start work on it immediately!", I reply, unable to contain my laughter.

Maharaj continues: "Now is the time for the world to hear this knowledge. Now is the time! This knowledge is not the property of this Sampradaya Lineage. It is "Universal Knowledge"! Make it simple and attractive, so that it becomes popular. This knowledge is for everyone. We have to help others come out of suffering. We have to put an end to their suffering! It is our duty to show them, how to wake up from the dream, and be free!

While we must never force this knowledge on anyone, at the very least, we can try to make people aware! By presenting them with an alternative viewpoint, or a different way of perceiving themselves and the world, we can help to bring them out of the illusion, and free them from suffering! All we can do is plant the seed, and then let the rest happen spontaneously. Whether they accept it or not, that's up to them. We cannot force them! So, go ahead! Go ahead!"

Shortly after, Maharaj had expressed his wish to spread the teachings, I had a vision of a wildfire spreading throughout the lands, from country to country, in an unstoppable manner!

I understand what Maharaj is saying, and what he wants to achieve, through this next book. Put simply, we have been conditioned, to know and enjoy, only one meal or dish. We eat from the dish of illusion. We do not know that there is another dish, until we are told. When we become aware of the possibility of an alternative, and, if we are ready, we can choose to eat from the dish of reality!"

I love the new book title, *Who Am I?* reminiscent of the great Bhagavan Ramana Maharshi's little book of Q & A's entitled *Nan Yar* in Tamil, (*Who Am I?*) published in 1923.

September – Maharaj and Anvita travel to the USA, to stay with their son. Once settled there and rested, he will offer *Satsangs*. Charles is in charge of organizing Maharaj's trip. He gathers donations from devotees around the world and books their air flight tickets.

Here is what Maharaj posted, to introduce himself to the American seekers:

"*Jai Guru*! As you know, I don't wish to deliver discussions on spirituality. I strongly expect that all seekers should have Practical Spiritual Conviction. As you are aware, meditation is a strong base that leads to Spontaneous Realization. Without any expectations, I would like to share Ultimate Truth amongst all the seekers. I strongly feel that everyone should have complete spiritual happiness, peacefulness, a tension-free life, and a fearless life.

To have the Spontaneous Spiritual Conviction, the seeker's sincere and deep involvement is necessary. Approaching different Masters, reading endless spiritual books, or merely dry spiritual discussions, will not help you to have Spontaneous Conviction. In the light of the above, I would like to implant Ultimate Truth amidst the Spiritual Heart of all. For this, your devotional participation is strongly expected.

With regards and blessings to all. My affectionate spiritual feelings towards all seekers. *Jai Sadguru*!"

These *Satsangs* took place in Silver Spring and Columbia. Here is a selection:

Talk A – "**Maharaj**: Do not underestimate yourself. Carry out your responsibilities, as if you are acting in a drama or movie. In the illusory world, we have many relations. We are mothers, fathers, aunts, brothers, sisters, grandparents, etc. We play so many different roles. Act them well! All our relatives came with the body-form, and they will disappear with the body-form. Take care of your family, but at the same time, know that all your family members are a big illusion! All our needs and all our requirements came along with the body. We only need spiritual knowledge because we have forgotten our identity. There was no spiritual knowledge prior to beingness? We are not beggars, yet we behave like beggars, pleading: "Oh God, bless me. Do something for me. Help me!" Wherever you go, you are bowing down to someone else, something other. The Master says, "Why are you bowing to everyone else, but yourself? Bow down to yourself! Bow to Selfless Self!" You are the only Power. After Conviction, you will not bow to anyone. This is not to say that you will disrespect anyone, but, you will know that you are the central point of the universe. Everything is within you. There is nothing else.

Q: You say it is not difficult to achieve this Ultimate Truth?

Maharaj: Of course, it is not difficult!

Q: And yet, it takes time for most people.

Maharaj: Suppose it has been dark in a cave for five hundred years. If you enter with a light, will the darkness say, "I have been here for so many years, I cannot leave immediately. It will take some time?" Of course not. Enlightenment is instant. When the light of knowledge shines on the darkness of ignorance, the change is instantaneous.

Talk B – "Q: Maharaj, why are we so scared to find this Ultimate Truth?

Maharaj: It is not like that. Because we have had so many concepts engraved upon us, we have accepted that "I am somebody", "I am a man" or "I am a woman". After Conviction, you will know that you are not the body at all.

Q: So, we are all *Brahman*, the *Brahman* itself. Is that correct? That is the premise?

Maharaj: It is more than a premise. It is a fact! Stop measuring yourself as the body-form. The bodies have different appearances.

Q: No problem, so that is the premise. So the question that goes begging is: Why is one *Brahman* willing to harm another *Brahman* if we are one and the same?

Maharaj: Because this is body-based knowledge. *Brahman* is not harming anything. Does the sky harm any other sky? Does the American sky harm the Indian sky? Sky doesn't know, "I am sky", Presence doesn't know, "I am Presence", *Brahman* doesn't know, "I am *Brahman*". *Brahman* is a word given to that Ultimate Truth that you are. The Invisible Listener within you is Ultimate Truth. It is called *Brahman*, *Atman*, *Paramatman*, God, Master. It is not an individual. There is no duality at all.

Q: So, can one say that it is okay for this *Brahman*, to harm that *Brahman*?

Maharaj: No, no. There is no, "I am *Brahman*, I will harm another *Brahman*". There aren't two different *Brahmans*.

Q: Okay, so it is one *Brahman*. But there are two separate bodies. If I harm this body in some way, do I just turn around and say it's okay because we are all one and the same?

Maharaj: Egoistic concepts are there: "I am someone". Erase that "someone". *Brahman* does not harm, cannot harm, anyone else.

Q: But if harm should happen - and I think you said earlier, that nothing is really being done - then no deeds are being done, ultimately.

Maharaj: There is no doer, and there is no deed. We are measuring ourselves in the body-form, and therefore, all these concepts appear. I am talking about that Invisible Presence within you, where there is nothing. Nothing is there: no thoughts are there, and no concepts are there. The concept *Brahman* is also not there. And as I told you, *Brahman* is just the name given to that Ultimate Truth. Except for your Selfless Self, there is no *Brahman, Atman, Paramatman*, God, Master. So, *Brahman* is not harming some other *Brahman* – like*,* "this *Brahman* is different from that *Brahman*".

Q: Okay, so in other words, what you do to others, you are doing to yourself, right?

Maharaj: As long as you are considering yourself in the body-form, these concepts will keep appearing. There is no other. No other exists! It is only because we are measuring ourselves in the body-form, that the concepts of "he" is there, "she" is there, "it" is there, and, therefore, they appear. Prior to beingness were any of these concepts there?

Q: But, if somebody harms someone?

Maharaj: When did you come across another, a someone? Prior to beingness, was there "someone" there? And, after leaving the body, is there going to be someone there?

Q: Okay, what if this body harms another body...?

Maharaj: I am shouting. I have to keep shouting at you! Because you are measuring yourself in the body-form, therefore, you are under the impression that there are different bodies. There are different houses, but the sky is one. This is called a bungalow, and this is a cottage. They are called by different names. If all the houses collapse, what would happen to the sky? Nothing! Stop considering yourself to be a separate entity or individual. It is because of this misidentification, that all these concepts keep on appearing, and causing you problems.

Spirit or Presence is One. It is only our bodies that are different. It is the basic thing. Since we are measuring ourselves in the body-form, all these concepts appear. It is only the bodies that are different.

The human body is an opportunity for you to identify yourself. Every moment is very important, very valuable. Complete concentration, complete involvement is most important. We are not accepting this. Everybody knows, "I am not the body at all". Everybody knows that. Some day or other, willingly or unwillingly, we are to leave this body. What remains?"

Talk C – "Q: Can you please say something about a practice that is silent, without words, that supports the aware Presence in recognizing itself?

Maharaj: After Conviction, there will be spontaneous silence. At present, there is no silence, only violence, because we have too many body-based concepts, clambering, and chattering continuously. Directly, or indirectly, we have become victims of our mind, ego, and intellect. To identify yourself in a real sense, intense meditation is needed.

Q: Should the *Naam Mantra* be recited continuously, after initiation?

Maharaj: Recite the *Naam Mantra* at all times, continuously, at every available moment. You need not sit in one position to do it. Attend to your duties, your work, and while you are doing this, keep reciting the Mantra at every opportunity.

Q: And will it still the mind, so that the mind is not all over the place?

Maharaj: The mind is always stinging you, pinching you from behind. Concentrating on the *Naam* is a kind of cleaning process. The mind will not let you concentrate on yourself. So, perseverance is needed at the beginning.

Q: *Vipassana* Meditation does not use a Mantra. It is basically about observing the breath and observing the bodily sensations. What are your thoughts on that?

Maharaj: It provides temporary relief. You can practice *Vipassana* for a time - one week, two weeks, or one month, but after leaving the *Vipassana* Centre, you will be back where you started. Again, you will find yourself at the same place.

Q: But what if you practice *Vipassana* every day? I mean, what are your thoughts on vipassana versus...

Maharaj: The principle behind *Vipassana*, or any practice, is to identify yourself in a real sense. Whatever practice you are doing, is based on the principle of identifying yourself, in the true sense. These are processes. *Vipassana* is a process, and meditation is also a process. But meditation is a strong process, through which, you can identify yourself, within a short time. It enables you to discard all the illusory concepts, and uncover your identity in a simple, quick and direct way.

Q: But in *Vipassana* meditation there is no mantra.

Maharaj: Go ahead, do *Vipassana* meditation if you wish, but you are posing yourself in the body-form, and then, doing some *Vipassana* meditation, therefore, it is meaningless. "I am somebody who is doing *Vipassana* meditation". This is egoistic meditation. You are to forget about your bodily identity. "I am doing some *sadhana*", "I am doing some meditation", That "I" must dissolve. The process of meditation will dissolve that "I".

Through the meditation, you are inviting the attention of the Invisible Meditator within you, that you are Ultimate Truth, you are Final Truth. You are hammering yourself, non-stop.

Q: In *I Am That* Sri Nisargadatta Maharaj says, "A quiet mind is all you need. When the mind is quiet, all else happens, as it should". Does it matter, therefore, how one quiets one's mind?

Maharaj: After knowing your Selfless Self, the mind will not remain. The existence of the mind appeared upon your Presence. The existence of the mind, ego, and intellect appeared upon your Presence. Presence does not have any mind, ego, or intellect. And therefore, try to identify yourself in a real sense. These are the words. I am conveying this to you, through words. After Conviction, the mind, ego, and intellect will not remain. Where was the mind prior to beingness? Where will the mind be after leaving the body? The mind does not have an independent identity. You have given birth to the mind, the ego, and the intellect. Without your Presence, how can you identify these?

Through meditation, you will be able to control your mind. The mind will be controlled spontaneously. Eventually, you will be thoughtless, as you were prior to beingness.

The mind means the flow of thoughts. Continuous thoughts are flowing which you define as the "mind". The thoughts enter the mind and travel to the intellect. The intellect makes a decision, and then the ego implements that decision.

This is the process, the functioning of the mind, ego and intellect. It is of no concern to you because you are separate from all that."

Talk D – "**Maharaj**: Yesterday we were talking about the principle of spirituality, and the purpose of spirituality. You know that the purpose of spirituality is to identify oneself in a real sense. What is the reason behind identifying ourselves in a real sense? We identify ourselves as the food-body, and that is not Reality. The body-form is not our Reality.

I am not saying that you are to neglect your food-body. This is the medium through which you can identify yourself. There are so many concepts from childhood till today: "I am born", "I am a man or woman", social concepts, religious concepts- and within this circle, we are living our life.

After identifying yourself perfectly, dramatic changes will take place within you. These are called the signs of Realization. Spiritual Science teaches that there are six signs, or symptoms, of Realization. Seekers often ask: "How can I identify whether I am Realized or not? What is the sign of Realization? What is the sign of Enlightenment?" After Conviction, after absorbing the knowledge of Reality, some changes will take place.

Shama means to forgive and forget. If anything happens against your mind, you will not get irritated, or become angry. *Dama* means tolerance or patience. Tolerance will arise spontaneously from within. Where petty matters used to irritate us, where there was even some violence inside us, now, patience will take its place.

You will feel it. If an incident happens against your mind, you won't be irritated. There will be tolerance and patience.

Titiksha means just to know the Reality. You are eager, anxious to know the Reality - "Who am I?" Suppose someone is talking about Reality, *Brahman*, *Atman*, *Paramatman*, God, Master. You have the ability to discern, the capacity to discern what you are listening to, calmly and quietly.

Uparati means that there is no longer any attraction for the world. There are so many worldly attractions: publicity, or power and fame, money and sex, etc. After Realization, there will not be any greed or attraction to the world. You are living in the world, but there is complete calm and quiet.

And then there is *bhakti* which means devotion, total devotion. After knowing the Reality there is total devotion. And finally, there is *shraddha* which means full trust and faith. You can use these as a barometer to gauge your progress.

After Spontaneous Conviction, these changes will occur. Prior to, and after beingness, at that time, there was no anger, nothing was there. These signs will appear spontaneously. You will be very calm and very quiet.

I sometimes tell this story, the example given by Gautama Buddha, which you may know. The story goes that there was a lady, who took on the challenge of irritating the Buddha, and so, she began abusing him with foul language. Gautama stayed calm and quiet. Eventually, the lady grew irritated, and said, "Why are you not getting angry? Why are you not getting irritated?" And he replied, "Oh mother, you have offered me something, and I have not accepted it. With whom does it remain?" This means that the abuse stays with the abuser. It is up to you whether you accept, or reject these illusory concepts.

There is a similar story, here in Maharashtra. There was a saint called Saint Eknath. He was a very calm, and quiet saint. So, one person took on the same challenge, "I will succeed in making him irritated".

Every day Saint Eknath went to the nearby river to bathe. On his way back, this person would spit on him. Calmly and quietly, Saint Eknath went back to the river. This happened forty times. Eventually, having failed to irritate Saint Eknath, that abuser became irritated and eventually bowed down to Saint Eknath. What did Saint Eknath say? "I bathed forty times because of you." This is patience and tolerance. Saint Eknath then invited him for lunch!

What am I trying to convey with these stories? There will be a big change! Any violence that is there just now, will disappear spontaneously. It can happen. There will always be silence and no violence. You will feel it, after Conviction. You will feel it. That is the principle of spirituality. Listening, talking, and approaching different Masters will not help you. It will confuse you. Some changes are needed. Only then, will real silence and peacefulness permeate. There will not be any tension. You will be free of the illusory circle in which you were living your life.

Why is there tension? We have expectations, and if they are not fulfilled, tension and irritation appear. Everybody has so many expectations, from family, from friends, from society. It is the nature of the mind.

All expectations and needs came along with the body. Body-based knowledge is not tolerable. It is a food-body that will survive, for as long as you supply it with food and water. It is an open fact that this body is not going to remain constant. Spirit or Presence, wants to continue living. That is its nature. Your Presence only knows itself through the body. Meditate! It is only through meditation that you can identify yourself, and have Conviction. No meditation = No Conviction! Knowledge will be absorbed totally. And, therefore, I am repeating: dry knowledge, dry discussion on spirituality are all meaningless. Even if we spent months or years talking together, it would all be meaningless. It is your identity that you need to uncover, not the identity of *Brahman*, *Atman*, *Paramatman*, God or Master.

No one but you can identify yourself. And this can only be done through meditation! The Master reminds you of your identity, but the rest is up to you!"

Talk E – "**Q**: In your book, *Selfless Self,* you said that meditation is like a spiritual broom. It is a nice image.

Maharaj: Yes, correct, correct. It is the anti-virus software. Our files are corrupted files. There are so many concepts in them. Though we know our identity, and though we know Reality, there are still some concepts around. Because of some internal weakness, these concepts continue to flow and exploit us.

What exactly is it that we want from spiritual knowledge? What is the principle? You want peace. You cannot find peace. Negative thoughts are always infiltrating. There is violence within us. We say, "Oh, I'm okay, I'm really okay", but there is something inside that is burning. That burning should stop.

For a long, long, time we have been posing as a man, or as a woman, in the body-form. You have totally accepted that "I am the body". But now you know that you are not the body at all, and never were! The purpose of spiritual knowledge is to identify yourself. When you identify yourself, there will be an abundance of peace and happiness.

Knowledge is meaningless. There was no knowledge prior to beingness, and there will be no use of it, after leaving the body. Knowledge means just to identify oneself, in a real sense. We are identifying ourselves in the body-form, and that is an illusion. And again, I reiterate that identification is not possible without meditation. To remove one illusion, we need the help of another illusion. To remove one thorn, we need to use another thorn. Then, we will throw both thorns away."

Talk F – "Q: So you do the *bhajans*, you do the meditation, you do the practice, and eventually it occurs… the penny drops - that you know who you are. You know you are not the body, and you know that the world does not even exist. And then you don't care, is that right? You don't even care what happens? So, if the body hurts, or if the body has great pleasures, or if the body is angry, or the mind is angry, it has nothing to do with who I am. And that is the end, that is the finality?

Maharaj: All these actions and reactions are there because we are not identifying ourselves. The moment you identify yourself, nothing will be there. The body does not get angry. If there were no Presence, then how can a dead body get angry? Prior to beingness, did you know about anger? And, after beingness, will there be any anger there?

Q: For me, sometimes, if there is anger in the mind, that anger has nothing to do with me, because I am the ocean, not the individual. And so I see that certain things I take the touch of, like...

Maharaj: Thoughts are flowing inside, and you are taking on ego. You are witnessing the thoughts - good thoughts and bad thoughts. Who is the witness?

Q: Be the witness of the best and the worst.

Maharaj: Your Spontaneous Presence is the Witness, the Invisible Witness. Your Spontaneous Invisible Presence is the Witness that is witnessing all these things. Everything appears upon your Presence. Presence does not have any anger.

Q: I guess what I am trying to say, is that pain and anger, do not seem to be of any concern.

Maharaj: Of course! Selfless Self has no concerns. You are totally different. These feelings came with the body. Prior to body-based knowledge, there was nothing. We did not know what anger or anxiety was! Nothing was known to us. Who wants peacefulness? Who wants happiness? Who wants a fearless life? Does the body want a fearless life?

Q: The "I am" wants peacefulness. "Paul" wants peacefulness.

Maharaj: That "I am" concept appeared upon your Presence. If your Presence were not there, who will have anything to say about "I am"? That Invisible Presence, Power, Energy, is needed for you to say "I am". A dead body cannot say "I am"!

Q: Correct, yeah.

Maharaj: If the Seer is not there to see the world, the world cannot be seen. Everything that is seen is reflected out of your Spontaneous Presence. To say, or do, or think, or feel, for any action to take place, your Presence is needed. I am calling it by the name "Presence". To identify something you have to use some name - *Brahman*, *Atman*, *Paramatman*, God, or Master - these are the names given to the Supernatural Power within you.

I am inviting the attention of the Invisible Listener within you, that has been called by many different names. But remember! You are that Supernatural Power. You are not separate from That. You Are That!

Do not underestimate yourself. You have great power, tremendous power. But all the time, we are measuring ourselves in the body-form, and that is an illusion. It is not your fault, but because of your long association with the body, you have become one with the body.

You are Ultimate Truth. It is a fact. You are unborn. Birth and death are connected to the body-knowledge only, and not to you. But the problem is that you are not accepting the facts. To aid acceptance, meditation is needed, and your deep involvement.

Do not torture your body. Why torture the body, in order to know your identity? Take some time out for you. Be involved! Look at you! "Yes, I want to know myself! Who am I? If I am not the body, who am I?" Ask the question. Find the answer within! Find the courage to find the answer."

Talk G – "Q: In your book, you said, "Be yourself and everything is okay". How do you "be yourself"?

Maharaj: Yes, it is a fact! You have accepted body-knowledge. "Yourself" means Selfless Self, through which you are talking just now, and identifying some concepts. Self is not separate from you. "Yourself", "myself", these names have been given. It is Selfless Self. These are only words.

There are so many Masters saying things in many different ways. Instead of analyzing the words of these Masters, pay attention to what they wanted to convey. Understand the message they were trying to give.

The message is "Except your Selfless Self, there is no God, no *Brahman*, no *Atman*, no *Paramatman*, and no Master". That is the gist of all spirituality.

194

Remember this! It is a fact! Be bold! Have the courage to accept the Reality! You will find dramatic changes taking place. As I have told you, the six qualities of Realization will appear within you. Where you feel some irritation and violence, there will be complete silence, complete silence and peacefulness. Your tolerance will increase. There will no longer be an attraction for the world. Why be attracted to the world, when it is illusion? This can happen. The only thing you have to do is devote some time for yourself, for Selfless Self, not for any *Brahman*, *Atman*, *Paramatman*, God, or Master. Knowledge is free of charge. Value it! If someone charges five thousand dollars or something, you will say, "Oh, he is a great Master."

One seeker came to me. His Master was a Hatha Yoga Master. His Master charged him five lakh rupees in foreign currency. Why? He had pierced his ear, and done this, and that. Why is this needed? Wearing different clothes, garlands, and so on, decorating the body? Or, a pierced ear! Why are they decorating the body? Prior to this world, did you come with a decorated body? Or, a pierced ear!

I am not criticizing anyone. This happens because we depend on others, to be able to know ourselves. We are not trying to know ourselves. We are not trying to know, "Who am I?" This is the main question. That question can only be solved within you because you are the source of this identity. Therefore, I define it as "Unidentified, Invisible, Anonymous Identity". There is no name; you can't guess what it is. If I am talking about something, that Invisible Listener is listening. There is a flow of thoughts. You are witnessing those thoughts. Who is that? And therefore, I have told you, "Be with you always" because your Presence is Ultimate Truth.

Do not accept illusory thoughts. Thoughts are flowing - why struggle with the thoughts? We are struggling with the thoughts, "Why this? Why that?" It is the nature of the body.

Q: But that's difficult...

Maharaj: Why is that difficult? You can identify thoughts. Those things which you do not accept, forget about them! If a number of dishes are given to you, you say, "I don't want this, I don't want that, I want this food only," correct? Do not flow along with the thoughts. Don't follow the mind, let the mind follow you. This will happen through the meditation. Give yourself some time for You! Reading books, and listening to everybody else, will not work. Listen to your own voice, your inner voice. You must listen to your own voice. It will happen if you are calm and quiet.

Q: But how do you know that the inner voice that you hear is not from your body?

Maharaj: The body is only a medium. You are witnessing thoughts. You are witnessing the dream, you are watching the dream. Who is watching that dream? You are asleep, the body can't watch. Who has created the dream-world? Have you decided, "Today I'll see this dream, and tomorrow I'll see that dream"? You see the sky, the oceans, the gods, and so many things. Who has created that dream-world?

Similarly, when the Presence clicked with the body, you were able to see this dream-world. The body does not create any dreams. It is the combination of

Presence and the body, just like the combination of the matchbox and the stick. When the matchstick strikes the matchbox, you see the fire. Fire is everywhere, just like the five elements are everywhere. American water is not separate from Indian water. Is the American sky different from the Indian sky? Because there are different bodies, we say, "This is one, and that is another one." Presence is One."

Talk H – "**Q**: My mind keeps asking, "Why am I here? To be of service? Or, "Why am I here in the physical body if I am already *Brahman*?"

Maharaj: That which says "my mind", is different from the mind. You are not the mind at all. You are watching your mind, identifying your mind, experiencing your mind. The mind is separate from you. You are supplying energy to your mind. You can control your mind. It happens, it is the nature of the mind. The thoughts are flowing. You are separate from the thoughts. You are thoughtless.

Q: Maharaj, over the last couple of years, my *sadhana* has progressed quite a bit. More so just sitting in *dnyana*, seeing the seer, knowing the knower. Basically being able to pivot the mind backwards, in the state of awareness. There is a statement by Nisargadatta Maharaj: "Patience and perseverance are most important at that stage". So, I have been continuing like this for the last couple of years, and now I can do it for about two hours a day. What next?

Maharaj: There is no next. No next is there, nothing is there. Does the sky have any "next" or "first", or "earlier"? Think about it. Your Presence is just like the sky or the space. It is everywhere like the five elements. Mind, ego, intellect - these concepts appeared upon your Presence. I am inviting the attention of that Presence through which you say, "my mind, my ego, my intellect." All relations, all requirements, all needs - who wants all these things? Where was that mind prior to beingness? There was no ego, and no intellect, prior to beingness.

I am placing before you various words in different ways. Try to identify the principle behind these words. This is not dry, spiritual knowledge. It is the Listener's Truth. The Listener is Ultimate. You are Ultimate Truth. You are the destination. The Absolute is within you."

Talk I – "**Maharaj**: Meditation is the base. Though it is not Ultimate Truth, it is the base, the foundation, which is absolutely necessary until you have the Conviction of Selfless Self.

Literary knowledge and oral knowledge, will not help you, because you are holding this human body. Even though we are formless and shapeless, we started considering ourselves as body-forms. Your Spontaneous Invisible Presence is like the space or the sky. But that Conviction is missing. And, in order to have this Conviction, one should undergo intense meditation. Meditation is your base, your foundation. Don't make excuses. Just do it!

The body is not tolerable. Body-based-knowledge is not tolerable. To make it tolerable, we resort to material things like power, money, and sex, and all sorts of other things. In them, we find temporary relief! To come out from these body-based concepts, meditation, and reciting the Mantra, are most important. Although the Mantra is a concept, these Sanskrit words have a lot of power. The efficacy of the *Naam Mantra* has been proven, time and time again, by our great lineage Masters, as well as by the immediate effects, often visible in the majority of seekers.

In the process of your meditation, involvement, and your strong devotion, sometimes miraculous experiences happen. They may be positive, or negative, miraculous experiences. I will give you an example from Sri Nisargadatta Maharaj. It will help your focus.

Early on, Nisargadatta Maharaj was very rich. He owned about ten shops. His finances were in very good shape when in 1933, or so, he came across Siddharameshwar Maharaj. One of his friends took him to see Siddharameshwar Maharaj. At that time, he said, "I will not believe in any body-based Sage or Saint. I am not going to bow down to him". But he went there, listened, and then experienced a miraculous inner change. His base was already solid. He was so deeply impressed, that he bowed down to Sri Siddharameshwar spontaneously. His association with Siddharameshwar lasted for about three years.

I am describing Nisargadatta Maharaj's experiences to help you focus on your devotional life. After 1939, or thereabouts, he left his routine life and set out to experience the Spiritual world. He faced so many unbearable problems. He left his family and everything else behind. He had numerous shops and apartments which were rented out, etc. But, he was driven to experience this spiritual knowledge. In the course of his spiritual adventure, he faced many negative experiences. He had no money, and he was wandering here and there, physically exhausted.

At one point, he found himself in some barren land where there was no water. There was nothing! Completely exhausted, he said he thought it was going to be the last moment of his life. But then, in that desolate, barren land, he could see a cottage, in the far distance.

Here, I am talking about devotional experiences, that appear when you are deeply involved in spirituality. Though it is not knowledge and not Reality, this kind of miraculous incident does happen.

He had seen this cottage, and so, with great difficulty, went there. There was an old man there, who gave him some food, bread, and water. Soon after that, he left. After taking a few steps, he looked back. The cottage was nowhere to be seen. It had disappeared.

Nisargadatta Maharaj rarely gave us examples of his miraculous experiences. But I learned from him. After this experience, he wrote a poem: "My Master became a cottage for me. My Master became food for me. My Master became water for me". This can happen to anyone. Your Master can manifest in any shape or form when you are in difficulty. But you must have strong faith, within yourself, and in your Master. When you have strong devotion and deep involvement, then this kind of miraculous experience can happen.

They can be positive or negative. "Negative experiences" mean that you will have some negative or depressive thoughts. There may be difficulties, just like in Nisargadatta Maharaj's case, where he faced so many problems in his life, so many problems, beyond one's imagination. But, he never ever lost his faith in his Master. His knowledge was very strong, exceptional, firm. He had total Conviction.

He had other positive, miraculous experiences, as well. He rarely talked about them, but one day, while he was sitting at his shop, he started pouring water from his teapot to passers-by. People started forming queues. It turned out that they were being healed and cured by that water. But Siddharameshwar Maharaj warned him, "What are you doing? This is not knowledge. It is not Reality. It's distracting you from Reality". So he stopped doing this!

In this dialogue, what I am telling you, is that after a time spent in meditation, reciting the Mantra, and absorbing the knowledge, with strong devotion, there may be some miraculous experiences. It is not knowledge. It is not Reality. It is not the Ultimate Truth. The point is that you could be distracted from Reality. If there is any ego still lurking, you may think, "Yes, she has had this miracle because of me". Or, maybe when you are with someone, a miracle takes place. You may then think to yourself: "Oh, I have so much power!" Beware! This will inflate the ego even more. Be careful! Take precautionary measures in the process of your devotional spirituality.

If during your devotion, such experiences occur, do not give them too much importance. All miraculous experiences appear upon your Presence. That Presence, that Invisible Presence, Anonymous Presence, is Ultimate Truth. Miracles have no value. It is the nature of our human body, of the human being. If you see miracles performed in front of you, you may bow down and say, "Oh, you are a very great man." But no one is performing those miracles. They are within you. You have tremendous power, but do not take on any ego around them. Nisargadatta Maharaj did not take any credit. He did not accept any prestige, "If it happens, it is because of my Master. I am not doing any miracles." He never took on any ego.

The reason I am drawing your attention to this is that because of your strong devotional life, these things may happen. Recognize them as progressive steps, and keep going. Don't be caught by them. Do not indulge in them for long. Do not stop there, keep moving forward, climbing until you reach the mountain peak. Involve yourself in devotion and spirituality till Conviction. I am alerting you, making you cautious, in the process of your devotional life, your spirituality. Ignore these experiences - they are not Reality."

Talk J – "Maharaj: We have so many desires. "I want this, that, and the other thing". Human beings don't come to the world with any pockets. They do not leave the body with pockets either. Therefore, why fill your pockets in between?

This means that prior to beingness, there was nothing. Now there is so much anxiety, greed and hedonism, for want of a better word: "I want this. I want that". Who wants all these things, and what do you want them for? How long do you imagine you are going to use all these things? You are after money, sex, power and many other material wants. These are all temporary solutions to alleviate your unease. They offer only a brief respite from body-knowledge discomfort.

Q: The Conviction, the Spontaneous Conviction, can happen at any time. It does not necessarily happen during meditation. Is that correct?

Maharaj: It happens spontaneously. After Conviction, all the body-based knowledge dissolves. It is very, very interesting. Go deep and deep and deep within Selfless Self, and you will find peacefulness, "Oh! I Am That!"

Q: Deeper and deeper into meditation?

Maharaj: After meditating, using these sacred words, all the concepts will melt. Your body-identity will be dissolved. And you will see within yourself, "My beingness is everywhere, and in every being. My Presence is everywhere". That Spontaneous Conviction will appear within you."

These Talks were received extremely well by Maharaj's American audience! Afterwards, many had the good fortune to receive the *Naam Mantra*. Long queues formed for initiation! Hamid, who had become a good friend of ours, finally managed to see Maharaj in Maryland. He only managed one night, due to work pressures, but one night was more than enough! Uniting with Maharaj is forever engraved in his heart!

December – Charles is not feeling well. Today, at breakfast, he started coughing uncontrollably, after eating a piece of toast. As he attempts to eat another piece, he seems unable to swallow. He starts choking. I am patting him on the back hard, until finally, he manages to bring the food back up. Something is not right, that's for sure. We will book an appointment with the doctor soon.

End of December – The doctor has arranged an endoscopy for Charles in January. We don't focus on the "what if's" at all. In the meantime, I prepare soft, easily digestible meals.

2017

January – When challenges come along, they offer us a "True Test", as to whether Truth has been established, or not. Our test is coming soon….

15ᵗʰ January – We attend the hospital and Charles undergoes an endoscopy. Following the procedure, he wants to know the results. The nurses do not wish to say, and tell him to wait for a letter. But Charles' persistence pays off. He is told that he has a mass in the oesophagus! Now that he knows what is affecting the body, he is very matter of fact about it. Charles is very strong and seems prepared, whereas "I" need a little more time to come to terms with the news.

20ᵗʰ January – We Skype with Maharaj who has returned from the States and is looking much better after the trip. Charles tells him about the cancer. Maharaj responds with, "Don't accept any diagnosis!", in a strong tone of voice. It is wonderful, pragmatic advice! We can see that if there is acceptance, then, that will only feed the "I" again. Nothing is happening. Cancer or any other disease may touch the body, but not Selfless Self!

      After looking at the images of the tumour, the doctor tells Charles that the cancer is very advanced. He is given about one year, at the most. His choices are either to have surgery, or do nothing! If he has surgery, there are high risks: the body may expire on the operating table, as the odds are not good. And if he survives, he will spend the foreseeable time, going in and out of the hospital! He knows what his priorities are, and exactly how to face the situation. He will use the time to make absolutely sure that the knowledge is absorbed, to ensure he is well-prepared! This diagnosis does not change anything fundamentally. We will carry on with the work and service to our Master!

23rd January – Today we treat ourselves to a fresh strawberry and cream fruit tart, cut it in half, and share it. It is delicious!

24th January – Today Charles can't swallow anything. Unbeknown to us, yesterday's heavenly sweet-tart turned out to be the last one, he would eat! Now he will need a feeding tube for liquid food only!

February – We hear that a French devotee, Gopal, who has been staying at the ashram for a long time, is setting up a live link from the ashram. This wonderful initiative will enable everyone to hear Maharaj's Talks and the *bhajans* in real-time! He is recording the current Talks for the next book of Q & A's! His *seva* to Maharaj is appreciated by all!

As we listen to Maharaj speaking, we notice he is coughing a lot more. That said, some of his Talks seem more direct than before, if that's at all possible!

March – Today I tune into Maharaj's Talk which is all about the importance of keeping the sacred *Naam Mantra* a secret. He says:

"You must not disclose the *Naam Mantra* to anyone because it is the order of *Sadguru*! The practice is a discipline given by *Sadguru*. If you disclose the Mantra to everyone, it will lose its importance because it will become a common word. The *Naam Mantra* is only for those seekers/devotees who have become disciples! So, you need to maintain the secrecy of these words. If you tell others, and it becomes public, it will become meaningless. The Lineage gives strict instructions that you are not to reveal the Mantra to anyone, because it is *Sadguru*'s order. Do not disclose it to anyone, in any way, or in any public place!

The words of the *Naam Mantra* are not ordinary words like "Ram" or "Krishna" that are used in our daily vocabulary. They contain an exceptional value that you are to preserve. It is so important to view it in this way. This Guru Mantra is not an ordinary word, but it is inbuilt with power and value. Therefore, you must make sure you keep and preserve its value, otherwise, it will become meaningless. As long as it is kept secret, private, respected and valued, it will work and be effective. If it is made public, that will be a tragedy, as the effects will diminish. Its value and power will be diluted, and basically, over time, it won't have any effect at all!

These powerful words were first given by Dattatreya, and continued by the "Nava Naatha", (The "Nine Masters"). When you received the *Naam Mantra* during initiation, you made a promise to the Master to keep it a secret. You have a duty to maintain the secrecy of these words, and to never make them public!"

Maharaj sounds very serious, as he speaks about the sacred *Naam Mantra*. When we are initiated, the Master entrusts us with the Mantra. Through it, there is an unbreakable link with him, as well as with the whole Lineage. If anyone reveals the *Naam Mantra* to another, it will not work for either of them, because he has effectively broken the sacred bond of trust with his Master/Guru.

April – We Skype with Maharaj. We tell him that when we first started Skyping with him in 2013, we used to feel scared, as the clock approached 4 pm on a Tuesday! Maharaj looks very surprised. He says: "No! You were afraid of me!" Maharaj could not conceive that anyone could be scared of him!

Charles tells him about a new project he has begun. He is designing a new version of *Selfless Self* that will resemble a beautiful, Bible-sized edition, using elegant fonts. Maharaj is very happy to hear this. Charles' body may have cancer, but his Spirit is elevated and dedicated to the work.

We have always recognized the enormity and impact of the Knowledge transmitted by Shri Ramakant Maharaj. It is Knowledge that is beyond Knowledge! Through the grace-filled genius of Maharaj, the indescribable is described! We see *Selfless Self* as the Bible for our time! It deserves to be presented in a striking, outstanding and beautiful format, resembling a tome-like edition, that is alive and ablaze with Ultimate Truth!

Each morning, Charles makes a little progress with the book, and then, as he tires, puts it down for a rest.

I prepare liquid food for him, at the same time that I prepare my meals. Every time we eat, we give thanks for another day and the food!

May – Humour has never left us! We recognize how fortunate we are to know Maharaj – very timely. Our state is "empty". There is no anxiety or fear, no sadness, or anything else, for that matter. We are not attached to one another. The love is impersonal, boundless and free! It is a privilege to serve Charles, and to attend to his physical needs. He did the same for me in the past, during a long illness. Maharaj always said: "Do your duties", but where there is love, there is no question of duty. It flows spontaneously, energetically. (I reflect on our relationship. We do not have a "relationship" as such, because we live as one, in oneness. Interestingly, I always carried an image of the two of us moving through life, positioned, side by side. It is only now, that this image has changed. Due to circumstances, we are now facing each other, so that I can play the role of the "carer"!)

July – Charles is needing more blood transfusions. We go to the hospital together, and I sit with him overnight. These days, I notice he is shining more. As the body grows weaker, Charles appears lighter, more radiant and untouched by anything. We are sustained!

September – For some months, we have been discussing the possibility of Maharaj travelling to the U.K. to offer *Satsang* and initiate sincere seekers. We prepare a schedule and send the information to Maharaj. The plan is for Maharaj and Anvita, (health permitting), to fly to London first, where they will stay for a few days, and then travel to the world-famous "Findhorn Spiritual Community" in Moray, Scotland, and perhaps, finally stopping in France. Maharaj expresses his delight and enthusiasm for the planned program.

27th October – Miracles do happen! Charles' feeding tube becomes blocked. We go to the hospital to fix the problem. Here is his Journal entry for that date:

"Just in case anyone finds themselves on the operating table, feeling a little nervous and aware of how things can go wrong etc etc., perhaps the following might be useful. Even the Surgeon was confused as to what to do, as he was working blind without scopes etc. The tube was removed from the stomach. Eventually, he failed to be able to insert a new tube.

I asked *Sadguru* for guidance: Called on all the Masters. 1. Ramakant Master visuals were used for a long time. 2. Then Nisargadatta. 3. Siddharameshwar. 4. Bhausaheb. Finally, *Sadguru* took control of proceedings and the surgeon asked little me (!) to guide the tube through the tumour by my own hand! And then down the gut and into the stomach! And lo and behold in 2 secs. like a mini-miracle, it got through the tiny hole in the centre of the tumour and the rest of the op was able to go ahead! I beheld the Power within, so to speak. Selfless Self was overseeing and was the main protagonist here for certain. I stayed with Selfless Self and NOT with fear and pain and was rewarded with a great outcome for fleeting body continuation. "I am not the body, I was not the body, I will not remain the body" ....With homage and endless gratitude to *Sadguru* and immense gratitude for all the prayers and blessings sent to me from all who read this *Jaisadguru*."

We are very fortunate to be part of this Lineage Family because the Masters are with us at all times. When the time draws near to exit the body, the Masters will be with us, too. They will always be there to receive us, guaranteed!

31st October – On Skype today, Maharaj expresses his deep affection for Charles and gives thanks to him for his dedication, devotion and work. He thanks him for enabling so many seekers to travel to see him, for all his assistance and generosity of spirit!

Charles replies: "Thank you, Maharaj, but there is no need to say anything, as it is a privilege and joy to serve you. Isn't it, Ann?" "Absolutely", I add. "There is nothing more important than serving you", he says.

Maharaj beams a loving smile, and tells Charles to take care and rest. "And meditate?", he asks. Maharaj says: "No, you don't have to meditate!"

7th November – The palliative care team returns today. They are amazed at Charles' peace, calm, contentment and humour. They are not used to seeing this very often, in the so-called "terminally ill". There is no agitation, fear or anxiety. Nothing!

10th November – We announce Maharaj's visit to the UK and Findhorn on FB. The plan is for him to visit London, from 9-18 June 2018, and Findhorn, from 20-27 August 2018.

15th November – Expect the unexpected! Change of plan! Maharaj informs us that, due to a recent downturn in health, it is now looking very unlikely that he will be able to travel!

Shreefal Tula Function Nashik Ashram,
8ᵗʰ July 2018

2018

8ᵗʰ January – [As it turned out, two weeks before leaving the body.] The blood transfusion is not happening today because Charles is too unwell. The consultant asks him if he would like to go to the Hospice now, or attempt to receive a transfusion at the bigger hospital nearby? There is still some life in the old dog, so he chooses to go to the hospital. The Hospice staff seem a little put-out. They are eager, maybe a little too eager, "to make him comfortable", as the saying goes!

Two hours pass by. Charles is sleeping. I feel this is such a beautiful night. There is something very special about the energy around us. Is this night the last? Or is it only the dress rehearsal?

"I told him often that I will be with him every step of the way, and I meant that literally! On this beautiful night, the ward seems ultra-quiet. Everyone is asleep. When Charles opens his eyes again, I feel the light all around us, and the Presence of the Masters. At this moment, I thank him for everything, for his friendship and love, and express my love to him, once more. He smiles; I smile. Everything is perfect. Charles falls asleep again. I am overflowing with gratitude for this night that endures forever. It feels like a deep transformation from night to day – but much, much more than that! This night is the big night – special, flowing with grace, as we are touched by the Masters. The two of us as one! One with the Masters! This is the night of transition. I am so happy!

It is now 5 am. I have been at his bedside since around 10 pm. Charles appears to be going, "in and out of consciousness". He has had his transfusion and the doctors are taking a "wait and see approach". Every so often, he opens his eyes, looks at me, smiles, then closes his eyes again.

Two hours later, Charles comes to. It is a new day. He made it through the rehearsal! Looks like we still have a little longer to go, though tonight there was a true and deep sense of completion. I will always remember the absolute, stunning, silent beauty and perfection of this angelic night!"

Charles is looking a little baffled that he has lived to see another day. "I know", I said, "me too!" because we both knew the body had gone beyond its expiry date! Whatever follows after today, will only be about going through the final motions.

The next day – There is pressure, again, from the Hospice to admit Charles. We tell the staff that we are going home. The Hospice team is keen to put their system in place, while we just wish to let things unfold spontaneously.

12th Jan – A few days later, Charles is back in the hospital. One doctor says, looking at his file: "I thought you wanted to die at home?" Charles says, "No!" Anywhere is good. It is not pre-planned!"

You cannot put a free bird in a cage to suit whoever, whenever. Charles always avoided authoritarian figures or authoritative people who, "told him what to do" or, "what he should be doing", (apart from Maharaj!) And now, at this very important moment, even more so. Everything will happen, the way it is meant to happen, without interference from those who think they know better.

20th Jan – Charles is in hospital with pneumonia. The doctor plans to send him back home, as soon as an oxygen tank has been delivered. We speak on the phone. Charles tells me that Nisargadatta made an appearance, and that he has been speaking to him, laughing with him, saying: "Remember to welcome the difficulties", with a wry smile. "Have I not had enough difficulties?" responded Charles.

I understand, also, how crucial it is for us to be apart at this juncture. At this very important time, any subtle attachments can be further loosened, and we can both concentrate, be with Selfless Self, and stay receptive to the Master's guidance. Charles is already prepared. His body has moved from the waiting room to the departure lounge! All that's left for him now is to leave the body!

We are back home again! This *lila* is like a game of musical chairs – going back and forth to the hospital. But we know it's only the body that is moving. Nothing else moves, nothing changes!

21st January – Today, Charles is looking at me so tenderly, with his big, loving puppy eyes. As I pass by his bed, he takes my hand and keeps repeating, "I love you, I love you, I love you", about ten times or so. He wants to let me know how grateful he is for the way I have looked after him. He says: "I could not have asked for more!" It is so sweet!

Later today, although his body is very weak, he has not lost his sense of humour. We share a poignant moment! He says: "Maharaj used to say, that without Presence you cannot lift a finger. Well, look! With Presence, I cannot lift a finger!" We laugh together!

We are nearing the last scene. It is the last day. We make the final trip to the hospital. He is on IV antibiotics to treat pneumonia, and is falling asleep, on and off.

22ⁿᵈ January – He is still poorly. There is no improvement with the antibiotics. Late morning, he is moved to a side room.

"It is wonderful to have the room to ourselves for this final, crucial scene of the drama. It is quite a large room which quickly fills up with the Lineage Masters, who have gathered spontaneously around his bed. His true, eternal family members are there for him. As I see them, I bow. When they start clapping, I join in and clap along with them, in this sacred, timeless moment.

With one hand, I hold Charles' hand, while placing my other hand on his heart. As he is leaving the body, I whisper the *Naam Mantra* in his ear, to assist him on the journey. His eyes are peaceful, transfixed on the beyond. The transition is effortless and smooth – from the form, back to the formless, our eternal home.

I am filled with inner joy for both Charles and myself. We were able to put the knowledge into practice all the way, right up to this eternal moment. There is no disconnect between "knowing and being". The teachings are well-absorbed. They did not remain theory, but are practically applied! The proof is in the pudding, as the saying goes. It is all very beautiful! Sublime!

Next, I sit quietly beside him in meditation, for the next few hours. In the meditation, I am his travelling companion, journeying with him through space. I am in awe and thankful for the gift, grace and blessings, for all of it!

At some point in the afternoon, a doctor knocks on the door to officially pronounce him "dead!" He communicates the usual line: "I am sorry for your loss!" Like some crazy, ecstatic *sadhu*, I reply with a huge smile: "No! Don't be sorry. There is no loss! It was beautiful!" He must have thought that I was either deranged, or in denial!

I feel so amazingly thankful because "living with cancer" for a year, did not shake our foundations. It did not take a toll on us and resulted in a smooth, joyful and graceful exit. And, what's more... the Masters came! Well, they are here all the time! Unfortunately, we don't remember them as often as we should! At this moment of total freedom and return to the Absolute Source, it is unbelievably miraculous that everything flowed, and melted as soft as butter!

I give myself a thorough scan and check over: "Am I sad? No! What do I feel? Nothing!" "Am I clear?" Yes!" There is nothing but pure joy and gratitude. Truly wonderful!"

I telephone Maharaj in Phondaghat to tell him the news. "Oh!" was all he said. Then, practical as ever, he asks me when the cremation will take place? "When am I going to get rid of the body? Do it quickly!", he says. Typically, Maharaj is speeding things up at 1000 miles an hour! I manage to book the cremation for 3 days' time.

25ᵗʰ January – Another miracle happens on cremation day! As we are singing the *bhajans*, I see Shri Nisargadatta again. He is showering Charles with deep red, rose-petalled flowers, blessing him. Then, the two of them spiral together and merge, before vanishing! Again, I feel so thankful and blessed. When Maharaj phones me a few minutes later, I cannot contain my joy. I utter something really stupid to Maharaj: I tell him what has just happened, saying, "Maharaj, you will never believe this, but Nisargadatta has just appeared!"

Maharaj's reaction is matter-of-fact, saying: "Of course! The Masters are Reality. They are always here with us".

Excitedly, I continue: "Maharaj, his transition was so beautiful that now I am going to prepare for my *Mahasamadhi*!", I blurted out. Maharaj brings me down to earth with a bang, saying, "No, you will not! You have a lot of work to do!" Now Charles has passed more responsibility to you! Quickly, he brings me firmly back into the body and my pending work, including finishing the book, *Who Am I?*

"Remember", he says, "Everything starts from you, and everything ends with you!" In other words, what he is saying is: cremation over, back to work, move on!

After the "great death", a few people, including some advanced students of Maharaj, commented, "You must be very sad". There was no sadness, but I tried to cry anyway. However, each time I tried to cry, I burst out laughing! It is ridiculous to cry! Who is crying? And, for whom, when nothing and no one exists? Charles has not gone anywhere. He is with me always.

27th January – Today I am resting in bed, when suddenly, I have a vision of Nisargadatta Maharaj. He appears in a kind of chariot that is moving steadily past me. He wants to show me that he is holding an urn that contains Charles' ashes. And he is holding them very close to his heart. It is a mini-movie but very beautiful. I bow and give thanks to Nisargadatta Maharaj!

End of January – I phone Maharaj and tell him I have written a 10-page letter to him describing Charles' end process, that I would like him to read. He is happy to read it and tells me to send it!

Early February – I notice that in the last few weeks - or did it start just after Charles' passing? - I am not sure… that I have been bursting into fits of uncontrollable laughter! They occur spontaneously, and can last for a few minutes! These episodes of laughter are a new phenomenon.

Mid-February – I phone Maharaj to arrange a Skype call. Maharaj is moving with the times… he says he doesn't use Skype anymore, only "WhatsApp" which is straightforward and faster! Maharaj tells me to come to Nashik! I tell him I will make the necessary preparations.

23rd February – Brief call with Maharaj. He says he has read my letter thoroughly. Smiling, he says, "I have read it very carefully, all of it, and I see no attachment! There is no attachment there at all, not in Charles, and not in you!" His words are immensely valuable. I thank him from the bottom of my heart. He says he will send a longer message, later on in the day.

Later in the evening – I receive a beautiful message from Maharaj:

"*Jaiguru* Dear St Ann, I have gone through your letter with spiritual overwhelming feelings. Really it's a spiritual miracle that happened in your spiritual life. Both of you have thrown yourselves into spirituality. And not even that, I found no body identity remained. Ultimate Truth totally absorbed within you and hence our dearest Charles was totally happy and peaceful while leaving the illusionary body. Also our Lineage *Sadgurus* have taken possession of our beloved Charles.

It's fact some or other day everybody has to take exit from this illusionary world for which there is no fear, no attachment. There is spontaneous peacefulness and happiness. Your letter is narrating each and every moment of practical spiritual feelings. It's a wonderful spontaneous experience of conviction. Words are not enough to explain the spirituality absorbed within our Charles. Really he is an exceptional, sincere devotee living the spiritual life. Now he has left some spiritual responsibilities to be followed through you.

Blessings of our Lineage Masters are always with you. I will definitely try to contact you. At present some problems with internet network. However, it will be solved within a couple of days

Take care of your health. With Blessings to you *Jai Sadguru*"

Late February – I stay with a couple of friends, Andrew and Michelle. I take one of my favourite, and most recent, photos of Charles with me. On the first night, I place the picture next to me on the bed and fall asleep. After a few hours, I woke up and felt my cheek moist! As I came to, I realize that Charles' Spirit had made himself known by kissing me on the cheek! What a beautiful visitation!

During my stay, I experience several spontaneous explosions of laughter. As my friend witnesses these episodes, she says, jokingly, that she hopes I don't end up like some crazy, out of control ecstatic!

Beginning of March – Skype. I tell Maharaj about the ongoing work to finish the *Selfless Self*, deluxe Bible edition. It is nearing completion. I hope to get it printed soon and plan to take one or two copies to Maharaj, when I travel to Nashik.

I will be there for my birthday which is auspicious. Maharaj says, smiling: "It will be wonderful to celebrate the birthday of a saint!" I emit a silly, embarrassed laugh before mentioning that our three birthdays - mine, Charles and Maharaj's take place exactly one week apart on 24th June, 1st July and 8th July, respectively. It is lovely! I joke with Maharaj that we are like the 3 musketeers, or the holy trinity! Maharaj laughs, even though I doubt he understands what I am talking about!

Mid-March – I speak with Maharaj: He tells me that visitors to the ashram have nothing but praise for the book, *Selfless Self*. I tell him about the guidance, miraculous Presence and the events that took place, during the writing process: the words of instruction that were transmitted as the book unfolded, the text moving on the screen, the light all around, etc. Maharaj is all ears!

"You said it yourself, Maharaj, that the book is a miracle! It was written by Selfless Self, for Selfless Self!" A long pause follows before the call ends.

1st April – I am travelling by train with Jasper, (my stepson), when, suddenly, laughter arises. The train is packed, and there is nowhere to hide! This time the laughter lasts for a very long time. Some passengers are looking at me. Jasper tells me to stop laughing. I try, but I cannot stop! I use my scarf to help subdue the laughter and muffle the noise. Eventually, the laughter subsides. Boy, am I relieved, and Jasper, too!

15th April – I asked Maharaj recently when he was going to be at the ashram, so I could plan my trip. Today he tells me that he will be available from 15th June till 31st August! [Maharaj's words came true, as he attained *Mahasamadhi* on 31st August!]

19th May – Maharaj is attending the "Inauguration of Dr Dhiraj Sarvadnya Hospital". Dhiraj has built this hospital, which includes a Meditation Room, beautifully adorned with pictures of all the Lineage Masters.

Early June – I communicate with a devotee-friend, Jeff, and tell him Maharaj has told me to come to the ashram. He is a great support and offers to help me financially if I need it. He tells me to look after myself as I'm travelling alone, and to keep in touch with him. I am touched by his caring!

3rd June – I had written to Maharaj a few days ago, expressing my delight and amazement that Charles' illness and transition had not thrown me off course. There were no wobbles or shaking of the foundations. I explained that I feel as solid as a rock. Today I receive a reply from Maharaj:

"Dear St Ann, After reading your message it reflects without your knowledge that spirituality is totally absorbed within you. For example, when the doctor gives antibiotic medicines or injections to the patient, it results in all the bacteria disappearing from the body. And the body becomes disease-less or pure. Similarly, before association with the Master, our food body was having a lot of subtle bacteria in the form of various illusionary concepts and we were unhappy depressed. No peace and happiness. But when the Master gives the *Naam Mantra* it is just like strong antibiotic injections and all concepts dissolve instantly.

I am fully aware and notice that you are an exceptional, sincere devotee and spirituality has been totally absorbed within you. This is not a dry appreciation but a keen observation. You have seen good days and very, very bad days but you are totally stable. Particularly when our beloved Charles was suffering from an incurable disease, even under such serious conditions you have not lost your spiritual confidence. You became stronger. That means you are having spiritual courage. In brief, there is no words for appreciation. With blessings *Jai Sadguru*."

8ᵗʰ June – Even though Maharaj's health is unstable, he is managing to attend various functions. Today a devotee, Rahul is privileged to welcome Maharaj for a Program at his home. Many devotees gather there!

15ᵗʰ June – Return to Nashik. Although it has been a long time since Charles and I had left Nashik, we never felt that we were separated from our Master, not for one moment. Maharaj had captured our hearts. He knew we had surrendered to Him. He knew our devotion to Him is eternal, beyond space and time.

It is a little daunting to be travelling to India, travelling anywhere, in fact, on my own. I have not done this for decades! I need to be strong, so, I call on Charles to accompany me! Unsurprisingly, Charles' Presence is strongly felt during the flight. Excitement and waves of bliss wash over. I am feeling the melting love, of, and for, the Master.

16th June – On arrival at the hotel, I find a beautiful message from Maharaj to welcome me:

"Dear St Ann, After long time you will visit Nashik. At this time, we are feeling the absence of our beloved devotee Charles. But perhaps it is the spiritual wish of our Lineage *Sadgurus*. However, it's a fact that because of both of you only, this rare spiritual knowledge has been brought to attention all over the world. We strongly welcome you. Today you take rest and come tomorrow morning for *Kakad Arati* or morning *Bhajan* starts at 11 am. We will have a talk tomorrow. With Blessings, *Jai Sadguru*."

I am touched! I don't feel I can wait till tomorrow. I need to go and see Maharaj tonight! I call Maharaj and ask if I can come and see him? He says, "Yes! Come!"

At his home, I find Anvita, devotee Vijay and Maharaj! It is beautiful to reunite with Maharaj. Maharaj says, "Such a long time!", and, breaking protocol, we hug. Then, I present Maharaj with the new edition of *Selfless Self*, which has been inscribed on the first page by Charles and myself, as follows:

"*Jai Guru*! To Our Dearest Master,
We came for the *Naam Mantra*
And we left with unimaginable treasure,
Beyond our wildest hopes and dreams.
You guided us back to our original place – Home at last!
You guaranteed us 100% happiness, and we are 1000% satisfied.

There is abundant peace, happiness, fearlessness and no tension.
We thank you from the bottomless bottom of Reality
Where our hearts melt and meet in one Heart.
We bow to you in total gratitude.
With all our love and affection always.
From Ann and Charles. *Jai Sadguru!*"

Vijay takes pictures of this special moment. Maharaj looks at the book, (dedicated to Charles), with admiration, and reads the words carefully. He loves the presentation and says: "Now with this book, we will remember Charles even more!"

Maharaj is looking well, though, I notice he has lost some weight. I offer a box of chocolates to Anvita. We have chai. Then Maharaj tells me to "take rest". He says we will meet again at 6.30 am for the *bhajans*.

The next day – I take a rickshaw to the ashram. There are not many westerners here, one Australian, Dimitri, and two French, Gopal and Guillaume. I am introduced to Ramzi from Jordan. It turns out he is staying at the same hotel as me. We have a connection and quickly become friends, travelling together, to and from, the ashram. I arrive early, to bow to the Masters, offer *puja*, and give thanks to them all, for all! Maharaj enters. I hurry to bow at his feet.

As we start singing the *Kakad Arati bhajans*, instantly, I feel as if I had never left! After a few more *bhajans*, I strongly feel Charles' Presence. He is standing beside me, next to my right shoulder, singing and clapping along with me, too! The *bhajans* lift the Spirit higher and higher, and within a short time, I am bursting into paroxysms of laughter – an instant rewind to 2013/14!

Later that day – Maharaj sends me another message, expressing his delight about the "Bible-style edition" of *Selfless Self*. He instructs me to post his quote on the "Selfless Self Website", www.selfless-self.com. It says:

"I have seen the book cover specially designed by our Charles. It is exceptional and very attractive. The choice of colour is beautiful and impressive. I am very much pleased with this fresh volume of the book. Along with all the memories, our Charles has left this fresh memory which will remind us all the time. With blessings, *Jai Guru*."

Next day – I meet with Lyall, a devotee from New Zealand, who is also staying at my hotel. We sometimes walk together to the ashram.

A few days later – The Guru is very protective. Like a mother, he is always looking after us. This morning, I experience an awkward encounter with the owner of the hotel, where I am staying. As a result, I miss the early morning *bhajans*! When Maharaj asks me why I did not attend earlier, I tell him what happened.

Maharaj expresses his anger, saying: "No one mistreats and takes advantage of my devotees!" He is livid. Then, he tells me to leave the hotel immediately and instructs a few devotees to assist me. Ever pragmatic, I am impressed at how attentive and protective he is of me, in my situation!

A few hours later, I settle into my new hotel. After a couple of hours, there is a knock on the door. I leap out of bed. It is Maharaj, accompanied by Vijay! He enters, and I bow at his feet. He wants to know if I have settled in, and if I am feeling safer now? I said yes, and thank him. I am always amazed at his caring, personal touch! I was still in a daze that Maharaj had actually visited me in my room, when he left!

*23*rd *June* – Maharaj tells me a secret. He says, "Ann, we have a surprise for you! Tomorrow, we will celebrate your birthday in the ashram!" Like an excited, innocent child who is unable to keep a secret, Maharaj spills the beans! Anvita is not pleased, saying, "Maharaj, now you have spoiled the surprise". He ignores her comment… I respond with, "What a blessing! What an honour! Thank you". I bow at His feet!

*24*th *June* – My Birthday. It is a Sunday when the ashram is at its busiest. Only a couple of devotees know that it is my birthday. They wish me a "Happy Birthday", during lunch. We have the usual tiffins and eat in the sheltered area above the ashram.

Getting ready for the 5.30 pm *bhajans*, I decide to dress in white again, wearing a white dress and shawl, with matching white leggings for this day. White is traditionally what the men wear in the ashram, while the women wear colourful saris etc, but I have always liked wearing white, possibly a throwback to something that was engraved in my heart, at my "First Communion" aged 7! I still have the photo, and remember clearly the significance of that day! I shared it with Maharaj some time ago. And when he saw it, he remarked, "Excellent!, I can see the saint in you!"

We sing the evening *bhajans*, and then Maharaj asks us all to sit down. After saying a few words to one devotee, Deepak, he quickly leaves. Following this, a few devotees place a table and chair in front of the altar, before making their way to the kitchen. After a few minutes, Deepak returns. In a slow procession, holding the special edition of *Selfless Self*, with reverence, he approaches the altar and bows, before placing it in front of the picture of Shri Nisargadatta Maharaj. The devotees are looking at each other, wondering what all the commotion is about.

Maharaj gives a Talk in Marathi. I hear him mentioning "Ann" and "Charles" a few times, and *Selfless Self*. When he does, some of the devotees turn around and stare at me! Before Maharaj's Talk has ended, two ladies whisk me away to the kitchen, and tell me they have a new outfit for me to wear for my special day. Then they quickly undress and re-dress me. They wish me a happy birthday! Anvita has chosen a beautiful, green, long top and matching pants.

The ladies push me out of the kitchen. Anvita beckons me to come forward. The table now has a huge cake on it! With all eyes on "me", self-consciousness arises! As I hear a few voices saying, "Go, go,", there is no escape! My first and only impulse is to walk directly towards Maharaj's chair. I bow at his feet and thank him from the bottom of my heart. Our smiles, joy and happiness unite in an ecstatic explosion of oneness!

There is no time to linger, as I am quickly guided by Anvita to sit at the table, facing a packed ashram of devotees – quite a challenge for one who prefers invisibility! Anvita hands me a knife to cut the cake, then scoops one spoonful and puts it in my mouth, following the tradition. At this point, everyone starts singing "Happy Birthday!" The cake is decorated beautifully, with ornate lettering "Ann".

What a memorable day! As we are all leaving, I thank Maharaj again, for the beautiful event. Later on, I ask a few devotees about what Maharaj had said in his Talk. They explain that he was telling everyone about the "English couple" who came to see him, stayed for a long time, and then facilitated hundreds of western and Indian devotees, to travel to see Maharaj! He talked about our recordings, the work on the book *Selfless Self*, and that this special edition was beautifully designed by "Charles", who did the work, while his body was affected by cancer. The Talk was a tribute to us both, a big "Thank you"! It was also a double celebration of our birthdays – Mine today, and Charles', on 1st July!

After the ashram celebrations, my friend, Ramzi, took me for a birthday dinner at our local restaurant. Everything is absolutely perfect! On cloud nine, I don't feel it can get any better than today! Can it?

25th June – The next day, Maharaj calls me. He wants me to start initiating "the foreigners", on his behalf, when I return to the UK… and it was only yesterday that I thought it couldn't get any better!

Maharaj has recently been in touch with various foreign devotees who cannot travel to meet him, due to illness or various other circumstances. So, Maharaj instructs me to serve him in this way!

Maharaj says:

"It is confirmed that practical spirituality is absorbed within you. This is not dry appreciation but it reflects from your total involvement and strong devotion. I am extremely happy. You will continue your spiritual responsibilities successfully. You are not alone. The blessings of all the Lineage *Sadgurus* are with you always."

He says he will message me further about it, later in the day. I am blown away! What a gift for my 65th birthday. "A gift, yes", says Maharaj, "but also a big responsibility!"

I receive a message from Maharaj:

"When you give the *Naam Mantra* to needy seekers, just confirm the person is really interested and not expecting the Mantra for miracles or to solve his family problems. With long experience, you know better. So, in brief, when you accept the responsibility of Master you have to follow certain rules and regulations, ie, no commercialization of knowledge. Go ahead with full spiritual courage. With Blessings. *Jai Sadguru.*"

26th June – Maharaj informs me that a few devotees have been putting his recent Talks together for the next book, however, he is concerned about the errors. And after *Selfless Self*, he does not wish for it to be published, as it stands! Our discussion leads to us talking about publishing *Selfless Self* in India, first, before the second book. I help Maharaj with this proposal and draw up a simple Contract with "Zen Publications" for the "Indian Rights" to *Selfless Self*.

Maharaj is happy to hear that *Selfless Self* will soon be published. This will buy us some more time to edit the second book which is to be called, *Ultimate Truth*.

27th June – In the afternoon, a few of us gather for a Talk. Maharaj announces: "The master editor has arrived", looking at me. "Make the book as attractive as *Selfless Self*! Later on, when I am alone with Maharaj, I express my concern, saying, that if I start editing the text, it may cause problems, like upsetting those who have already been working on it!

Maharaj dismisses my comments with a wave of his hand, and hands me the manuscripts. (There are two – one covering the "Talks from Nashik", and the other, the "Talks from his USA" visit). Maharaj says, "It is your book now!" and with a hand gesture, tells me to "start the work!"

I thought, ok, the Master has instructed me to take on this work, but I don't wish to tread on anyone's toes, or upset the apple cart.

I am happy to begin working, although I had no idea I was coming to Nashik for this reason! Instead, I had imagined a beautiful meditative stay, singing *bhajans,* without any pressures at all! Lol! I was wrong! There is always another plan! Shortly after Maharaj had assigned the work to me, he told me that I had approximately 2 months to complete the book. No pressure!

I begin editing *Ultimate Truth*. Maharaj wishes a "Q&A" format for this book. He wants to make sure that all the questions, any questions that seekers may have, will be answered satisfactorily!

28th June – Illness strikes! I must have eaten something at the hotel that did not agree with me, or maybe I have caught some kind of a bug. There is vomiting and diarrhoea. I rest for half an hour, hoping it will pass. Then, there is more of the same. Here's hoping it goes away quickly. There is much work to be done, and I need energy and strength to accomplish it all.

Maharaj advises me to go and see the doctor, round the corner from the ashram. I see him, and he prescribes me antibiotics. Afterwards, I attend the ashram, but have to leave in the middle of the *bhajans,* to get some fresh air. I am feeling very dizzy!

29th June – Maharaj messages me telling me that a devotee-friend, Richard from the UK is unable to visit the ashram, and that he is deeply interested to have our *Naam Mantra.* Maharaj sends me a copy of his message to Richard, as well as Richard's reply:

"*Jaiguru* Dear Richard, Are you from England? If so, then there is good news for you. I authorize ANN SHAW to give the Lineage Mantra on my behalf. At present, she is at Nashik Ashram, India. She will be back by the middle of August. So, don't worry. With blessings. *Jai Sadguru*"

"*Jaiguru* Dear Maharaj, This is WONDERFUL and exciting news – my heart is full of joy! Thank you Maharaj, for your kindness and great blessings! I think Ann must feel very humbled. Now I will be able to receive the *Naam Mantra* and feel even closer to you and the lineage – and to immerse myself in the repeating of this holy treasure! *Jai, Jai, Jai Sadguru*! Richard."

We are all very happy!

3rd July – A devotee called Nitin arrives from Jaipur, Rajasthan. He is very friendly. We chat for a little while. He wants us to go and eat, but I explain I have not been feeling well for a few days, and can't keep any food down. He is kind and offers to walk me back to my hotel, where I try to rest. The antibiotics don't seem to be working yet.

4th July – Maharaj comes to visit me at the hotel, to see how I am. I attempt to bow to him, but he says, "No"! He tells me that, Deepak, will bring me some tonic, electrolyte fluids, which will help. Then, never missing an opportunity, he asks me how the book is going! Aha! Suddenly I get a flashback to the old days when I worked on *Selfless Self*. I reassure Maharaj that I have started the work, but it is going slowly at the moment. Maharaj never allows anything to interfere with the real work! Whatever goes on in the body must never block the perennial flow!

In the afternoon, Nitin is very direct with me, saying, I look awful, very ill. He is not the first one to comment. Sudheer, another devotee, had earlier commented that I was looking very thin and pale!

"How about we go to the hospital to get you checked out?" proposes Nitin. Reluctantly, I agree! Fortunately, the hospital is nearby, on the same street as the hotel. We go together. I am grateful that Nitin can translate for me. Blood tests are taken. We wait, and then, I am admitted. I am given a bed to lie on, but no gown to change into, before being hooked up to a couple of drips.

My main concern is that I will not be able to work on the book. I know how important it is to Maharaj, and I have no wish to disappoint him. But, at the same time, Maharaj always says, "we need to look after the body". A few things are going on: a bacterial infection, bleeding from the back passage, dehydration, etc. Feeling very weak, I resign the body to the treatment.

A Dutch couple, Saraswati and Florin arrive. Maharaj tells Saraswati to visit me. He also sends a few Indian devotees to check on me, including, Dr Dhiraj, and a couple of other medics, who look at the drips I am on, as well as my notes, to report back to Maharaj. Nitin is very kind and returns regularly, speaks with my doctor and updates me.

After three days in the hospital, I am still feeling weak. But it is Maharaj's big birthday celebration tomorrow. I must be there! I feel it is really important. I have to attend! I ask Nitin to ask the doctor if I can go tomorrow? The doctor wants to wait and see how I am in the morning. If my blood results improve, he may allow it, if not….

8ᵗʰ July – Maharaj's Birthday. In the morning, I beg the doctor to let me go to the ashram, if only for a few hours. He is reluctant. He asks me if the bleeding has stopped? I nod my head! It is a little white lie, but I have to get him to agree to let me go. Finally, he gives me the okay, as long as I return to the hospital in a couple of hours, as promised. The doctor removes the drip, but leaves my IV cannula in for my return. Nitin helps me gather my things. We return to the hotel. I feel shaky, weak and dizzy but I am going to Maharaj's Birthday Party! Yay! I wear the new green outfit that was gifted on my birthday for this special day!

Today Maharaj's body is 77! It has been decided to carry out the "*Shreefal Tula Function*", ("Coconut Scales"), as happened on Ranjit Maharaj's last birthday, before he left the body! (Is this Maharaj's last birthday?)

Full-sized scales are used for the *Tula*. On one side, Maharaj is seated, and on the other, coconuts are placed by the devotees on the scale. First of all, Maharaj sits on one scale and is weighed. Then the coconuts are piled up on the other scale, until both scales are in equal balance. Each coconut placed by a devotee is a symbolic offering of the ego. After this ritual, the rest of the celebrations follow.

I am seated at a distance from the platform, observing the display, when I hear my name being called… one person says, "Ann", then another, and so on. Maharaj told the devotees who were standing beside him, "I want Ann. Where is Ann?" Far away from the platform where Maharaj is seated, it took a little time for them to find me. Then, I am told to go to Maharaj. It is difficult to walk through the hundreds of devotees, who are gathered there, and mostly seated on the floor. I am also very wobbly.

"Eventually, I reach Maharaj and carefully climb onto the platform. Maharaj is looking radiant. I bow at his Holy Feet, spontaneously place my head on his lap, take hold of both his hands, look directly into his eyes, and with a gigantic smile, I say, from the bottom of my heart: "A very happy birthday, Maharaj!" At this magical moment, Maharaj and I are blissfully one. He smiles, I smile… one smile, union. Time stops and there is only ecstasy! I am definitely in heaven. This experience is one of the most precious, blessed and wonderful ones! In the knowledge of "I am That" and "Maharaj is That", we merge!"

I stay for a couple of hours longer, beginning to feel very wobbly and out of the body. Suddenly, I hear someone calling my name, then I hear it again. The announcement is calling "Ann Shaw" back to the hospital. "Will Ann Shaw return to the hospital immediately!" The doctor is concerned that I had not returned at the agreed time. Nitin accompanies me back to the hospital. It has been a crazy, magnificent, wild and wonderful day… What a glorious birthday, dear Maharaj! Thank you, thank you, thank you, from the bottom of my heart. *Jai Guru*!

I am in the hospital for several more days. Apart from the infection, the light-headedness and dizziness continue. Because of this, the doctors suggest an MRI scan of the brain. When Maharaj hears this, that they are planning to do something with my "brain", he does not like the sound of that at all, and wants me out of the hospital, fast!

The doctor at the hospital, advises me against leaving, and makes me sign a declaration, to say I am discharging myself, against their medical advice! Nitin is a great support to me and very kind, even insisting on settling the hospital bill.

Maharaj, caring as ever, arranges for me to go and see another doctor, who starts me on a different course of antibiotics. He tells me to finish the course, and then rest for a few days back in the hotel. Maharaj also arranges for me to see his Ayurvedic doctor, Kiran. During this time, Maharaj tells Deepak to help me out, and do any shopping that I may need. He is very kind. I try to continue working on the book, but only manage a page or so, before feeling sleepy.

9th July – Maharaj is so caring, that he will even take the time to tell me which foods to eat, and which not to eat. Today Maharaj messages me telling me to avoid milk products, no paneer. Buttermilk is ok, okra is ok but not spicy foods, etc. After listing the foods, he adds:

"Take care of your health. You have to do a lot of spiritual work, sharing of spiritual knowledge all over the world and publishing books. I am quite sure you are fully capable to shoulder the job! You have to observe a lot of spiritual duties for which sound physical and spiritual health is most important. With Blessings. *Jai Sadguru!*"

I smile at the job list that strikes me as huge, particularly now, when the body is weak!

10th July – Maharaj messages me again, saying, he has complete confidence in me.

"You are deserving of the new spiritual responsibilities. I am quite sure you are already blessed by all the Lineage *Sadgurus*. Considering your strong devotion and strong trust, the head of our Lineage, *Sadguru* Shri Bhausaheb Maharaj gave you the Master's crown and confirmed it. And now I give you the spiritual authority. It is a great spiritual and devotional job and I am sure you can handle the responsibilities with all success. Go ahead! Go ahead! With Blessings. *Jai Sadguru!*"

I thank Maharaj for his trust and encouragement!

12th July – I make an effort to attend the *bhajans* this morning, even though I am not feeling well, and still a little "out of it". At some point, a western devotee whispers in my ear, saying that, as I have not seen Maharaj for some time, I should go and bow to him now. She pushes me forward in his direction. I did not realize that it was at the special moment, when no one is allowed to cross the lines that run down the ashram floor.

I walk across the lines, and, start bowing to Maharaj. He is furious, and says, "No! No!" He tells me to stand behind him. So, I go behind and remain at the "men's side" until the *Arati* ends! I am not pleased with the devotee who knows the rules! (Trust this to happen, so soon after Maharaj had entrusted me, with so much!)

During the *Arati*, there is the concept that, all the Lineage Masters appear and make their Presence felt, at this specific time! It feels as if, I have committed a mortal sin! Afterwards, Maharaj asks me what had happened? Fortunately, the instigator confessed that it was her idea! Why? I don't know!

Unfortunately, due to a limited amount of energy, I was not able to spend much time during this trip, with the other foreign devotees who had arrived for Maharaj's birthday. Plus, I was always rushing back to the hotel after the *bhajans,* to work on the book. But, I did speak with one devotee, Lauv, from Mauritius, who struck me as sincere and devotional. He had visited a few times before, and spoke highly and respectfully, of Maharaj.

13th July – Today, Gilles arrives. He is an exuberant, French devotee, whom I had met briefly some months before. When he messaged me recently, he told me he was planning to come to Nashik, but was uncertain if it would actually happen. So, I was very surprised when he checked into the same hotel. Weakened by the illness, and feeling the pressure of the work on the book, at first, I was not so excited about seeing him. I did not return Gilles' calls.

Eventually, however, he knocks on my door and, as I see his happy, smiling face, and feel his beautiful energy, it is really lovely to see him again! He gives me a big, bear hug that almost crushes my frail body! I tell him I cannot go for coffee at that moment, as I am working on a book for Maharaj, and there is a deadline! Instead, we arrange to meet downstairs, in the restaurant, at 3 pm.

We meet, and choose a table far away from the entrance. Now, feeling a little better at having done some work, I can meet him properly.

I learn that Gilles has been travelling to India, every year, for around 16 years. He has visited many different parts of India, including Tiruvannamalai.

He tells me he that he is amazed to meet the "editor" of Maharaj's book, *Selfless Self,* which, he tells me, "spoke to him directly and transformed him"! Unlike many other seekers, Gilles had not read Nisargadatta's *I am That* book. For him, *Selfless Self* was the only hammer needed to crack the ego nut!

I tell Gilles that Maharaj has not been very well since his birthday. He has lost quite a lot of weight, and these days, he is not attending the ashram in the mornings.

Gilles is full of joy! It is not just a *joie de vivre*, but he is a pure bundle of joy! It is not long before the laughter begins, hysterical laughter. What a character he is! When we are together, the energy is explosive and timeless. We are laughing at lots of silly things, at everything. Being in his company is like inhaling huge doses of laughing gas!

We feast and celebrate, like two innocent freedom-loving children, for nearly two hours. After that, we have to hurry to get to the *bhajans* on time. We decide to make our meetings, which he calls "*Satsangs*", regular, at the same place, at the same time. After spending time with Gilles, I feel much better. He is a tonic that works instantly, unlike the antibiotics I have been taking for weeks!

The next day, I invite Gilles to my room, before we eat. He notices a picture of Charles that I have pinned to a wall. I tell him that it is only about 5 months since he left the body. Spontaneously, which is the way he lives, Gilles kneels on the floor, and bows to the picture. It is a lovely gesture! Then, we go out to feast together. Again, we talk and laugh and talk some more, and laugh, and laugh, some more. Before we know it, we have to dash to the *bhajans* again. Gilles says, "thank you for another beautiful *Satsang*!"

Maharaj has not appeared for a few days, and the devotees are beginning to look anxious. In contrast, Gilles and I somehow feel that Maharaj has brought us together. Through Maharaj, we are united in joy, during a period that appears dark, for many of the devotees, who are falling into worry and depression, as they anticipate the worst!

I have not been attending the early morning *Kakad Arati bhajans*, as I find that the best time to work on the book, *Ultimate Truth*, is in the early morning, when I have more energy. If I can work from 5 am to 9 am, there will be progress. Maharaj has also asked for a section of the book, to contain the experiences of devotees. I start emailing them, asking if they wish to write something about their time with Maharaj.

Mid-July – I take a rickshaw to attend a clinic, for my first ayurvedic treatment. When I meet with Dr Kiran, we instantly feel a connection between us. The massage is both invigorating and relaxing. She tells me that she usually goes with her husband - who is also an ayurvedic doctor - to treat Maharaj, in the evenings.

14th July – I receive another message from Maharaj. He is preparing me, grooming me to take on bigger responsibilities:

"*Jaiguru* Dear St Ann, Really I am having a lot of spiritual expectations. I already told you to represent spirituality amongst mass seekers. But avoid struggle. There are some elements that may try to test your spiritual knowledge or capacity. Don't be confused. You can spontaneously convince the listener that spiritual strength is already with you. Go ahead! All Lineage Blessings are with you. *Sadguru* Shri Siddharameshwar Maharaj told his disciples PUT FORWARD YOUR FRONT STEP I WILL LIFT YOUR BACK STEP AHEAD. It's having tremendous energy and Confidence. So don't worry. You have got self-generated spiritual power supported by all Lineage *Sadguru*. With Blessings."

I reply:

"*Jaiguru* Maharaj! Thank you for yours... perfect words and just what I needed to hear. Self-generated spiritual power... yes! I have full confidence that the Masters are guiding and blessing 'me' all the time. I am happy that you have high expectations of me, as it is my duty to be your 'super' agent, and spread these rarest of teachings, far and wide. I am entirely at your service. With thanks. *Jai Guru*!"

19ᵗʰ July – A Greek couple, publishers of the Nisargadatta books, based in Athens, arrive at the ashram. They have just finished translating *Selfless Self* into Greek, and have brought some copies with them. They have come at the right time, as Maharaj's health is going downhill, rapidly. They are fortunate to be initiated on the same day!

20ᵗʰ July – Today, Maharaj appears. He is very frail but determined to speak. This time, during his Talk, he does not say the usual, "accept the Reality!", but instead, "Please accept the Reality!" When I hear his heartfelt plea, I take it as a sign that Maharaj does not have much longer in the body, as he has never before pleaded in this way! It is a very touching and poignant Talk because even though it is evident that Maharaj is weak, there is great strength behind his plea. Here is the Talk:

FINAL PLEA FROM Shri Ramakant Maharaj – *"Please Accept the Reality"*

"My Dearest Devotees,

Yes, my dear friends, we will have a short discussion. There is one basic thing: as long as you are counting yourself as the body-form, it will be highly impossible for you to accept the Reality. It is an open fact, that this body is not your identity at all. I am shouting this out all the time, in different ways. Listen to me! I am talking about Presence. Keep your attention on Presence, and not on all the illusory layers, that have covered over your Presence, your Reality.

Now that you have the knowledge, listen to your own Master, that Invisible Presence within you. Self-Realization will only arise if you discard all the dust with a

242

spiritual broom. Are you ready to remove all the dust, that you have accumulated? All I am requesting from you is that you undergo meditation. It is the only way, the only medium, through which you can remove all this dust, all the garbage of the illusory concepts.

You are happy to accept quotations from the great teachers and Masters and indulge in re-quoting their words, parrot-fashion: "So and so, says it like this, and so and so, says it like that!" The fact that you are happy with all these second-hand quotations is a dangerous thing. You are hooked on the words! As you know, words are not Ultimate Truth, they are only indicators or pointers. You say, "I read *I Am That* every day. I have read Ramana Maharshi a thousand times". You are inflating the ego by making these claims. That ego is dangerous for your spiritual career. Please don't do this! Because even if you have read so many books, and taken the Mantra from me, it is totally meaningless. **You either accept the Reality, or you do not. There are no halfway measures!** There should not be any duality. That is the drawback of the human being.

Read the Reader! Read books, but don't become addicted to them. If you have read all these spiritual books, why are you coming here? It means that whatever knowledge you have, is only theoretical knowledge. It has not touched you. You have not yet identified yourself. Don't become a Master of spirituality, become a Master of Selfless Self!

The body is not your identity at all. When it is your time to leave the body, there should not be any concept of "I am dying" around. Prepare now! The purpose behind spirituality is that you should be fearless. Be strong, and stand on your own feet! You are Ultimate Truth, but you are not willing to accept it.

You are to dissolve the concept of "body-attachment". Start from you! Everything starts from you, and everything ends within you. You are the central point of this world. If that Invisible Presence within the body were not there, what value does the body have, and what is the value of all your relations? There is no value. There are no relations! Please just accept the Reality!

You have to teach your mind, teach your ego, and intellect. Become their Master! It is very simple. Always remain with your Selfless Self. Ignore the mind and the thoughts. Don't waste your energy, by giving these things attention. If you follow my instructions, meditate sincerely, and recite the *Naam Mantra*, all the dust will be removed. And, you will be delightfully surprised at the transformation.

After knowing the Reality, forget about all the illusory concepts! Because they are all decorated notes, fake currency, that has no value in the market. Use this approach to throw everything out. You are not fake notes. You are Reality! You are Reality!

When I am sitting here, talking with you, there is a flow coming from my Master which I am sharing with you. This can happen to you also. It is not impossible if you become one with your Master, and totally accept the Reality that the Master is conveying.

After Spontaneous Conviction, there will be permanent happiness and peace, fearlessness and a stress-free life. You will not need any material cause to make you happy, or peaceful. Happiness is your nature. Peace is your nature.

Don't underestimate yourself! You are not a little, insignificant thing. You are Great! That Greatness is already within you. Stop ignoring it! The human body presents you with a golden opportunity to finally know who you really are. So, please don't waste any more time!

Just, please, accept the Reality!"

27th July – *Guru Purnima*. Maharaj's health has rapidly deteriorated in only a few weeks. Now, he can hardly walk, without it causing pain. He has to be helped to stand and sit down. Valmiki, a devotee, is his right-hand man. He is a great support, always looking out for Maharaj, making sure he is steady on his feet. Maharaj should have been in bed, but he would never have agreed to that, especially on the biggest day of the year, when the Guru is given thanks by his devotees and disciples. It is a sad event seeing Maharaj's body so debilitated. And yet, at the same time, there is a teaching there, too, for us all: how to be courageous in the face of intensely, debilitating and excruciatingly painful, bodily struggles!

During the Program we sing the new, uplifting and heartfelt *Arati* to Ramakanta, composed by devotee, Mayuri Dhangar. Here is the English translation:

"O Master Ramakant!
We here adore you with *Aarati*.
You have always been gracious to us.
The moments of your memories always keep us
Away from all the fears and worries in our material life.

Refrain

Arati Ramakanta, *Sadguru* full of grace.
Your name keeps all fear away.
Your exceptional devotion to your Master
Was so intense that it led you to Self-Realization.
We are your ignorant devotees.
We earnestly pray at your feet for that
Inconceivable, divine power.

Refrain

You have uplifted the world by removing
Their ignorance of spirituality and by
Giving them the knowledge of the Selfless Self.
Oh Lord! You are really the idol of knowledge
And your grace always protects the devotees.

Refrain

O Beloved Master!
The moment we perceived your formless essence
Was the dawn of our fortune.
We bow down to you with boundless gratitude
For opening the doors of the treasury of
Spiritual bliss."

29th July – After *Guru Purnima*, Maharaj's appearances at the ashram became very few and far between! However, on rare occasions when he does show up, a few devotees now feel the need to increase their prostrations to him. Unprepared for Maharaj to leave the body, they seem to be trying to hold onto his form. On these occasions, Anvita deals with them firmly, telling them to stop it, and get up from the floor!

31st July – Maharaj sends a message:

"*Jaiguru* Dear St Ann, After assigning the great spiritual responsibility I am having a lot of expectations from you. First of all, you are 100% deserve to carry out spiritual responsibilities. Secondly, after prolonged involvement in spirituality, you will never find any difficulty to answer questions of seekers. Most important is that spirituality is totally absorbed within you. So don't worry. Before initiations or giving *Nam Mantra* just confirm whether the seeker is really interested and his spiritual background. Also, you plainly declare after getting *Nam Mantra* don't expect miracles. You know better how to tackle various seekers. Go ahead. *Sadguru* Blessings are always with you. *Jaiguru.*"

August – Today, I receive another treatment from Dr Kiran. During it, she asks me how many pages of *Ultimate Truth*, I have completed? At first, I thought she was just curious, but later on, she confesses that Maharaj wants to know how the work is going! He is also asking about my health! Maharaj even told her to offer me a treatment that would give me lots of energy, so that I would be able to finish the book quickly! I laugh, saying to Dr Kiran, "So, now you are his spy, passing on information!" She laughs, too!

Later on that day, I speak with Maharaj, about the procedure involved in initiation. After reminding me of the basics, as I cannot remember the details of my initiation, he explains that it will develop spontaneously, in my own way, and not to be concerned!

Another day – Vijay sometimes drives Maharaj to our hotel restaurant, to pick up takeaway food. Today, while Gilles is outside smoking, he spots Maharaj sitting in the car. Spontaneously, he approaches Maharaj. The car window is down, and Maharaj is resting his arm on it. Suddenly, Gilles seizes the opportunity! He takes hold of Maharaj's hand with both hands, stares him straight in the eyes, and announces with great force: "I love you". Maharaj is taken aback! Then Gilles skips away, happy as Larry! This beautiful moment encapsulates Gilles! Always spontaneous, one can never predict what he will do next!

6ᵗʰ August – A few foreigners have arrived: an American man, a German lady and another Japanese lady. Today, Mark, the American, is happy to see Maharaj for the first time, even though he is not able to speak. The next day, Maharaj makes an appearance, but again, he does not talk. And the next day, it is the same!

I have been witnessing Mark since his arrival, and I am impressed by his calmness and stillness in this situation. He keeps his cool, diligently attending the ashram, three times a day. He has travelled thousands of miles to hear Maharaj speak, and receive the *Naam Mantra*. Now he is not sure if either is going to happen, as time is running out. He is leaving in a few days' time.

7ᵗʰ August – Maharaj messages me enquiring how long the foreign devotees are staying? He proposes that I initiate them, if he is not strong enough, but if they are staying longer, then maybe he will be able to carry out the initiations. He says:

"All depends on my health. And if they like to have confirmation, then you may contact me. I will convince them that I authorize you to give *Nam Mantra* on my behalf. As you know *Sadguru* Shri Gurulingam Maharaj gave *Nam Mantra* to Shri Bhausaheb Maharaj through their disciple Raghunath Priya Maharaj. Also *Sadguru* Shri Bhausaheb Maharaj gave *Nam Mantra* to *Satguru* Shri Amburav Maharaj, through their other disciple… And hence if they are staying at Nashik 3 days or more I will give them *Nam Mantra*. At present too much weakness. Please convince them. There is no difference between you and me. The bodies are different, the invisible presence is one and the same. So go ahead. With Blessings *Jai Sadguru*."

9ᵗʰ August – Maharaj is still too weak to initiate the foreigners. He messages me on WhatsApp, instructing me to initiate Mark on his behalf. He requests that I initiate Mark at the hotel. He does not want anyone at the ashram to know at this moment, that he has given me his authority to give the *Naam Mantra*.

I inform Mark of Maharaj's instructions and arrange to meet him, in his room, at the hotel, later in the morning. I prepare myself with a long meditation, to make sure I am as empty as possible, so that Maharaj can come through this vehicle called "Ann".

This is my first initiation. It is all going very smoothly, until I whisper the Mantra in Mark's ear. Suddenly, Mark interrupts me, saying, "Sorry, but I am deaf in that ear. Can you whisper in the other one?" We laugh at the situation! Then I whisper in his good ear!

In the evening, Maharaj is feeling a little better. I had missed a couple of calls and messages from him, when I had gone out earlier to see the doctor. Maharaj wants to know if I have initiated Mark? As Maharaj had not heard from me, he tells Anvita to bring Mark for initiation. Mark is elated! Maharaj initiates Mark. Auspiciously, that day, Mark had a "double whammy!"

Thereafter, when Maharaj finally receives my message, he announces in a buoyant tone, "I express my congratulations. Today is an historical day because it is the first time a Master and his disciple have initiated someone together!"

Then, he continues, enthusiastically, "Go ahead! Go ahead! My blessings are always with you. *Jai Guru*". We are both celebrating the special event! Following this, he makes what appears to be two contradictory statements: "Keep it quiet for now, but as soon as you reach London, start initiating!" "I will, Maharaj. Thank you. *Jai Guru*!", I say, while at the same time, wondering how that will work out!

Shortly after – I tell my friend, Richard, who is desperate to receive the *Naam*, that I will be able to initiate him very soon. Richard informs me that Maharaj has already told him the news! Maharaj can never keep any surprises!

The body has been left in a weakened state since contracting the bacterial infection. With the deadline for the book fast approaching, I must keep pushing hard to finish the work. After visiting the doctor, Maharaj asks to see me. He suggests that I come and stay at his home with Anvita, where I can help out and support Anvita when Maharaj is poorly. I would love to attend to Maharaj, but feel that my body is already stretched to the limit! However, I am very touched that Maharaj made this request. What a privilege it would have been, to care for him physically, even once!

10th August – While some of the devotees are feeling a sense of doom and gloom, and overwhelmed by sadness, as Maharaj's health continues to decline, Gilles and I are both untouched. In contrast, there is so much joy between us – a blessing from Maharaj, we feel! Often, when excessive, uncontrollable laughter arises as we dine at the restaurant, the staff members would come running in, to check if everything is ok!

Gilles enjoys listening to popular music. Sharing our musical tastes is revealing! We find out that when we listen to love songs, we both substitute the boy-girl love/romance, with the divine love/romance! We are both excited to discover this about each other, as he thought he was the only one who did this, and likewise, I thought I was the only one who did it!

There is no end to our laughter! In his room at the hotel, he used to merrily dance and prance around, in pure joy. This brought me to my knees in hysterical laughter. One memorable song he enjoyed playing, was Mel C's, *"I Turn to You"* from the 1990s! *"I turn to you, like a flower leaning towards the sun/I turn to you./Cos you're the only one/when I'm upside down/I turn to you… Where would I be? What would I do? If you'd never helped me through"….*

After his performances, we continued to party. Together we are like the happiest children, totally fulfilled with a bottle of "Thumbs-up", an Indian version

251

of Coca-Cola, and a couple of cream biscuits! Together, we find an abundance of perfection in the simplicity!

11ᵗʰ August – While the ashram is quiet, Gilles and I discuss visiting the "Shirdi Temple", which is not far from Nashik. We book a taxi for 5 am the next morning. Shirdi is a very popular pilgrimage site. To avoid long queues, we set off early. Shirdi Baba, (circa 1838-1918) is a great saint, revered by both Hindus and Muslims. Many accounts of healings and miraculous testimonies surround this saint. I owe a great deal to him, which is why I wish to visit!

"In the early 1990s, I was very ill for a couple of years, with a mysterious illness. After numerous tests and no diagnosis, I continued to lose weight and strength. Frustrated with orthodox medicine, and desperate for healing, Charles reminded me of what the Vedic astrologer had said to us, when he relayed a fascinating account of a past life. He told us, that we had lived in Shirdi and that we had met Shirdi Himself! We were his disciples. Not only that, but he also said that Charles used to look after the temple, as well as painting the artwork there! Reinspired by this story, we started re-reading the little biography of Shirdi which we had picked up in India. We had nothing to lose, so we prayed directly to Shirdi for healing. At this time, Charles also created a large picture of Shirdi Baba which he pinned to the wall, beside my bed.

Miracle or not, faith can move mountains! After only a few months of intense prayer, during which time, I experienced powerful rays emanating from the picture, the body began its road to recovery. As I got back on my feet, I thanked

Shirdi from the bottom of my heart. Although I never knew what the condition was, that had affected the body so badly, it did not matter, as it had passed! I felt indebted to Shirdi and could never thank him enough!"

Nearly 30 years later, I am given the opportunity to thank Shirdi properly, accompanied by Gilles!

We arrive in the early morning. At 9 am we decide to go for a coffee, at the café across from the Temple. We do not see much of a queue, so, we spend about 30 minutes at the café.

Then, we cross the road, collect our tickets, and join the slow-moving queue. Thankfully, the women are not divided or separated from the men. We shuffle along in anticipation. During the wait, I am telling Shirdi everything I want to say to him, offering praise and gratitude. It must have taken more than an hour to reach the wondrous, ornate golden statue and *samadhi* of Shirdi Baba. Now that we are near the altar, we are hurried along quickly, and only given a brief moment to bow to Shirdi.

Gilles and I bow together, at the same time, with reverence. Suddenly, I experience a rush of energy, like an indrawing breath, before being guided out of the temple. I ask Gilles if he felt anything, and he did, too! We try to describe the sound, the vibration. The energy made a sound like a sudden and dramatic inhalation! We are both very happy to have bowed at Shirdi's Holy Feet.

We decide to return to the café for another coffee. Something inexplicable follows. When I ask Gilles what the time is, he says it is 9 am! I laugh and say, it can't be, because that is when we first arrived here. He checks his phone, and it is 9 am! Time stopped during our pilgrimage!

When we get back into the taxi, to return to Nashik, Gilles starts to feel guilty about skipping the *bhajans*, anxious in case anyone has noticed he is missing. He is like a schoolboy worried about the consequences of having played truant.

When we return to the hotel and attend the *bhajans*, we hear from a devotee that Maharaj had not been well this morning, and so, at around 9 am, he was taken to the hospital for a check-up! I look at Gilles in amazement. It was the exact moment that time stood still!

12th August – Today, we are told that Maharaj and Anvita will be leaving Nashik, the following day. They are going to stay with Dhiraj at his home. Maharaj asks the devotees who are still at the ashram, to gather at his home, in the evening.

"We go in, one by one, and take our turn to bow to Maharaj. I am sitting next to Gilles. During Maharaj's "Final Talk" in Nashik, he forcefully says, "Don't change Masters! Your Master is like a mother. You don't change your mother!" There are maybe about a dozen or so of us gathered in his living room, drinking chai with our Master, for the last time.

Maharaj looks drawn, and it is an effort for him to speak. I tell him not to try, that it is enough to just be with him, but still, he carries on talking. Maharaj asks me about the book, and I tell him that most of the work is done. The "Talks from Nashik" are completed, and all that's left to finish, is a smaller section on the "Talks from the USA", which I reassure, him will take a maximum of two weeks. Maharaj is satisfied with that. There is nothing to say really, but it is nice to be with him this last time, a kind of rounding off, a completion, so to speak.

The next morning, some devotees gather in his home. Gilles and I line up on the street to say goodbye to Maharaj. It is lovely! We do not feel sad, because the Presence of the Master continues beyond the body. We have an eternal bond with Maharaj! We watch the drama unfold like a movie! However, there is an aura of sadness around Maharaj, as he knows he will not be returning to the ashram which has been his home for decades. He knows he will never be with his devotees again, physically. We wave them goodbye and return to the ashram."

The following day – The foreign devotees are beginning to leave now, including Gilles. Before he leaves, we exchange another big, bear hug. He is tremendous company. He is my spiritual brother! Now, he is leaving to go to Delhi, to visit his old friends. After his departure, I eat at the same restaurant, at the same table, at the same time. The occasion offers a necessary pause for reflection about Maharaj, Gilles, the Teachings, and finishing *Ultimate Truth*. However, today, our favourite dishes do not taste the same, because Gilles is not with me!

I stay on for a few more days, before catching my flight home, and visit Dr Kiran a couple more times to complete the ayurvedic course of treatment. We have formed a very strong bond. She is my spiritual sister!

Return to the UK – I have still not recovered from the illness, and have lost quite a lot of weight. My return to Nashik proved to be a wonderful, whirlwind event! Even though the body is pretty exhausted, the Spirit is soaring! There is no time to rest and recover, as I need to finish editing the book. Only two weeks left!

Maharaj asked for a section in the book to be dedicated to contributions from devotees, detailing their experiences with Maharaj. I had emailed many of them, but still had not received all the replies. So, I chase them up. The title for this section arises: It will be called, "How the Master Changed my Life".

I work solidly for the next ten days or so, and finish writing an "Introduction" to the book, which Maharaj had asked for. The Introduction contains a valuable teaching, as it explains how the Master's words always come true. When Maharaj assigned me the task of editing, I was doubtful that it could be done in such a short time. But now it is finished! I format the manuscript and email the print-ready file to the publishers, "Zen Publications".

I message Nishad, Maharaj's youngest son, and ask him if he can let Maharaj know, that the book has been completed. The publisher immediately prints a copy to show to Maharaj. I receive help with the book cover, deciding on a deep red colour since Maharaj loved the Bible edition in that same colour!

Maharaj's body has been hanging on, perhaps to ensure the completion of *Ultimate Truth*. This book is very important to him, as he wants to leave behind a book that contains all the answers to all possible questions, that seekers may ask!

I send one final message that arose spontaneously, to Maharaj, via Nishad: "Dear Maharaj, don't worry! I will continue the work of *Sadguru*. I am your servant……" When I read it the next day, "I" could not believe I had written these words! (I did not write them, the Spontaneous Presence did!) Never mind, what was said is true! I have every intention of continuing the work for Maharaj!

30th August – I receive communication from Nishad. He asks me to contact the western devotees, and tell them to prepare for Maharaj's *Mahasamadhi*. And, if any of them wish to travel to India, they should plan to do so now, as Maharaj has entered the final stage. I contact as many as I can, by email. Sonny, in the USA, decides to travel. [Sadly, he will not make it in time!]

31st August – Nishad messages, to let me know, that Maharaj attained *Mahasamadhi* at 11.36 am and he requests that I let everyone know!

The first person I contact is Gilles, hoping that he will share with me, the task of emailing everyone. But Gilles is stunned by the news, no, he is broken, by the news! In a shaky voice, he says, he will speak with me later. He is in no fit state to help me with the practicalities! I contact as many devotees as possible and also post the news on FB.

Later today, I hear the preparations for Maharaj's *Mahasamadhi* are already underway. Unfortunately, the celebrations will take place this afternoon, making it impossible for any westerners, who are not currently in the area, to get there on time.

Fortunately for me, my friend, Nitin, tells me he will attend the *Mahasamadhi*, as long as I accompany him online, in real-time. He is feeling a little shaken and unsteady, still trying to absorb the news! Of course, I agree!

Nitin arrives in Mumbai and makes his way to "Banganga Crematorium". When the Program starts, he communicates the sequence of events as they unfold, one by one. At some point, later on, Nitin grows quiet, as he witnesses the preparations of the pyre. I have to repeat his name a few times, to bring him back! There is no doubt that the whole occasion is very emotive!

Eventually, Nitin tells me that Maharaj's body has just been set alight. At this precise moment, as I close my eyes, Maharaj appears! The atmosphere is misty and ethereal. Then, Maharaj passes his arm through the ether and places his hand on my head. He says: "Follow me!"

Now it is my turn to be stunned! I am so amazed and touched by this, that all I can do is fall to my knees and prostrate.

Nitin continues to relay what is happening next, but I can no longer focus. I can no longer listen, whilst still in the process of absorbing the miracle, that has just taken place. Eventually, we say goodbye!

I meditate and reflect: I knew Maharaj would connect with me soon, but surmised, it would be in a few weeks' time or thereabouts. I never thought he would appear immediately, though, the events were so fast-moving, I never really had any time to think! "I am feeling very, very blessed! Thank you, Maharaj! Thank you!" I utter.

7th September – Maharaj is appearing in my dreams, communicating messages and offering his guidance. Last night, he said: "I want you to keep in touch with six devotees", and he named them all. When I woke up this morning, all I could remember was: "I want you to keep in touch with six devotees!" When I told this story to a few people, they usually asked if he or she could possibly be one of them?

I always replied affirmatively, with: "I am sure you are!" Within a matter of weeks, six had become sixteen, and then, even more!

18th September – Nisargadatta's "Death Anniversary", (*Punyatithi*), takes place today! This is the day Maharaj had always wished, and planned for, the publication of the book, *Ultimate Truth*! And his wish came true!

I notice that several changes have been made to the text and the book cover. However, in due course, some of the alterations to the text were reversed. The "Introduction" was partially reinstated! Oh well! Here is the original introduction:

"'*Sadguru* has arranged everything. The Master Editor has arrived!', exclaimed Maharaj, with a big smile on his face. I had just arrived in Nashik, India, when Maharaj sprung a surprise on me: I was to edit and prepare for publication, the existing draft manuscripts of *Ultimate Truth* by 1st September 2018! Feeling somewhat pressured, I wondered about the sense of urgency. Later on, I realized that Maharaj must have known that He did not have much time left in the food-body!

"Just glance at each page. Make it as attractive as *Selfless Self*", instructed Maharaj: At the time, the task seemed daunting, however, the miracle happened. It is now done, according to the Master's wishes! This challenge acted as an important reminder - that whatever the Guru says will happen, will always happen. Never doubt Ultimate Truth!

Equally amazing, is that the completion of this work occurred on the very same day, that the Master's food-body expired. Today, 31st August 2018, He took *Mahasamadhi*. Though the body has gone, He is with us, closer than ever before.

Ultimate Truth consists of 3 parts: "Talks from Nashik Ashram", between March and November 2017, and "Talks from the Master's U.S.A. visit" in 2016. (Bold text has been used to hammer home the teachings.) The final section, "How the Master Changed my Life" contains personal sharings, from seekers whose lives have been transformed forever by Maharaj's teachings.

There are around 250 questions. Those ultimate and fundamental questions of our existence, as well as more commonplace, everyday ones, are answered with uncompromising power, clarity and directness, that leave nothing to the imagination. There is no hiding place from Truth! These profound teachings, that take the reader beyond knowledge, are conveyed in a simple, light and effective way. *Ultimate Truth* leaves no stone unturned, till all the questions posed by seekers are finally exhausted. How to achieve Self-Realization is presented simply and logically, flavoured with the Master's unique brand of humour!

Our most humble and compassionate Master, tirelessly shared these teachings, again and again, expecting nothing in return. He had one wish only: to put an end to our needless suffering, once and for all! Even in his Final Talk, when he was visibly frail, and his voice was very feeble, his focus remained steadfast: liberation for his devotees. With great poignancy, he pleaded: "Please accept the Reality".

I humbly bow, with deep and overflowing gratitude, at the feet of my Great Master, Shri Ramakant Maharaj: *Ultimate Truth* is a timely gift to the world! *Jai Sadguru*."

In the evening, I start reading the section entitled, "How the Master Changed my Life", which includes some very touching contributions, from many devotees. Here are a few:

"When you hear the Master, Sri Ramakant speaking, you know it is Truth. He found me at last, after searching for over thirty years. I finally found a living Realized Master, and life has not been the same since. I am happy and contented all the time, full of laughter and joy."

"I missed Nisargadatta Maharaj. I was not around for Ramana Maharshi. I wasn't going to miss Sri Ramakant Maharaj. In His Presence, I was left speechless. I took the *Naam Mantra* and it literally, blew my mind! I am empty, thoughtless and beyond happy! I cannot say any more, except that I am eternally grateful to my Master."

"As Truth is beyond words, there's not much to say about Sri Ramakant Maharaj, but if I were to try to put it into words, I'd say that it was a beautiful thing seeing silence speak. That meeting in Oneness is imprinted in my Heart forever."

"Ramakant Maharaj is the first Master I have ever bowed to. That says it all!"

"He is always with me, in my heart. Trusting the Guru, and his instructions is everything. *Om Shanti. Jai Guru* Sri Ramakant Maharaj!"

"I have been searching for decades, but now my search has ended with Ramakant Maharaj. I have met so many Masters but He is the only one who has shown me that the answers are all within me. His teaching showed me, that all the knowledge and concepts that I had accumulated, were in fact, blocking the Truth. Thank you Maharaj for helping to discard this illusory baggage. Now I know what Maharaj means when he says 'You are a free bird!'"

"Hopefully, my testimony will inspire sincere seekers around the world, as so many of us have lost faith because of the hardships of life. My greatest encounter in this existence is Sri Ramakant Maharaj. Finally, I came face to face with the knower of all hearts manifesting Himself in a physical body. Having received the *Naam Mantra* felt like the detonation of the atomic consciousness inside of me.

My seeking came to an end. The supposedly heavy cloud hanging around my head started to dissolve slowly, but surely. My power and faith were regenerated. It is a matter of great grace and merit to come across such a rare one.

There are many mystical experiences from the meditation – colourful and bright light! The circumstances around me suddenly became very favourable – from having no job, I am now doing the job of my dreams, and my physical health is improving a lot."

"Words cannot express the transformation that has taken place, since discovering Sri Ramakant Maharaj: There is no longer a sense of time. The days and nights, weeks and years, just flow spontaneously. Everything flows, and unfolds, with a heart that is bursting with joy, and peace, that surpasses all understanding. There are no thoughts, only a vast emptiness that is filled with pure happiness, ecstasy and laughter. I did not know that it was possible, to be empty and full at the same time. I used to think I knew so much. Then, I discovered that I did not know anything at all. Knowing that there is nothing to know, is the greatest liberation! I bow to my great, and humble Master, with immense respect and gratitude!"

October – The body is "not co-operating", as Maharaj used to say. I find myself sleeping for around 13 hours per day. I visit the doctor several times, and she arranges all sorts of blood tests, to pinpoint the source of the fatigue, weight loss and various other symptoms. Most of the tests come back negative. The main culprit seems to be the remnants of the bacterial infection, or maybe, some unidentified secondary condition, that has developed from it. Whatever it is, it does not seem to be something the doctor can help me with!

Early November – Jeff is very kind and reaches out to me. With his useful nursing background, he tries to identify my health problems, asking me about all of my symptoms, to see if he can join up the dots. So far, we haven't come up with a diagnosis. He continues to be a great support during this period, for which I am very grateful.

Mid-November – One day, I pick up the printed pdf of *Jean Dunn's Diaries* and start reading it again. I love Jean Dunn! Whenever I read her diaries, I am always inspired by her deep devotion to Nisargadatta Maharaj. Spontaneously, it comes to me, that her highly personal account of being with her Master, deserves to be published in book-form. I visualize a small, cute, journal-sized book, in the same colour of orange, that was used for *Seeds of Consciousness,* one of the books she had edited for Nisargadatta.

1ˢᵗ December – The *Jean Dunn Journals* book is published, just in time for the festive season. It receives a very favourable response.

Mid-December – Dear Hamid, phones again. He is one of my closest spiritual brothers. We talk for two hours. Our conversations are ever-fresh, though we frequently retell and relive the same stories, time and again – as if they are brand new! Even though we have not met in person, we share a strong connection, filled with laughter and a deep love for Maharaj. Hamid's life as a musician takes him all around the world. He is always on the go, which means there are few opportunities to meet up. We long for it to happen soon!

End of December – What a glorious year it has been! My companions, Charles and Maharaj, are with me always, guiding, protecting and supporting this vehicle, called "Ann". There is love in abundance! Spontaneous laughter arises once more. There is pure joy! Laughter has been my companion throughout 2018! What a blessed year. I am filled with immeasurable gratitude!

2019

8th January – I receive the sacred ashes of Maharaj. It is incredible to hold them! Maharaj's Presence is strong. The room is sacredly atmospheric, and feels even more like an ashram now.

During this period of physical weakness and fatigue, I experience Maharaj's Presence strongly, and constantly. In fact, it is often felt so explosively, that I frequently wonder whether I might combust! This phase of virtual immobility is simultaneously, one of fulness and overflowing grace, replete with many significant experiences. In particular, there is one profound experience, where I witness my own death:

"The first night, after receiving the ashes, I have a powerful vision where I leave the body. I am suspended above my body. I have separated, disconnected from the body-form. Then, I hear a voice telling me, "This is the complete you". It is amazing! I have left the body, and can view clearly that, the body is nothing more than a shell. I am fully alive, everywhere, vast and taking up the whole of space."

Now that the ashes are here, the "*Naam Mantra* Initiations", as instructed by Maharaj, can begin in earnest.

"Joanne" is the very first one to be initiated in the UK. She has been following Maharaj, since she discovered his book, *Selfless Self*, in 2015. Both Charles and I, kept in touch with her over the years, responding to her questions and establishing a deep friendship, in, and through, Maharaj. She is a beautiful example, of someone who is deeply devoted to a Master, with whom she has never even met! She may not have had the opportunity to be in his physical Presence, nevertheless, she experienced his Presence strongly, and an unbreakable bond was established!

19ᵗʰ January – Joanne is arriving at 8 am. She will stay for one night! The altar at my home has been carefully prepared, with fresh flowers and incense burning. We have not yet met in person, since she first made contact, five years ago. All our communications took place via email.

When she arrives, we hug each other warmly. She is in awe of the centrepiece altar, which displays a huge picture of Maharaj, wearing a pink turban. Below it, there are several smaller pictures of the Masters: Bhausaheb, Siddharameshwar, Nisargadatta and Ranjit Maharaj's.

She is eager to know all the details about Maharaj, what he was like, etc. She asks about Charles, too, and I show her a couple of photos of him. We talk for a couple of hours.

Later on that day, we both prepare for the Initiation. I give her a beautiful white kurti, pants, and a shawl to wear. Then, she asks me if she should wear makeup, which she only wears on special occasions. I say, "Of course! Today is a big day! A special, special occasion, your True Birthday".

I remind her of a quote from Nisargadatta, who said: "The Mantra reminds you of your true identity. Your parents gave you a name and everyone called you by that name. Mantra is called *Nama* – Name, calling yourself as you are, in Reality!" Joanne's eyes light up, and she runs to the bathroom, excitedly, to put on her make-up.

"As soon as she is ready, we stand together facing the altar, and fully prostrate to the Masters. Then, we begin to sing the *bhajans*. Joanne is very happy, as ecstatic as a child, exuding great innocent joy. Then, she sits on the floor, and the Initiation takes place. We meditate together! It is a beautiful day! I prepare a space for her to sleep in front of the altar, in the company of the Masters. She is blissful. She leaves early the next morning. What a beautiful celebration it has been with Joanne. The seed that was planted in 2015 has grown into a mighty, exceptional tree, blooming with devotion! Beautiful! If only, all of Maharaj's devotees were like Joanne!"

The next day, Chris arrives from San Diego. He is staying for a few days. After getting over the jet lag, we meet, and talk about Maharaj, before his Initiation. He is a serious seeker which is why he has travelled so far, to receive the *Naam Mantra*, which will help him with his meditation. We have a beautiful ceremony, and then take photos to commemorate his special day!

26th January – I return to work on the book, *Who am I?* It is a challenge to construct it into a "mainstream" book. How to go about compiling it, according to Maharaj's twofold requirements? Present the teachings in a simple, direct way and, at the same time, intermingle them with western culture! I ask Maharaj for guidance, before continuing from where I had left off, a few months ago.

End of January – I reflect on my recent visions of Charles. In the past, there were still memories of him, but now, there is no division between us, therefore, there are no memories of "someone else"! I no longer think about him, or see him, as anything other than love.

Later – I reflect on Shirdi Baba, who visited this morning. It was lovely! It was the same kind of experience I had, when Gilles, and I, bowed to the big golden statue in Shirdi. The texture was absorbent, absorbing me. Shirdi continues to draw me in. Thank you for the blessing!

February – Death experience:

"I am lying awake in bed when I have a vision. My face appears in front of me. I witness the ageing process speeded up. My face is getting older and older. My cheekbones are jutting out, and then the face that I see, transforms into a skull. I witness the elemental form of this face dissolving in front of my eyes. It completely disintegrates.

As this energy comes closer to me and is about to disappear, I stretch out my arms, embrace the decomposed material, and take it into my heart. This is another direct experience of death, showing that the body form is insubstantial – there's nothing to it. There is complete detachment, no emotion, no nothing."

March – I receive complaints about the publication of the *Jean Dunn Journals*, regarding an issue over copyright! I was not aware that there is any copyright issue, as the pdf has been circulating online for decades. Jean, herself, had shared it freely with her devotees. There is certainly no breach that I can see, nor any copyright infringement.

The Masters in this Lineage all share a deep wish, to openly spread the teachings, for the benefit of all. They have never been possessive of the knowledge, or made any claims of ownership! Sadly, my original and spontaneous impulse, to publish the *Journals,* has attracted a different kind of energy: the potential threat of legal action, if I do not remove the book! These worldly threats are the opposite of Jean Dunn's open, free Spirit! I am forced to withdraw the book! What would Maharaj say? "These things happen. Forget it!" And so, I did!

End of March – These days, when I get into bed, I feel that I am in a "divine sandwich"! It is so blissful and wholesome! Since receiving Maharaj's ashes, many things seem to be happening, even though I know that nothing ever happens! It feels like there is a lot of electricity around, like fireworks fizzling and sizzling in my head. The electricity is surging upwards to the crown chakra. I often laugh out aloud at what is taking place. Today, I feel like one of those cartoon characters on TV, whose hair is standing, frazzled on end, after receiving some kind of electric shock! Lol! There seems to be some things going on in the nervous system. Am "I" being rewired?

Magical things are definitely happening during this period, like several amusing coincidences and synchronicities. This particular series of events began with an intuition, where a stream of words arose spontaneously from within. I capture these words on paper:

"I am going to be wed in the most beautiful temple, the most stunning cathedral, the inmost sanctuary of the Heart. It is the culmination of the divine romance. It is the fulfilment... union! "The Wedding" refers to the transformation into the Divine Self."

Immediately after, I am inspired to buy a white dress, for the forthcoming occasion in July, of Maharaj's "Samadhi Installation Ceremony". Almost instantly, I go online and find a suitable dress, that is loose, layered and flowing. I purchase it.

A few days later, the dress arrives. When I look at the designer label, and see, "Ann Self", I burst out laughing! Following this, I go out to buy a pair of sandals. It is only when I return home, that I notice that they are called, "Bliss Sandals!" Again, I chuckle to myself, thinking, how everything is happening spontaneously, and magically. The third of three happenings, comes two days later, when, I receive the necklace I have chosen to wear, along with my outfit for Maharaj. It came in a little blue velvet pouch, with imprinted, white letters: "Hoo Am I"! I am amazed, as I am currently working on the book entitled *Who Am I?* These are not coincidences. There is no such thing! Throughout these spontaneous occurrences, I feel Maharaj's strong Presence, his beautiful energy, smiles and humour. I am certain that I can hear him chuckling!"

April – My stepson, Jasper, is planning to visit India next month, and travel to Tiruvannamalai. He has also arranged to meet with the Vedic astrologer, Charles and I had seen, and raved about, for many years! He feels that maybe, he can receive some guidance, regarding his life's direction. Jasper is the closest son to his father,

Charles, and is like him in many ways! I have known him since he was a young boy. We have always been close, and get on well with each other. Over the years we have grown even closer!

We talk about the trip. I ask him, if I can go with him? There is a longing, stirring in my heart, to pay my respects to Ramana Maharshi, and prostrate before him in Arunachala. My connection with him has always been strong. He even used to appear in my dreams and visions. It is my firm belief, that he has been one of several guides and protectors, throughout my life.

Jasper is keen for me to go. However, he is at the same time, cautious about my health. Nevertheless, I need to go. I reassure him that I will be fine, adding, that it may be the only chance I will ever have, to go to Tiruvannamalai! We book our flight tickets for May.

Before leaving for India, a few more initiations take place: a musician, Ed, from the U.S.A and Nepalese born, Paban, etc.

1ˢᵗ May – I tell Gilles that I will be going for a short trip to Tiruvannamalai, but will be back in time, to travel to Nashik, for Maharaj's *Samadhi* installation, in July. He tells me, to take care of my health, especially at this time of year, when the climate is incredibly hot!

Mid-May – Jasper and I set off on our pilgrimage to India. A friend of his recommends that he visit Auroville and Pondicherry, during the trip.

We make our way to the abode of Shri Aurobindo, (1872-1950), the philosopher and poet who developed a system he called, "Integral Yoga". I was an avid reader of Aurobindo's books during my twenties, before moving on to other teachers!

21st May – On our first day in Pondicherry, we visit Shri Aurobindo's ashram. That first night, I have a dream in which Shri Aurobindo appears. I recognize his distinct face, long flowing beard, and his gazing, intense eyes. He speaks a few words: "Welcome! It is a privilege to work with you". His message gladdens my heart!

We visit the community in Auroville for a short time. I am interested in receiving more Ayurvedic massage, and here, it is on offer in abundance! The body needs healing, so I decide to book in for several massage sessions at the nearby healing centre. My stay here is health-giving, like being in a health spa resort. The food is excellent, and, there is also a bakery with fancy cakes, as well an array of sweet delights!

22nd May – We visit the "*Matrimandir*", (Temple of the Mother), which we have already seen from a distance. It looks like a spaceship! We read that it took 37 years to build, from 1971 until 2008. It is the heart of Auroville and symbolises the birth of a new consciousness!

We join the queue to obtain tickets. As we enter the Mandir, we see various figures dotted around, dressed in strange white, space-like clothing. Each one waves his hand forward, with a strange gesture. The silence is palpable. We stop to put on a pair of socks that we are all required to wear, before proceeding to the big hall, where we find a little spot, and sit down.

"My meditation is very light and "I" quickly dissolve into space. The space expands into infinity. After a little while, the lights in the hall are switched on, signifying that our 15 minutes are up! Without any words spoken, we follow each other, remove the socks, and exit the building.

The silence experienced is powerful, and I do not wish to break it. We walk to the bus stop and wait. As I am standing there, I hear and feel, what sounds like a crack, or crackling, on the top of my skull. I look up at the tree above me, and in a kind of shock, I ask Jasper if a coconut has fallen on my head? It must have sounded strange... Then, when I touch the top of my crown chakra, it is moist and damp, as if something is leaking out. I lean my head forward and ask Jasper to look at my head. He looks, and says he cannot see anything! I am perplexed at what I have just experienced. What did this crack mean? Was it an opening of the crown chakra? What was the moist sensation? Could it have been an experience of divine nectar that I've read about? It is beyond my understanding, and so, I accept the experience as another blessing, this time from Shri Aurobindo."

Our next stop is Tiruvannamalai!

8th June – We arrive in Tiruvannamalai, in the scorching heat. After checking into a hotel, close to the ashram, we rest and recover from the flight. From my bedroom window, I can see the magnificent, imposing holy mountain of Arunachala!

The following day, we visit the small Meditation Room, which is already quite full. I bow to the picture of Ramana! "At long last, you have brought me here!" I whisper. After half an hour, I am forced to leave, as the heat is rising in the unventilated room. We realize that next time, we will have to go to the meditation room much earlier in the day, when it is cooler.

Later on, we explore the big hall, where some people are circumambulating the statue of Shri Ramana, and others are scattered around, sitting quietly. We continue walking around the grounds, taking in the peaceful atmosphere.

We stop outside the well-preserved "Nirvana Room", where Ramana spent his last days. I can feel the strong, saintly energy here. While standing at this power spot, the door suddenly starts rattling by itself, as if a strong wind is causing it to shake. There is no wind! I like to think that Ramana is welcoming us! I bow to Ramana and say a few prayers.

9ᵗʰ *June* – We prepare ourselves to climb up the mountain of Arunachala. We set off early, then slowly, slowly, follow in the footsteps of the endless pilgrims, who have come before us. Intent on walking carefully on the uneven surfaces, we are, however, very aware that time is of the essence. We need to get a move on, so we don't get scorched by the rising heat.

We stop for meditation, at the sacred cave where Ramana had spent many years. The longing to prostrate to Ramana, which has burned within me for a lifetime, is about to be fulfilled. From that deep and intense longing, prayers of gratitude issue forth, prayers of thanksgiving to Ramana, for being a constant Light throughout my life, and for shielding me from harm.

I wait patiently for my fellow visitors to end their meditation and depart, so, that there is enough space for me to fully stretch out to Him, on this sacred ground. Finally, the opportunity arrives. I lie flat and submit myself wholly, in worship to

Bhagavan Ramana. He has given so much, that my only wish is to give back and surrender myself to Him totally.

After a brief pause to eat and drink, we set off back down Arunachala. Something extraordinary happens next. Suddenly, I experience a flash, an image, a vision:

"I see two Indians carrying a stretcher, which is made from two planks of wood and canvas. On the stretcher, I see my dead body! As I continue to walk down the hill, I try to look more closely, (as if I am concentrating hard on a movie scene). It is definitely my body! Suddenly, I am given an explanation for the strong connection, that I have always felt with Shri Ramana. Or, maybe there are two possibilities. I tell Jasper that I need to stop walking, to avoid stumbling, while all this is being revealed to me. I conclude that – if there is such a thing as a previous life – then I lived during Shri Ramana's time, and perhaps, my body had expired in Arunachala! What an awesome thought!

The other explanation that surfaces, is that the experience I am having is another profound "death" experience! However, the first explanation seems more fitting. Although I am somehow perplexed, the overwhelming feeling is one of being blessed. I thank Shri Ramana, and we, eventually, descend to the bottom of the hill. The next few days are spent in meditation and contemplation of this grace-filled experience."

We visit the ashram of Yogi Ramsuratkumar, (1918-2001) also called the "God-child of Tiruvannamalai". Yogi Ramsuratkumar credited three spiritual beacons for his realization, namely Shri Aurobindo, Ramana Maharshi and Swami Ramdas! Inside "Swagatham Hall" at Yogi Ramsuratkumar's Ashram, the atmosphere is electric! Pictures of numerous known, and unknown, saints are displayed on the walls. I have never seen so many saints gathered together in this way! There is nothing like it! Such a powerful energy coming from these images, as I stand in the centre, encircled by these extraordinary saints and sages!

Before we leave Tiruvannamalai, we visit a jewellery shop. I am prompted to buy a pair of earrings. I am shown two that interest me: one of "Ganesha" and one of "Shiva" in silver. Some years ago, I probably would have chosen the Ganesha earrings, to help me remove some of my many obstacles in life! But now, I find the perfect ones in Shiva. They will always be a reminder of the amazing event here in Tiruvannamalai!

Our final stop is a visit to the Vedic astrologer. Jasper is looking for guidance, for answers, and hopes the "Seer" can reveal them to him. I accompany Jasper to the astrologer, and recognize him from decades before. I had not planned to see him myself, but a strange thing happened. After Jasper emerged from his consultation, looking somewhat stunned, yet at the same time, very happy, the astrologer tells me to come in. I tell him I have not booked an appointment, that I am just waiting for Jasper. But as he insists, I do not resist. I follow him inside.

Just like before, he asks for my name, date and place of birth. He leaves the room, and after a couple of minutes, returns with the appropriate "inscribed palm leaves".

He is charming and humorous. Sensing his humour, I joke with him: "You told my husband over 20 years ago that he would live till he was over 80 years of age. It didn't happen. He was only in his 60's when he passed, so I would like a refund please!" I laugh, as I say it, and so does he! He goes on to explain that his work, is "prediction", while what transpires, is "destiny"! I reassure him that I am not serious, just "having fun"!

He starts the reading. Even though I had not asked for it, nor was I looking for anything, his accuracy strikes a chord, in the same way, it did, so many years ago! In the first reading, he had told me, that it would be some years before I would meet my true Guru! Now he is accurately relaying to me, that I have met my Guru, and that he has left the body!

He tells me that my Guru, Ramakant Maharaj, is using me as an instrument to spread his Teachings. He says my medium is writing, and reveals that I have written a book or two already, and will continue to write several more books, which are based on my Guru's Teachings.

He goes on to talk about my husband's journey, which is fascinating, as well as hearing him describe some of my current health issues. He also emphasizes my connection to two of Charles' sons, and that I am to guide them!

We thank him, offer a donation, and leave. Jasper is uplifted by what was shared. He informs me that the Seer told him that I am like a "Divine Mother" to him! He also said that soon, he would become more serious about spirituality, and find his way, with the help of my guidance.

We prepare for our return flight home to the UK. It has been an amazing pilgrimage that started without any expectations, and ended with a deeper sense of fulfilment. And most importantly, I did not fall ill!

20th June – It is time to reunite with my dear friend, Gilles. We plan our return trip to India, for the installation of Maharaj's *Samadhi*, in the ashram. We both feel the same strong pull, to be there for this very significant day. First of all, there are many obstacles to overcome, such as airline companies going bust, hearing of severe floods in Mumbai, etc. We discuss the changing events, but still reassure each other, that we will be there on time because Maharaj is calling us. He wants us both there! Every obstacle we face, is always to be seen as an opportunity to strengthen our foundations, rise to the challenges, and not be deterred by anything!

30th June – Femke, a Dutch seeker, arrives for initiation. She has read the Dutch translation of *Selfless Self*, and is eager, to deepen her meditation.

6th July – Gilles' flight leaves for India before mine. We arrange to meet at Mumbai airport. When I arrive at Heathrow, I discover that my flight has been delayed for 5 hours, due to bad weather in Mumbai! Already feeling tired, 5 hours seems like a lifetime. Eventually, I board the flight, and I'm on my way! At the other end, I send a message to Gilles. We do not manage to meet up till the next morning!

7th July – The day before the celebrations at the ashram, we decide – no - we are guided to "do the rounds" of a few important places. We visit Banganga Crematorium, and find the spot where Ramakant Maharaj's body was cremated. We speak with a caretaker there, who tells us that Maharaj's body was burned on the exact same section of ground as Nisargadatta's cremation in 1981! It feels important to be there, as we were not able to attend the *Mahasamadhi* celebrations last year.

Next stop, we ask the taxi driver to take us to Shri Ranjit Maharaj's home, which has been preserved since the days that he offered *Satsangs* there. His home is a humble abode, tiny, yet, it contains everything needed for life – including a basic shower for ablutions, and a cooking stove. The atmosphere is alive with Shri Ranjit's Presence. The room is fragrantly heavy with a beautiful peace. We spend some time there, in meditation.

Last stop! We make our way to Shri Nisargadatta's old humble residence, where he lived and taught, for many years. On arrival, we meet a couple of family members, who currently live there. They are used to visitors, wishing to check out the famous residence of Nisargadatta! There are various pictures on the walls. When we sit to meditate for a short time, however, we are not left entirely alone. We are aware of family members hovering in the background, causing a minor distraction! We thank them for letting us be there, and then leave.

8th July – Maharaj Birthday and the Installation of the Samadhi. We arrive in Nashik for the special event!

We meet with Anvita and Nishad, who wish to show us the newly set up room in Maharaj's home. There, we see beautiful glass case units, displaying Maharaj's personal effects, books, diaries, etc. The atmosphere is wonderful and the energy, buzzing! We spend a few moments in silence, soaking up the atmosphere, touched by the sight of our Master's familiar personal effects, such as his spectacles and watch, while also noticing, a few precious hand-written notebooks!

It turns out that very few western devotees manage to attend this memorable day. At last, I meet Sonny, briefly. We hug warmly. Unfortunately, he is not able to stay for the Program, as he has to return home for work. Hard luck, again!

This day signifies both Maharaj's body-birthday and his *Samadhi*. Herein lies another essential and valuable teaching, demonstrating once more, that there is no birth and there is no death. Everything is one. Maharaj never came, and he never went!

During this ceremony, devotees queue up in front of the *Samadhi*. We are invited to place our fingers inside the *Samadhi* column, containing Maharaj's ashes. What a blessing!

Shri Balwant is here. His joyful Presence permeates the whole ashram. We join the procession of devotees, carrying the sacred ashes of Maharaj, around the streets of Nashik. I have the privilege of carrying these ashes, too!

When we return to the ashram, I spot Shri Balwant dancing and smiling, still holding Maharaj's ashes. This celebratory aspect and joy, profoundly strike me on this day. It is another example of the highest teachings in action! Today, as the consistency and pragmatism of the knowledge is so clearly demonstrated, I can see clearly, how the knowledge is truly implemented and authentically lived! This Lineage does not teach dry and theoretical knowledge, but supremely practical, living knowledge!

The atmosphere is immensely uplifting! There is no mourning. Why mourn? Who mourns? For whom? For what? What is evidenced here are overflowing expressions of happiness, for liberation, for eternal life … giving thanks to, and rejoicing in, the miraculous presence of a rare *Jnani*, Guru, Master. We are celebrating Shri Ramakant Maharaj, a contemporary saint, who will be with us for all eternity!

Several Talks follow in the Marathi language, and then, we feast on food.

16th July – *Guru Purnima*, this year, is a little subdued, as it is the first year without Maharaj! However, something wonderful happened that evening! I have the honour of placing a garland around Maharaj's picture, above his *Samadhi*, with a fellow devotee. After doing so, I kneel down.

As I look at Maharaj's picture and bow to him, I experience intense energy. Then suddenly, in the empty space within, Maharaj places a prayer, which is, in fact, the one aspiration, and the highest aspiration, we can attain in our lifetime, Self-Realization. The prayer, which Maharaj installs in my heart, is truly the only prayer: "Make me a Master!" I thank him with total and utter reverence.

18th July – Gilles leaves to visit his old friends in Delhi. He gives me his usual big, bear hug. Joy is intermingled with sadness, at our parting. [Unbeknown to us, this is the last time we are to see each other!]

Late July – I stay in Nashik for a couple of weeks more, meditating in front of the *Samadhi*, and deepening my understanding of what was revealed earlier, regarding the symbolic "wedding". I am married to Shri Ramakant Maharaj. We are entwined. We are one. The act of placing my fingers into Maharaj's ashes, imprinted our union in my heart, dissolving any remaining separation between us. This ultimate merging, revealed to me more profoundly, that, "I am That!"

Early August – During this time, I have the opportunity to speak with Anvita, and share with her, that one year ago, Maharaj had authorized me to initiate sincere seekers, on his behalf! I show her some of the messages exchanged between Maharaj and myself, via "WhatsApp". I tell her that, earlier in the year, around a dozen devotees travelled from all over the world. They are now initiated with the *Naam Mantra*!

Anvita's response is wonderful, saying, she is very happy to hear the news! She is keen to keep the messages, and remarks on how beautifully Maharaj writes to his devotees! She has never seen that before, and is moved by his care and "personal touch"! When she reads the part where Maharaj requests, that I initiate the American devotee, Mark, at the hotel, she asks me if I did as Maharaj had instructed? I said "Yes!" She smiles one of her beautiful smiles.

I also mention that I have been contacted by a few devotees who tell me I have no right to be initiating. Anvita's response is clear and strong: "Why do you listen? Don't pay any attention! Do what Maharaj has told you!" Her guidance gives me strength. I thank her!

During our meeting, Anvita also relates something that is extraordinarily beautiful. She says that in the last few days, when Maharaj was in the hospital, she did not want to be around him, as she did not wish, to cause any distractions: "He was Maharaj before we married!". It is beautiful to hear her words reflecting her deep, lifelong devotion to Maharaj!

Later on – The *"Souvenir"* book of Maharaj has recently been published by Mandar Ghaisas, a devotee of Maharaj. Anvita asks me to take a suitcase full of them back to the UK, for distribution. I contributed a short piece to *Souvenir*, an attempt to describe how Charles and myself experienced Maharaj, and called it, "Dance of the Sacred Marriage":

"What was Sri Ramakant Maharaj like? He was ordinary, kind, humble, compassionate and humorous. He was such a beautiful being, so gentle, yet, at the same time, one could feel his power, his Presence, the sense of divine otherworldliness. When he spoke, the words flowed out of him spontaneously, and forcefully. He is a true *Sadguru*!

Maharaj often cautioned us: "Don't take my words literally, it is what I am trying to convey that is important". And it wasn't just the meaning behind the words that was highly effective, it was the power behind the words that was experienced as a transmission from Source. That power, energy or vibration was palpable all around Him.

There were so many timeless and transformative moments with Maharaj, though one, in particular, remains fresh. During this *Satsang*, Maharaj pointed to Charles and myself, who were seated directly in front of Him, and in an authoritative voice, he said: "YOU are Ultimate Truth. YOU are Almighty God!" When he stretched out his arm I could see the shimmering, vibrating waves of energy coming from (his) space, and then, it was as if, that energy behind the words entered (my) space. We both felt this transmission deeply. And, not only that, it had a lasting effect.

Being in the Presence of an authentic, Self-Realized Master like Sri Ramakant is key because the Master's Presence is like a magnet, that draws you into that invisible, stateless realm, enveloping you in its Energy and Power.

The Guru is transparent. Sri Ramakant acted like a mirror in which you could see your Selfless Self. In the Presence of this Pure Light, you feel compelled to surrender completely to the Master, who touches the deepest core of your being. He reminds you of your forgotten Identity, and increases your earnestness, propelling you forward to "remember" That, and Be That. The only response there can be is one of spontaneous, and complete self-abandonment - the endless desire to fully prostrate, and bow, before the Master's resplendent light.

Ultimately, there is no Master and no disciple, however, the illusory process and practice are like a beautiful dance, that takes place between the Master and the disciple. In this "Dance of the Lover and the Beloved", the Master leads the disciple through Self-Enquiry, Self-Knowledge to Self-Realization.

After attending the Master Class, the last dance commences. In this "Dance of the Sacred Marriage", the Spiritual journey culminates in the union of the lover and the Beloved - in Oneness.

Without the guidance of a Self-Realized Master, we are like the blind leading the blind, with only what Maharaj calls "body-based knowledge" at our disposal. It is an indisputable fact that many seekers from all over the world, have awakened through Maharaj's Presence, grace and blessings. How can we thank Him? By letting this river of knowledge, and beyond knowledge, flow to others.

What was Sri Ramakant Maharaj like? A rare, shining Light that continues to guide us. He is not different, or separate from us. We are One.

I am blessed for that rare opportunity to have been with Him physically. I am blessed for the unbreakable bond between us. I am blessed for the sacred communion with Him in the eternal now. Bowing to His Holiness with unceasing gratitude. *Jai Guru*!"

12ᵗʰ August – There is severe flooding in Nashik. Today, the roads are like rivers. I have to ask someone to help me across the road, to get to my hotel, as the water is knee-deep! When I get back to my room, covered in dirt and contaminated water, I quickly take a shower. The last thing I need now, is to catch another infection!

The night before I am due to leave, the hotel manager tells me there are no taxis available, to take me to the airport, due to severe flooding. However, if I pay double the amount, he will phone around, and try and find me a driver! I tell him that is no problem, and to please call me back soon. Later that evening, I am told that a taxi is available. The cost has increased again. I do not mind, as long as I can get to the airport!

I catch my flight and return home safely.

Mid-August – More visitors arrive for Initiation: Mario from Switzerland, Branko from Croatia, Jeremy, a long-standing devotee of Nisargadatta, etc.

Mid-September – I am experiencing strange symptoms of dizziness and light-headedness. I visit the doctor, who arranges for me to have a few blood tests. They come back clear. The next day, I am still not back to my usual self. The dizziness and weakness continue. I decide not to work today and retire to bed.

Since meeting Ramzi last year, we have kept in touch. Today I receive a small parcel from him. It is so thoughtful! He sent me a hot water bottle that has a soft woollen cover over it, to bring me some relief and comfort. It is very thoughtful of him!

October – I speak with Gilles – my unique, buoyant, crazy spiritual brother – regularly, on Sundays. His energy is always beautiful, and his laughter, contagious. Today, however, he asks me, to pray for his wellbeing. He tells me, he has not been feeling well! We are such close, kindred Spirits, who synchronise so well! Now it looks like we are also falling ill at the same time! Gilles shares various physical problems with me, which have suddenly appeared, as if, from out of nowhere. The doctor is investigating his symptoms, such as ear pain, neck pain and weakness! His health is suddenly, and rapidly, going downhill.

Mid-October – Antonio, a Spanish devotee, has been researching the Lineage. His book, *Yo no hago discipulos, hago maestros – Biografia alrededor de Nisargadatta Maharaj*, has been published this month.

November – "Expect the unexpected", says Nisargadatta. Well, for Gilles, this is happening in record time. I hear that he is now in hospital, in Paris. He does not wish to reveal his condition, adhering to Maharaj's guidance, of refusing to give attention to our bodily problems. We keep in touch via Whats App.

I recall, that when we were together in Nashik recently, Gilles said, "Maharaj wants you to give the *Naam Mantra*, and spread the teachings. What about me? What does he want me to do?" I replied: "This will become clear, in time!"

2020

January – My tests have all come back normal. Whatever is going on in the body, remains a mystery! The work has slowed down. The body's engine is like an old-fashioned train, that seems to be running out of steam! Although I don't give the symptoms attention, they are, at present, severe enough to interfere with the work. I am not able to write for the time being. Each time I try, tiredness and fatigue take over. Looking after the body means resting, and taking it extremely easy.

I witness all that is going on with the body, while at the same time, continuing to feel the strong and constant Presence of Maharaj.

7th February – Sean and Mel are arriving from New Zealand today. They are very earnest and sincere devotees. They know the importance of the sacred *Naam Mantra* and are making the long trip, exclusively, to receive it. After spending a night or so in a hotel to recover from the flight, they will come today, and then, return straight home. Mission accomplished! If only many more seekers had this kind of devotion!

10th February – It transpires that Gilles has nothing more to do. He is now very weak with cancer. There is nothing to be done! He is only in his mid-forties! I don't manage to travel to see him, as my health has also declined.

12th February – Gilles leaves the body! He stays positive right to the end, with Maharaj firmly ensconced in his heart, surrounded by pictures of the Masters, while listening to the *bhajans*.

Gilles is an only child. His mother is heartbroken and inconsolable. I reach out to her, via Gilles' WhatsApp account. Everyone is surprised by the news. Gilles was such a bundle of joy, so alive, that the news of his sudden departure is completely unexpected. However, his work is done! He is liberated. He will always have a special place in my heart.

Sometime later, Anvita messages me, asking after Gilles. She says: "Maharaj loved him". It is beautiful to hear this, and reminds me of the deep love Gilles had for Maharaj, and in particular, that occasion, when spontaneously, he grabbed Maharaj's hand, and told him, "I love you, Maharaj". Beautiful!

8th March – An American couple, Robert and Michelle from California, arrive in the UK for Initiation. When we meet and start talking, it is as if we have always been lifelong friends! Robert is a long-standing follower of Nisargadatta Maharaj. They ask me many questions about Maharaj, and what it was like to be with him.

Robert has a strange request! Tomorrow on the 9th March, he wants to be initiated at the exact time of his body's birthday. The aim of this, is that in some way, the initiation will annul, or superimpose, the exact moment of his "birth". We plan it accordingly, while at the same time, being fully aware that this arrangement, is nothing but a concept!

9ᵗʰ March – As soon as Robert receives the *Naam Mantra*, we both hear what sounds like drums beating. We look out of the window, expecting perhaps to see some kind of parade, but there is nothing! Robert is very joyful.

A few days later – Many flights have been cancelled, due to an emerging global virus, named Covid-19. Auspiciously, Robert and Michelle made it here, just in time!

April-July – I still don't know what is going on with the body. However, after a period of rest, my strength is returning, and I am able to focus my attention back on the important book, *Who am I?* I know Maharaj is waiting for it to be finished. I can almost hear his familiar words echoing: "How many pages?" The work continues!

It transpires that Robert and Michelle who came in March were the last visitors to be initiated due to the Covid-19 pandemic and the subsequent restrictions that were put in place.

31ˢᵗ August – During the last few months, I have been consulting with Maharaj, asking him about the possibility of offering Initiations online. Today, auspiciously, on the Anniversary of Maharaj's *Mahasamadhi*, Maharaj gives his consent. Loud and clear, he says: "Go ahead, go ahead".

Adapting the initiations and making them available online, will provide a wonderful opportunity, globally, for sincere seekers to receive the sacred *Naam Mantra*, in service to my Master. *Jai Guru Shri Ramakant Maharaj*!

10th November – The first online initiation is amazing! Maharaj's Presence is felt strongly. During the meditation, I can see Maharaj placing his hand on the recipient's head. When I ask her afterwards, how the meditation went, she tells me that she saw all the Masters standing around her. She also had a vision of Maharaj placing his hand on her head. He blessed her. Hearing this, made me very happy, and gave me great encouragement to initiate others.

12th November – Today, it is a great pleasure and honour to initiate Jim, a dear friend in California. He first became acquainted with Charles, back in 2015, when *Selfless Self*, was published. After Charles returned to the formless state, Jim became one of my spiritual brothers, and we began exchanging long messages on FB, etc. It is a beautiful, memorable day! After Jim's initiation, there followed many more, from the UK, USA, Europe and many from South America, and Argentina, in particular.

I am translating the information, for both the preparation and initiation-process meetings, into Spanish and French. I can manage these languages for those seekers who do not speak English… but that's my limit!

Interestingly, many emails are arriving from Japanese readers of *Selfless Self*. (The book took 3 years to translate, and I have been told by a Japanese seeker, that, "the translation is excellent"). Unfortunately, most of them do not speak English, so, I am unable to assist with initiations, for the time being.

Beginning of December – I have kept in touch with Mario, among several others, since he travelled from Switzerland to the UK, for Initiation. Out of the blue, he calls me, asking for my address, as he wishes to send me some Swiss chocolates as a festive gift! I tell him not to go to any trouble, however, he insists. I am very touched by these spontaneous kindnesses among the devotees.

End of December – "The body is not co-operating again", as Maharaj used to say. Since falling ill in Nashik in June 2018, it has been one thing after another: various symptoms come and go, and I cannot work out if they are related or connected – and neither, it seems, can the doctors. Despite what has been going on in the body, I keep pushing forward with the work on the *Who am I?* book.

2021

1ˢᵗ January – Today, an American lady, who has been practising and teaching "*Kriya Yoga*", for decades, receives the *Naam Mantra*. Afterwards, she emails me to say that she is very surprised at the power of the *Naam*, which she finds extremely intense!

Many Initiations follow throughout January and February. There are seekers from Australia, the USA, Europe and a few from India as well.

What is happening is extraordinary! Maharaj is sending sincere devotees from all over the world. Some of them have dreams about Maharaj, which then lead them to me!

Here is an email sent to me by one devotee, describing the lead-up to her initiation:

"...It was late 2020... I was trying to hold onto the teachings of Nisargadatta Maharaj, Ramana Maharshi, Anamalai Swami... which I read over and over and over again for hours in a row. It gave immense consolation... but waves of sadness and fear were not shaken off so easily. I could not meditate or concentrate. I missed having a support that was not only 'understanding' intellectually but something that helped me put it into practice. I used to watch all the videos I could that made me feel close to the Masters - physically. Feel their warmth and love. And I prayed so much to find a Master that could guide me "more personally". So I searched the web... I was not working, so I spent literally 14 hours a day reading

292

the teachings and searching for more documentaries...images anything related to these masters.

And then, at last, I found Ramakant Maharaj on YouTube... I Loved Him immediately. I knew he was a true Master in my heart. He was the Son of Nisargadatta Maharaj and there was not a word uttered from his mouth that was untrue to me. I saw all the videos!

Then I visited the website... then ordered the book *Selfless Self*... then made plans to go to the ashram...then purchased the *Dasbodh* and all the books Ramakant suggested. All this I did in a space of a week.

I read *Selfless Self* in 2 days! I felt so happy ... it gave me so much comfort and hope and happiness!! but also I felt sad because I did not have the *Naam Mantra*. I searched for mantras online and was reciting *Aham Brahamasmi*.

A couple of weeks passed by and I had a dream - in which I heard the name "Ann Shaw" repeatedly all night long - like a Mantra. I did not know who Ann Shaw was in my dream... I woke up with this name in my mind and my heart. And then found your name on the cover page of *Selfless Self*. So... I wrote to you... I told you about my dream... and the rest is history... you told me about the initiation... and on the 6th of February 2021 you initiated me into the *Naam Mantra* ...."

March – I hear the sudden and sad news, that Shri Balwant Maharaj had contracted Covid-19. He was hospitalized, and soon after, attained *Mahasamadhi*. It is a great loss, as he was such a beautiful Master and rare *Jnani*. Maharaj and Shri Balwant were very close. He travelled frequently, from Pathri to Nashik, to attend the various Program days. They had tremendous respect, love and caring for one another.

I recall on the morning of Maharaj's last birthday, a frail Maharaj bowing to Shri Balwant, (after Shri Balwant had bowed to Maharaj). At that time, due to weakness, Maharaj had difficulty getting back on his feet, so, Shri Balwant helped him up. Then he embraced Maharaj warmly! It was beautiful to see!

A couple of days later – More sad news reaches me today. I find out that Kesho (affectionately known as "Mama"), who was Treasurer of Nashik Ashram, left the body, due to Covid-19. He tirelessly dedicated himself to running the ashram activities, administration and programs with the utmost devotion.

April – After all the starts and stops, by the grace of Maharaj, the book *Who Am I?* has finally been completed. I save the work on a USB stick and place it on the altar, bowing to Maharaj, and asking him to bless it. A prayer issues forth: "Dear Maharaj, may your wishes for this book be brought to fruition and bring peace to all those who are suffering!"

I just need to proofread it, before searching for a publisher. Finding one may well prove challenging, as the world in which we live, brainwashes us into believing that we are "somebodies"! It teaches us, "I am somebody", whereas *Who Am I?* is all about realizing, "I am nobody!"

May – Some of those who have been initiated through this vehicle, would like to meet up in a group. We establish a Skype group entitled, "Social Devotion". (In

2014, Maharaj had asked Charles and me to form a group in this name, but we did not manage it at that time.) Intuitively, the perfect format for these meetings arises. Its focus will be collective meditation on the *Naam Mantra*! How powerful that would be! I suggest starting the meeting, with each one singing a *bhajan*, or part of one, as they are all familiar with the ones that are used for the pre-initiation practice, Then, we could meditate for 30 minutes, followed by a reading from *Selfless Self*. Finally, we would end the session with the *Arati* to Ramakanta!

June – Last night, I had a beautiful dream, after one of those days, when the body had caused a great deal of pain. The dream reminded me somewhat of Yogi Ramsurat Kumar's laughing fits. He used to get thrown out of the ashrams, because he would spontaneously roll on the floor, in hysterical laughter.

Well, in my dream, I was rolling on the floor with great laughter. And then, I was flying in the air, singing one of the *bhajans*, *Anandu Rei*, meaning "Bliss is all around". I am bliss. Bliss is everywhere! And this morning, as I emerged from the dream and awoke, I experienced the body "clicking back in", with a kind of "ka-chung" sound. It was a great dance of Spirit – totally free of pain!

8th July – There is a spontaneous "whoosh", like a fountain that has just been turned on, and beginning to spray! An inspiration arises to write an account, of what it was like for Charles and me, to meet Shri Ramakant Maharaj. There is not much recent literature around, offering insight into the Guru-disciple relationship, and the essential process of undoing the ego, under the guidance of an authentic Master. We kept diaries and journals during our time with Maharaj, as well as beyond. I start reading these for the new book. I am not sure what the title will be at the moment, but I'm sure it will arise spontaneously, in due course.

10th July – I receive a communication from devotee Rahul, who sends Anvita's beautiful composition of the *Kakad Arati* to Shri Ramakant Maharaj in Marathi. Rahul sent the English translation as well. Here it is:

"Wake up O dear Maharaj! It's dawn! Open your eyes of
Knowledge and give me your blessing...
And, accept this musical adoration as an offering!

Oh Sun (of Knowledge)! Spread the rays of Knowledge
and end the night (darkness) of ignorance..
Waiting to see you and offer their flowers of devotion,
are all the devotees of yours!

Eyes are impatient to see your beautiful smiling face!
And, the ears are eager to listen to your words
full of sweetness!

The nectar of your teachings is bringing salvation
to your devotees...
To fly in the sky of Consciousness, give power
to our wings!

Let my mind always be with my Selfless Self,
It's my Prayer to You…
Anvita bows down at Your holy feet,
with immense Gratitude to You!"

Mid-July – More Initiations are taking place, with seekers from this country, and that one…. It is amazing to be able to reach so many. Maharaj once told me that, in time, I would develop my very own, natural way of initiating… and that things would spontaneously be added to the way the initiation takes place. How true! Now the Initiation, one's "True Birthday" has blossomed into a beautiful 50-minute Ceremony. It includes prostrations, *prasad*, shared meditation, singing *bhajans*, etc. The process is time-consuming, as I have a "Preparatory Meeting" beforehand, to ensure - on Maharaj's insistence - that the seekers are sincere!

23rd July – *Guru Purnima*. Anvita publishes Part 3 of the book *Selfless Self*, which she has translated from English to Marathi. *Jai Guru*!

29th July – A Chinese couple living in NY are initiated today! They are both translators, who spread the highest teachings of Non-Duality. They devote their energy to translating the books of the Lineage Masters, as well as those of Ramana Maharshi.

September – Dreams! I have had Maharaj appearing in dreams many times on his own, but in the last year or so, he has been appearing with Charles. In these dreams,

I see Charles standing behind Maharaj. They both appear to be very, very tall, gigantic, in fact! I feel that I have been graced, with the beautiful gift of two guardian angels, while at the same time, always being aware of there never being, a "two" or an "I".

Early October – Another amazing dream. Charles and myself are flying through space, similar to the famous animation *The Snowman*, from the 1980s: "*We're walking in the air, we're floating in the moonlit sky…*". All of a sudden Charles has to go, and I wake up.

17th October – The first Japanese lady is initiated today. This was only made possible because she has a sufficient grasp of English! It is wonderful to know, that Maharaj's invisible footprints are treading across the globe! *Jai Guru!*

Mid-November – The work on the new book has halted. The fatigue is back, and I am not able to do anything at all.

19th November –Mark, a disciple of Shri Ramakant Maharaj, messages me out of the blue on FB. It turns out that he lives in Japan and speaks fluent Japanese! We meet on Zoom, and he offers to help me with the Initiations of Japanese seekers! This is an example of the way Maharaj orchestrates everything!

1st December – There is still no energy. I am overcome with extreme tiredness, and also sleeping a great deal!

14th December – I have been in bed for 2 weeks now. Tired of lying in bed, and not able to work, I shout out a loud plea to Maharaj, "Maharaj, please help this poor, broken body! Please help!"

15th December – The next day, Maharaj answers my call! He wakes me up at 4 am. I can see him clearly, and feel a surge of energy. Thoughtlessly, I pick up the "Journals" book, (now called *Timeless Years with Shri Ramakant*), and start working on it again. Before realizing it, I notice the time is 8 am. I am really happy to have worked for the last 4 hours. May it continue!

Late December – The second edition of the *Souvenir* book is published. Mandar Ghaisas' *seva* to Maharaj is admirable! When he published the first edition, half the book was written in Marathi, and the other half in English. Now we have two separate editions, in both English and Marathi. The publication is a beautiful keepsake, filled with tributes from devotees across the world, as well as lots of information about Maharaj, and wonderful pictures of him!

I read Joanne's extraordinary contribution. For the last 6 years, she has been living proof that there can be oneness with the Guru, even if you have not had the opportunity to meet him physically! Joanne's experience is also another example of the living, Transcendental Presence of the Guru, that operates beyond time and space, beyond logic and reason, but according to its own spiritual law that transcends our understanding.

Here is an extract from Joanne's beautiful submission, describing how she prepared for the special celebratory day on 8th July 2019, the "Installation of the *Samadhi* of Shri Ramakant Maharaj, in Nashik Ashram":

"... A week before the *Samadhi* installation, I spontaneously felt an impulse to buy myself a small gold band to cement my commitment to Maharaj/Selfless Self. I planned a little ceremony for the actual day, and from that day on I would wear the ring. Two days before the ceremony I had the most vivid dream I had ever had. I had my hand placed on the 'Bible' deluxe version of *Selfless Self* when suddenly Maharaj placed his hand right next to mine. There was such a surge of power it woke me with a start, and all I kept saying was 'thank you, thank you. I just felt this overwhelming feeling of the unbreakable bond between the Master and the devotee".

When one reads Maharaj's biography, describing his upbringing, the hardships, poverty and struggles he underwent as a boy and young man, it is amazing! How did he overcome all the worldly-related barriers that he faced? And not only that, he grew into a Master, a *Jnani* – a rare, Self-Realized Master and Teacher!

"My life is a miracle", Maharaj often said, "because I know where I have come from". He is such an inspiration to us all. If it happened to Maharaj, if he can do it, and realize his true nature, then anyone can!

Mid-December – A group of Russian devotees living in L.A. contact me, enquiring about initiations. Tony, received the *Naam Mantra* from Maharaj in 2014 and has been spreading the good news ever since. The preparatory meetings and subsequent initiations are arranged for those in Tony's group, who do not have the *Naam Mantra*.

20th December – Anvita informs me that she has completed the translation of *Ultimate Truth* into Marathi. She has been tirelessly been working on this for some time. *Jai Guru*!

25th December – After Charles' body had returned to the elements, Maharaj instructed, no, he commanded, two of the sons to, "look after Ann". Jasper took his command very seriously. Over the last couple of years, he has been helping me out a great deal.

Christmas day is very special. It is filled with light. Jasper arrives in the afternoon. Although he was initiated by Maharaj in 2014, his practice has been quite wobbly. However, in the last couple of months, I have been trying to bring him back onto solid ground, hammering him with Maharaj's teachings, as well as asking Maharaj, to stabilize and strengthen him up!

"Today, we are graced with Maharaj's Presence. I start talking about Maharaj, his teachings, Charles, etc, when, suddenly, the whole room lights up. I can feel Maharaj in the room, and so can Jasper. Not long after, I become aware that Maharaj has infused Jasper with a droplet of nectar! The hours pass by unawares, and before we know it, it's about 7 pm – time to eat!

Since that day, Jasper has had two significant dreams, one where Maharaj and myself appear to him, and another one in which his father, Charles, appears. In both dreams, the emphasis on the importance of the teachings and practice is the main focus. When Charles tells him, "I love you", this, too, has a deep impact and elevates him. He also reiterates what Maharaj and I had said recently: Embrace this opportunity to know yourself now, otherwise, there could be another dream!

Afterwards, I thank Maharaj and Charles for the guidance they gave him, and its lasting impact. I also stress the importance of surrender and gratitude, which Jasper has taken on board, and is finding immensely helpful."

2022

January – Jasper is working on a way, by which Maharaj's teachings can further spread, across the world. After a start-stop attempt with one app, his research comes up with "Ramakant Maharaj Radio!" He usually prefers to complete tasks slowly, as if he were on a sleeper train. Now, however, it looks like he is on an express train. He completes the task in record time! I am amazed at how fast this project manifested itself. The radio station is up and running within a couple of days! *Jai Guru!*

22nd January – It is 4 years since Charles dropped the body. Now, that this book, *Timeless Years with Shri Ramakant Maharaj* is almost finished, on this auspicious day, I upload a post to FB, announcing its imminent publication.

"The writing of *Timeless Years* will end soon, but the bond with Shri Ramakant Maharaj will never end, for that is eternal! Now, nearly a decade after meeting my Guru, I can still feel his hand on my head, as strongly as I did on Initiation Day! I continue to be guided and blessed by Him. He is always with me.

While reliving those precious, timeless years, Maharaj's love permeates everything. Drawing me inwards to that spaceless, stateless, timeless zone, gentle exhilaration flows and unfolds, as together, beating to one drum, the pages are written. Each moment and experience with Maharaj arises afresh, alive, as if, lived for the very first time!"

23rd January – I receive an email from an Italian seeker who wishes to speak with me online, to discuss the significance of a dream he has just had, in which Shri Ramakant appears. He informs me that he has only watched one video of Maharaj. In the dream, when Maharaj appears, he tells him he has no peace and quiet. Shri Ramakant ignores him, and tells him that he will initiate him! The seeker panics and shouts, "No!", as he does not feel worthy enough. Maharaj ignores him again, and proceeds to give him the *Naam Mantra*.

The next morning, he remembers the dream but not the *Naam Mantra*! I tell him that when the Guru appears in dreams, it is always real, and not just his imagination. We will continue to speak, and slowly progress to Initiation!

3rd February – I find out it is Shri Bhausaheb Maharaj's "Death Anniversary" today. I have just finished *Timeless Years*, apart from the corrections. On this auspicious day, I offer the book to Shri Bhausaheb, and ask him to bless it! Our online group, (Julia, Lauv, Solange, Shanti, Rafal, Francis, Jasper), celebrates an impromptu program for this special day.

6th February – I recall that one year after Charles and myself were initiated, Maharaj said, "Today, you are 1 year old!" Well, today, I receive a communication from a close friend and devotee who is celebrating her very "First Birthday":

"On the 6th of February 2021, you initiated me into the *Naam Mantra*, (which by the way - it's TODAY!)

Oh! my dear Ann, it gives me great joy to recall all of this. Tears of happiness roll down my face. But, what gives me more joy is that since that moment my life changed (even more deeply than when I first read Nisargadatta Maharaj some 10 years ago and was mind blown… and for the next 10 years only read Nisargadatta and nothing more!)

It's like the culmination of a life of search finally gave its fruits in the form of the *Naam Mantra*. The Mantra is now my living Master, the Love, the Presence, the Consolation I was further looking for. THANK YOU infinitely. *Jai Guru! Jai Sadguru*! Much love."

7th February – I called on my Guru, Shri Ramakant Maharaj, on the 14th December 2021, to help me with the completion of *Timeless Years*. Every day since then, Maharaj has been my alarm clock, waking me up at 4 am to continue the work. By His Grace, today, it is finished! *Jai Guru, Jai Sadguru.*

Afterword

The timeless, universal and powerful knowledge, direct from the Source, which poured out of Shri Ramakant Maharaj, has been recorded in his books and audio/visual Talks. He is here with you always! Accept his teachings, not with your mind, but with your heart, your core, your whole being! Stay true to your Guru! Stay faithful! He has graced you with the nectar of pure Truth. He has given you everything. Don't be tempted to throw it all away for a "spiritual massage", for some diluted, second-grade, substitute! Don't fall under the spell of words again! Be silent! Stay silent!

Nisargadatta Maharaj says: "When the *Jnani*'s body dies, it dissolves into the five elements. If a disciple calls on the *Jnani*, his form will appear to him. His body is always present in the 5 elements, but not in concentrated form". Shri Nisargadatta Maharaj has not gone anywhere, and neither has Shri Ramakant Maharaj! You can call on him to ask for guidance, at any time, at any place.

"Have *Satsang* with yourself!" This means: be in the company of the one, (Selfless Self) who is always in your company! Surrender and pray, until your "Inner Master" reveals Itself and guides you.

Keep bowing to the images of the Masters, knowing that the egoless you is bowing to itself, to Selfless Self! There is no duality. There never was!

Keep asking Maharaj for blessings, until you can bless yourself with confidence and strong conviction. As Maharaj used to say: "Why do you ask others for blessings? Place your hand on your head and bless yourself".

When you dare to let go of the dream with all its illusions, and accept the Reality, you will be free from all fear, stress and suffering. And, as the river of life spontaneously flows, causeless, permanent happiness and peace will be yours in abundance! *Jai Guru. Jai Sadguru*!

Further Reading

Shri Ramakant Maharaj books:

Selfless Self, (2015, pub. Selfless Self Press) Ed. by Ann Shaw, (also available in French, Spanish, Dutch, Japanese, Korean, Greek.)

Be With You, (2016, pub. Selfless Self Press) Ed. By Ann Shaw, (also available in French, Spanish, Dutch, Portuguese.)

Ultimate Truth, (2018, pub. Zen Publications, Mumbai.)

Souvenir Tribute book to Shri Ramakant Maharaj, (2021, pub. Mandar Ghaisas, Mumbai.) Available in English and Marathi.

Mahasamadhi of Shri Ramakant Maharaj,
31ˢᵗ August 2018

Printed in Great Britain
by Amazon

79418724R00187